LOVE LIFE

A story of self exploration through sacred teachings, solitude and sex.

To Our Dear Sweet Rose.
Thank you for being
a feather in the
wind & a
Root in our
hearts ♡
xo Niki

◆

To Flore Dawn
Thank you for giving this project wind and wings.

To my Spirit guides
Thank you for hearing my highest thoughts
and wielding my wildest dreams.

To the Universe
Thank you for co-creating this beautiful story with me.

Niki Trosky
Love Life

Copyright © 2015 Niki Trosky
www.lovelifeproductions.com

ALL RIGHTS RESERVED. This book contains material protected under International and Federal Copyright Laws and Treaties. Any unauthorized reprint or use of this material is prohibited. No part of this book may be reproduced or transmitted in any form or by any means, electronic or mechanical, including photocopying, recording, or by any information storage and retrieval system without express written permission from the author/publisher.

Cover Design and Layout: Lucas c Pauls

This book is dedicated
to every single woman
who has ever looked for love.

"Your task is not to seek for love,
but merely to seek and find all the barriers
within yourself that you have built against it."
– Rumi

Introduction by Chelsea Brunette

Niki Trosky's manuscript was touching, bewildering at times, and deeply honest. The heroine of the story, Trosky's character of "the girl", immediately grabbed the reader's hand, giggling and smiling and pulled us along for an unexpected journey, an ambitious adventure of self-discovery, of trip-ups and bruised knees and the triumphs of self-awareness.

The memoir was written directly from the heart, an unchaining of things held on, of dreams and tears spilled, and of revelations exposed, a beautiful soliloquy of inner thoughts and considerations. The language, the expressions and comparisons used, moved me and will sway future readers into the unknown. The carefully chosen words that filled page after page with colourful descriptions of faraway lands and unique friendships were felt deeply; they encouraged the reader to live and participate in every moment.

In provocative script, "the girl" takes us around the world with her. She recounts the moments of intense loneliness, includes us in homesick letters, the feelings of confusion, both in love and intimacy and the isolation of her complete removal from all things expected. "The girl" settles into the sand with the reader, on the beaches of India, toes in sand, recounting memories and thoughts bubbling to the surface. Tales of intimate conversations and spontaneous adventures that come from simply "allowing" herself to take part; from smelling the rich, dark coffee brewing on the banks, to the many friendships formed and lost along the way.

The inconceivable growth that occurs out of the inner turmoil "the girl" experiences, as she evolves into Zahira, the wise woman of confidence and creativity, will embrace readers. The beautifully, calm and enlightened Zahira invites us, the reader, into her deepest thoughts and conflicts and tugs us into profound, exotic situations, situations that will leave us questioning our own self-determined, expected roles in life.

I believe I was intensely touched by Zahira's words because the challenges she faces within herself, the internal conflict she overcomes, may well be something that we all struggle with at some level. The rebirth of the author, one void of social expectations, was inspiring. Zahira shed layers of the past, left them crumpled and deserted on the floor and emerged as a self-aware, enlightened and accepting woman, guidance in her prose, something we can all strive for.

As a reader, I felt a great connection to "the girl" and envy for the woman Zahira. I finished the book with an impression that a profound friendship had been created between Trosky and myself, as she was able to write in a manner that readers can relate to, and described herself in a way that readers will fall in love with.

I was saddened to reach the end of the book, the end of an insightful, intimate relationship between the author and herself, and the author and the readers. Her display of independence and courage, personified, and desire to self-improve, was both refreshing and inspiring.

This book is not to be quickly devoured and forgotten; it should be savoured, reached for at times of hunger and wandering. Each chapter and story, every delicate layer of "the girl", should be peeled down to the very core, and absorbed, every succulent fibre of honesty revelled in, held between grinning teeth. Every bite celebrated, with juices dripping down skin, not to be wasted, as every last drop, every last word, is essential and wonderful.

Warning Label

You are about to read an intimate diary written in the third person. It is not a perfect manuscript. It was never meant to be a glossy over-edited work that emphasizes grammar over natural expression. It is a raw memoir that unfolds with more honesty than proper punctuation. Sometimes the tense sways from past to future to present. That's what naturally happens when writing in the moment. Memories will always be in the past and hopes will always dream of the future. Read it with a little grain of salt (and maybe some lemon and tequila?!)...

LOVE

LIFE

Prologue

◆

The End (of a stale idea)

"I am tired of waiting for a lover to go to India," the girl whispered to the moon and the old oak tree.

For some forgotten reason the girl had always linked India to a lover. For over a decade she convinced herself she needed to wait for the man of her dreams to go with her. Part of her felt it was romantic the other part felt it was practical. Wouldn't she need someone to hold back her hair while she puked? She just assumed everybody got sick when they travelled through India.

To be clear, the girl has no fear of getting off a plane by herself. Truth be told she *loves* it. She adores being able to do whatever she wants whenever she wants to. She can surf the cusp of time and let the abracadabra unfold.

So how did India become reserved for a partner? Who was making up these rules anyhow? Hey, wait a minute...

"I don't need to wait anymore. I can go alone!" she said half surprised at this obvious realization.

Flicking this simple switch in her mind triggered a deep shift in her being. It felt as though a stale bubble had burst and million little heart shaped bubbles were drifting up into the night sky. She let out a loud cackle. The same one that always ripples from her belly when the truth sets her free. She instantly felt lighter.

She was alone in the woods.

It was her birthday.

◆

3 Months Later

"The forces that are guiding to you to India at this time are big. You have been destined for this one. India will be humbling and empowering. It will teach you much, but know you have much to teach India. You are far down the path and you have much to offer," said the Ayahuasquero who is also one of her best friends.

"Oh no!" she replied. "I am planning on going quietly. I want to sink into the background and observe. I want to be invisible."

"And that is exactly what a master would do," he smiled.

The girl started laughing hysterically and then hugged her friend for a long time. He truly sees her. He meets her moment for moment. He knows her every move. He is her shadow of light. She is beyond grateful to have him in her life, she is relieved.

"This trip will be huge for you," he smiled and hugged her, "huge."

"It's time," she said picking up her backpack.

"It is time," he reflected with a knowing smile.

◆

Got to Goa

The girl arrived to Goa under the light of a full moon. She knew instantly what needed to happen. She slipped into the night and out of her clothes for a skinny dip in the Arabian sea. It wasn't as romantic she'd hoped. The waves were heavy and full. She got knocked around in the dark and found herself scrambling for balance. It was still a significant way to greet her favourite healer. She has an undeniable affinity for the ocean.

The girl sat quietly in the sand and let the sounds of the water soothe her. She was *and* is proud to be here alone. She has chosen her own company. She feels both empowered and fragile. In her vulnerable moments she slips into longing for her last lover. It has been over a year since they have been together, but he still creeps up in waves of unexpected sadness.

Today she felt a new appreciation for his resurfacing. Instead of heartbreak she felt gratitude. For the first time she could appreciate the pain that spurred her path to peace. Their breakup was brutal, but it was also compounded by a series of tragic events. In one week the girl lost a close family friend to cancer and then almost lost her uncle in a severe car accident. Within the same week one of her co-workers dropped dead next to the photo copy machine and her high school sweet heart ended his own life with a shot gun.

This series of events led to intense suffering which in turn lead her to a new realization. In the depths of her despair the girl discovered that ***nothing matters if she is not at peace.*** This realization spurred her to graciously surrender all of her goals, hopes and dreams for one year. She wiped everything clear from her calendar. She erased her entire list of things to do. Her only mission became a path to peace.

This path to peace lead her to the woods to be alone on her birthday. It also lead her to the realization that India was calling her with or without a lover. It lead her to this very moment where she finds herself alone and in the belly of the unknown. Her broken heart allowed her to hit rock bottom. It was from this grounded perspective that a new clarity prevailed.

She gave up on life as she knew it

to find life as it should be known…

◆

Let's Talk About Sex

"Is this draining you?" asked the Bubble Masseuse with a thoughtful touch.

He was referring to his deep inhales of her skin. He was pressing his nose up against her flesh taking long deep breaths and then exhaling with a sigh.

"Not at all," she laughed completely entertained by the whole thing.

"Good," he grinned, "because it's giving me such incredible energy. Your presence alone is like putting flowers in a room."

The girl has made a new friend. They met a few days ago while swimming. He dove beneath her and released a giant exhale. It showered upward bubbles and tickled her whole being into delight. He did it again and again just to please her.

The Bubble Masseuse is sweet and intriguing. He has renounced the life of a regular joe to follow his personal flow. He is borderless and poetic by nature. He is so much fun to spend time with and the two find themselves laughing freely. They did however share a moment of frustration surrounding sex. He was hopeful and she withheld.

This sent the girl wheeling through familiar feelings of guilt. She was bombarded with voices that told her she was being too picky, too superficial, too egotistical. They chastised her for being too prudish. They taunted her for isolating herself into an entire year of celibacy. She let these voices boil and settle to the same conclusion they always find:

When it's on it's on. When it's not it's not.
There should never be feelings of obligation surrounding sex.

"I'm sorry if I am sending out mixed messages," she started to explain, "to be honest I really like you. I just have a hard time sharing my body. Sometimes I feel like I've built a fortress around myself. I have managed to isolate myself into an entire year of celibacy. It's confusing as hell. I feel guilty when I don't have sex, like there is something wrong with me."

"There is definitely *nothing* wrong with you," the Bubble Masseuse pursued with an eager tone. He was still hopeful she would change her mind.

"Thanks, but I think we need to negotiate sharing a bed and not our bodies," the girl persisted with a gentle tone.

The Bubble Masseuse accepted her conclusion gracefully. He was mature and wise enough to not take it personally. He was open to explore their relationship without sex. They spent three days laughing easily until it was time to part ways.

"I wish I could order a six pack of you and me to go," he smiled as they were saying goodbye. "It would make the train ride seventh heaven."

"Did you just say you wished you could order a six pack of you and me to go?" the girl laughed hysterically. "Yer hilarious. Thanks for being so great and for easing me into India. Your open heart has me off to a great start..."

◆

Secret Talent & Story Telling

The girl left the Bubble Masseuse to enjoy the sunset. She was happy to be alone. It was a perfect chance to melt into her surroundings. There was a serene and seductive quality to the elements. The wind and the water felt slow, warm and luxurious. Even the sand felt like soft velvet on her bare skin.

She stretched out on the beach and swept her fingertips through the loose gold earth. Her mind softened and her body did too. She got lost in the swaying motions of her hands. They were making unconscious symbols in the sand. She melted into the moment with an effortless awareness.

When the sun dropped completely into the sea the girl sauntered home with one thing on her mind. She opened the door to her beach nest where the air was thick and damp. She turned on the fan and felt a great romance for her scene. She was all alone and she was humming with anticipation.

It was on.

She stripped down and draped her new sarong across her bare shoulders. It felt light on her skin in contrast to the dense night air. She made her way outside to find a seat on the balcony and perched her feet up on the ledge. There was nothing between her and jungle that was fading in the twilight.

The girl sat still for a long time. She tuned into the subtleness of the moment. She let the air around her brush her into arousal. She slipped into a deeply meditative state. Her body was utterly awake and her mind was lost. There was no more room for thoughts of guilt or loneliness. There was no more room for *any* thoughts. There was only room for a moment of divine love making.

With inescapable presence the girl orgasmed with nothing more than a feather like touch. It is a skill she has honed over her years of sexual isolation. She can turn herself on like nobody else can. She has learnt to connect to something greater than her body and can abandon herself in sacred sensuality. She can trace & tease her line of arousal and turn her pleasure into puddles.

The girl takes a pause from writing her story to appreciate her surroundings. She is in a small restaurant with an open terrace. The streets are still and she can faintly hear the echo of the ocean. Her skin is flush from the hot night air and her body feels loose from her love making. Her bare toes are resting on the seat next to her and she marvels at how quiet the scene is. She anticipated a noisier more hectic India, the kind she sees in the movies. Instead she has landed in a sleepy coastal town that makes her feel loose and natural.

Her laptop is balanced on her lap. It is nothing worth writing about, not like the romantic typewriters she has lugged on all of her previous journeys. Her handsome Eaton's Viking or sweet teal Olivetti naturally assumed their own characters in her stories. They were always written into her adventures due to their surprising presence in jungles and deserts, cafe's and coastlines. She can't imagine her mini purple laptop will draw much attention, but it sure is light and convenient.

The girl has been writing her story for over a decade. In fact she is the one who is writing right now. She wonders if that is confusing... but she can't help it. She identifies naturally with being a character. Documenting her life in the third person pushes her into all kinds of interesting adventures. She is more inspired to write about 'the girl' than to write from the position of 'I'. '*She*' somehow seems more interesting than 'me'. 'She' is an elegant hobo while 'I' am a school teacher from Winnipeg on a leave of absence.

See what she means?

◆

One last (*very important*) thing before we take off...

The girl takes a sip of green tea and looks up to smile at Grandmother moon. She has a special affection for the moon and has recently received a song from her. She hums it constantly. It came to her in a moment when she was dreaming of being a mother. It sounds like a lullaby and it feels like being cradled. The girl often catches herself lost in this tune without knowing where and when it started. It just appears when she is content and at peace.

She once heard that all of the unborn souls of the Universe are kept in the belly of the moon. It is a First Nation story that she holds close to her heart. The girl wants nothing more than to find the love of her life and have a baby. She has tried fooling herself to believe otherwise, but *more than anything she wants to be a mom.*

She has been speaking to her unborn child for years. She feels she has a son who is waiting for her to catch up with him. She frequently has conversations with his spirit. She will often place her hands on her belly, tilt her chin to the moon and whisper,

"Choose your father wisely."

PART 1

Tantric Touchdown

◆

Love Letters from the Absolute for the Absolute

"Oh my God. Oh my God…oh my God…oh my God," the girl kept repeating, "Oh my God!"

She almost burst into tears when she saw the Golden Beach. It was like walking into a postcard from heaven.

"Oh my God," she said again and again. "I'm never leaving here."

The girl started to write her own postcards home that began with; *my life as I know it is done. I will not be returning…*

She was greeted by the most stunning lighting imaginable. It felt as though she were opening a sepia-toned love letter that was carefully stored in the shoebox of her heart. The beach was instantaneous magic. The water was calm and clear and yet had the most inviting and playful waves, soft round gentle waves. She has never felt such a smooth and flat ocean floor. It felt like she was walking through an ocean prairie, wading in fields of water that were rippling with the wind.

There were a handful of giant boulders jutting out of the sea like tall and humble grandfathers. They were both silent and stoic. The beach was capped on the south side by a mountain of lush green jungle. There were palm trees colouring the shoreline with the most meticulous placements. It was like God had an exterior decorator come and dial the whole scene. The impresario in her was beyond impressed.

"I'm never leaving here am I?" she asked herself.

In the moment she could not recall a place that has floored her so quickly. She literally dropped to her knees in the sand and wanted to cry. The girl has been to many stunning parts of the globe, perhaps some even more beautiful than this, but an overwhelming feeling of home hit her like a ton of welcome mats.

It gets better. So much better it's kind of hard to believe. The girl is here to study traditional tantra yoga and she just met her teacher Bhagavan.

"I am really excited to be here," she said as she introduced herself.

"Welcome. What questions do you have for me?" he asked right off the hop.

"Well what is your initial read on me? Can you get an initial sense of anything I need to change that I might not be aware of?" she asked directly. It was a bold question, but if he was a true master could he not sense her well being (or lack there of it) in a heart beat?

"Ah this is a great question. This tells me you are already at a deep level of understanding. No, I cannot sense anything that you need to fix. I would prefer to speak to you on a professional level. I can see you attaining a very high professional level of tantra," he said with a smile.

"That leads me to my next question. What is your definition of tantra?" she asked him. "So far in my personal quest for understanding this word I have heard many definitions."

"I have a very simple way to tell you what tantra is," Bhagavan replied. "It is about honouring you. The woman is Goddess. You are the divine being. Tantra teaches men and women to honour Kali the Goddess, the one who brings us life."

The girl almost burst out laughing. She suppressed it in to a smile and then asked, "So the woman is divine and what about the man? Is it up to us to acknowledge that man is God or is he a mere mortal?"

"Mere mortal," Bhagavan replied with a straight face. "When humans can see woman as the divine it will eliminate all social, psychological and political problems. This is the tantric way. This is what I teach," said Bhagavan.

Wow! So wait a minute...not only has the girl found the most divine scenery, but she also she gets to spend her time being reminded that she too is divine. If the girl could write a fantasy novel about her life (apart from the one she is writing now) this would be it!

The girl has scored a tantric touchdown.

◆

Laws of Tantra

Be honest with yourself
Be honest with everyone
Participate fully in life
Believe in yourself

◆

Loving Letters

Hey mom & dad!
I have arrived in paradise. I think I said oh my God about thirty times in a row. My heart has fallen madly in love. This place feels like a love letter I wrote to myself in a past life. Not only is the beach like a postcard from God, my new tantric yoga teacher is all about honouring the Goddess.
He teaches his students to love and embrace life, to be the heroes in their own stories! So essentially I get to spend the next month in heaven learning to love myself more than I already do. I almost died laughing. How the bleep did i get so lucky?
I sent you some love through the moon. I hope you got it. Thanks for your endless inspiration!
Love your daughter.

~~~

Hello sweet pea!
This morning our moon was a very large and orange in colour. It was fantastic. I must have looked at it when you whispered my name. It was so low I don't think I would have seen it otherwise.
You are so right to say you are lucky. I could give thanks for hours
~~~

and hours about how lucky I am to have my family. You all fill my heart with such pure joy. It brings tears to my eyes. I am the most fortunate person alive!

I am thrilled you are able to experience your own personal joy. It is such an uplifting feeling. Carry this always and you will never feel old. Know you are soooo loved you will never feel alone. Enjoy your beautiful beach and your beloved ocean.

Talk to you soon, love mom

Oh wait...your dad wants to write something....

Well my dear let me just reiterate what the gentleman from California told you—your presence alone really is like putting flowers in a room. I'm glad to hear that the people there see you as the people here see you! A fresh bouquet of flowers that put a smile on everyone's face.

I miss you and my thoughts of you and what you are experiencing go through my mind every day.

~ Love you a lot! dad xoxo

◆

When it Rains...

"I think today is a day to give a goddess a four hour massage," said the hot buff yogi as they began to wake up. "Your skin is so addictive."

They were puddled beneath a pink halo fit for a princess. The rosy mosquito netting cast a soft light on their scene. The girl felt as though she were still dreaming.

"Okay!" she laughed.

How could she refuse? She was being held by strong muscles. Her head was melting into his heartbeat. She felt comfortable and safe.

The two new friends had lost the night together. They got caught in a rain storm and took shelter in his second story beach nest. It was meant to be a pit stop, a place to grab a dry shirt and carry on. The elements, however, had a different agenda. The rain swelled to monsoon proportions and the thunder decided they were not leaving. They fell into his bed and started talking.

Their conversation flowed as naturally as the weather, it was still pouring when the rain stopped. When they finally checked the time five hours had past. They were both surprised at the vortex they had created. It only made sense that she spend the night.

They fell asleep comfortably beside each other. It wasn't until the sun crept through the thatched roof that the girl rolled into his arms. The idea of getting spoiled by this man's touch was more than appealing. They made a date for her massage. She would return at sunset.

◆

It Pours.

"Thank you," said the girl when she returned to the yogi's beach nest, "I am really looking forward to this."

"Well," he began, "it is just an excuse to touch your soft skin so in my books this is a win win."

If anything the girl won won. She double won. He worked on her naked body with professional courtesy and skill. He practices Kahuna massage. It is a Hawaiian technique that feels like a wave rushing over the body. It washed her into drool mode. She surrendered everything to him. He was a perfect gentleman. It wasn't until he had finished his work that the play began. He brought new definition to a full body massage.

"Holy shit," she said more than once. He worked her into an actual real life orgasm (not one she was faking). She naturally surrendered everything to this man. She didn't have any feelings of doubt or confusion. It was clearly on. He pushed her buttons into bliss. "Holy shit!" she repeated.

Once again they fell into a vortex. Instead of talking this was all touch. The strands of moonlight filtering through the thatched roof painted their flesh with bubbles of light.

"It looks like the Universe on your skin," he smiled in the dark.

The girl pulled herself out of her puddle to observe their scene. It was beyond romantic, it was electric. Her animal instinct began to stir from deep within and she instantaneously let loose on this man. She couldn't stop touching and kissing him. It felt so good to desire and be desired. It was an absolute meditation of awareness. Every sense of her being was alive and present, savouring and indulging. It was a gift. He gave the girl a chance to be a woman. He opened her enough to turn on her most sensual self. It wasn't even a thought, it was just a natural reaction to his affection.

"Well Miss Universe, should we get you a cup of ginger tea?" he asked after their fifth attempt to detach themselves.

She laughed outright and agreed that she needed to pull herself into reality. Her tantra yoga training officially starts tomorrow. It is the same course that this man has just completed. He has transformed over the last month and she has just reaped the benefits.

They made their way to a beachside cafe for a late night meal.

"Oh shit," he said, "it's Halloween today!"

"Oh wow that's right! Well the tricks up your sleeve were the best treats imaginable. Sweeter than candy," she said with a playful wink.

The girl relaxed into the beach chair and sunk her toes into the sand. There was nothing more she could possibly wish for. The wind swept her hair across her cheeks like feathers. She felt perfect.

◆

Harvesting Pomelos

"Oh my goodness! That's a pomelo tree?!?" she half shouted. The girl burst into hysterics. Right outside her bedroom door is a blossoming pomelo tree. The fruit is so ripe and full the branches are bending under their weight.

The joke? (well it's an inside joke). One of her close friends back home made up her own rating system for men. It's based on fruits. A plum is sweet, but more cute than sexy. A mango is super hot and sexy, but a pomelo…a pomelo is the *bomb*.

The girl has been sucking the juice out of her very own pomelo, a man whom she can't get enough of. He is exquisite and delicious. She has been so consumed that she hasn't taken the time to write home. She lost her desire to reach out and is expressing her desire to reach in. They have exchanged body work. His first massage sent her into butter mode. She melted with his touch and he opened her gently, one sigh at a time.

Today it was her turn to devour him. She worked on his rock hard body with so much joy in her heart. It was an absolute pleasure to unleash herself on this man. She couldn't stop touching him. It felt so good to reconnect with an unbridled side of herself.

She spent time smoothing out the lines on his forehead and softening his face with firm fingers. Then she moved to his heart where she placed her forehead and began to hum. She rocked back and forth in a trance purring a soft lullaby.

When it was time to turn it on he instantly responded. Both of their bodies were rising to the occasion. She worked him entirely and she was amazed at his ability to restrain from orgasm. He was releasing his own subtle sighs and when she returned to his lips he sat her up and gently placed her on her back. It was her turn again. With nothing more than his tongue he reduced the girl to an absolute puddle of marshmallow bliss. Her muscles released every ounce of unwritten tension and she exhaled into womanhood.

As they were cuddling and connecting eye to eye he said, "Just so you know I try not to orgasm. It is something I have learnt through Taoism. When a man ejaculates he looses a lot of valuable energy, an energy that is extinguishable. Saving myself keeps me young and fertile...but don't worry you can have as many orgasms as you want."

"Wow," was her response, "I am impressed that you can restrain yourself so well."

He started laughing, "Believe me, I am impressed I was able to as well. That may have been the most challenging ever!"

Okay so wait...the girl is recalculating her fortune; she is living in a postcard from heaven, going to a tantric school to honour herself as a goddess and is currently devouring a pomelo who can restrain himself from having an orgasm so she can have as many as she wants to?

Fuck me! Please.

◆

Cease Fire

"Thank you, thank you, thank you," the girl whispered as she flopped on to her bed.

It was an unsuspecting moment of overwhelming gratitude. It came from a simple smile from the bread man. His sweet expression triggered a deep sense of joy within her. His eyes and his humble beauty crumbled her to tears. To be honest the smile was the trigger, but her entire current reality is what warrants the reaction.

Her tears of joy are coming from a body that has been pleasured beyond measure. After a year of restraining her body is celebrating touch. She is making love to a sizzling hot god. A god who has learnt to honour the goddess. A god who doesn't need to ejaculate. A god who lets her orgasm as much as she wants to. A god who puts her needs first.

It is a completely different phenomenon. She is learning so much about her sexual relationships, how she would succumb to pleasing her partners again and again. How she rarely climaxed and they always did. How she would work to please them and take that as her reward. The only moments where she has had complete attention on herself is when she has been alone. When she makes love to herself she is free to patiently indulge all of her senses.

She has heard whispers of men who have learnt not to ejaculate. She has read snippets here, over heard conversations there...but now she is directly in the line of cease fire. It is a lifetime of conditioning that is unwinding all around her. As her body is reaping the benefits her brain is trying to catch up.

She will be honest and say that it was an ego issue to start. She has never had difficulties pleasing a man. She did not realize this had created an invisible self-confidence, one that she was unaware of until it was stripped. It did not take long to adapt however. As soon as she listened to his reasoning she let the record of her body skip on release.

◆

Ego

Tantra does not believe in ego.
You are either living with clarity or with illusion.
There is no ego there is only confusion,
there is only the illusion.
You have to believe that you are precious.
When you believe that you are precious,
everyone else and everything else becomes precious.

◆

Pop goes the bliss ball

Woosh! The ball drops. The minute the girl writes home with glowing news about having hot sex in paradise the plug is pulled. The god who has been reading her like the sunday times has made a new announcement. It goes a little somethin' like this...

"Okay," the Pomelo said as he sits up to turn off the music, "I really need to say something."

"Alright," replied the girl. She instantly knew it was going to make her squirm so she crossed her fingers behind her back. She always does this when she feels she is about to be delivered unwanted news.

"Okay, well... this is hard to say, but I have to try," the Pomelo began. "I just really feel it is important to be honest with you. I really like you and I want this relationship to be based on truth."

He went on to explain his current situation. He is fresh from a break up with a woman he loved for four years. The girl already knew this and was not surprised to hear it, in fact she was more surprised they had carried on as far as they had to this point.

"I am really learning the importance of being truthful. It is the only way to create a foundation for a relationship. I don't want you to feel rejected. I can't even believe this is me saying these things, but I can't be sexual with you right now," he finished.

The girl felt her blissful bubble burst. Her expectations of this steamy romance instantly deflated her. She also felt his genuine struggle and was proud of his ability to dig up and express the truth. She was not upset with him; she was in fact impressed.

"I don't feel rejected," she replied honestly. "I am proud of you for being so real about all of this."

"It's not easy. I know I still have my own shit to work through. I could maybe continue sleeping with you if you weren't so great, but I have started to develop feelings for you. I feel like you deserve someone who is a hundred percent present," he replied.

The girl feels his genuine affection for her. Not only does she feel it, but she returns it. She is crazy about this guy. She has spent the last year alone, not willing to share herself with just anyone. This god before her came as a beautiful gift. In less than a week he has touched her being with great depth. She wants nothing more than to devour and digest every last morsel of him.

"So would it be better if I started sleeping at my place?" she asked.

"I still want to spend time with you," he smiled. "I really do honour you."

The girl was patiently watching herself. She could feel a swell of tears creeping up. She was unable to let them flow for some reason. She sat quietly with her head on his chest. She was waiting for the right words. She was completely aware of her own disappointment.

"Do you want me to do some work on your hip?" he asked.

"Sure," she said softly.

He has been working on healing her right hip. It has a deep and difficult pain to access. It prevents her from sitting cross legged in meditation. The Pomelo told her over lunch that the hips are where we store our sensuality. He explained that hips are connected to the emotions of sex.

"As I press on your hip, ask yourself what the connection is between the pain and your sexual being. Tell your subconscious that you accept the pain and are ready to release it," he said.

As the Pomelo began to work with expert skill the girl felt incredibly deep wounds releasing. She tuned into herself and the message was loud and clear. She has a lifetime of sexual frustration stored deep in her right hip. She started to cry and cry and cry. She was crying because the same man who was healing her frustrations was also currently at the root of them. The muscles pushing on her pain were the same ones that were able to give her true orgasmic pleasure. She was crying because she had finally found a man to unleash her most sensual self upon and now she would have to tie herself back up. As she was healing she was hurting both physically and emotionally.

"What is it that you are looking for?" he asked as he was still applying pressure.

"Well I thought that I had found it," she said trying not to sob.

"But this goes deeper than us. What are you afraid of? You can't fully rotate your hip to open. You are afraid of fully opening yourself. Why?" he persisted.

"I don't know. I always come back to the same place. I feel like I can't give myself away so easily. There needs to be an exceptionally strong attraction for me," she replied honestly.

"Okay what about meeting someone and finding a starting point? Can you open yourself to explore someone who has qualities that you are interested in? Why can't you allow yourself to be open to this idea? What is stopping you?" he continued.

"Maybe it is an ego thing," she replied after a long thought. "My ego doesn't let me give myself away with out a fight. Perhaps I am worried about what other people will think of me if I share myself too easily, but perhaps it is just myself I am worried about disappointing."

"I don't see your friends as people who would pass judgement on you. How is yourself stopping you?" he asked.

"Well... I come to the same conclusion every time. I feel like when it's on it's on. Everything else is just a distraction. I have lots of opportunities to sleep with men, but maybe that's the problem. I isolate myself by being too selective. I have also been with some incredibly beautiful men who have set the bar really high," the girl confessed.

"What is it that you are looking for that you can't find?" he continued with his line of questioning.

"I want someone that I am deathly attracted to. Someone who I can't stop touching and someone who can't stop touching me. I want to be with someone who truly sees me. I want to be with someone who connects with me beyond skin," she sighed with partial exhaustion.

"Why does it have to be so special?" he asked.

She hesitated, but persisted with her truth talking, "Because I'm so special."

"I find it hard to believe that you have not met anyone else this year who has been able to open you up," he said softly.

"But I believe what we are sharing is really special," she said with silent tears streaming down her face.

"It seems like this hip problem is also about not being assertive with your sexual needs. Have you been satisfied in your past relationships?"

"Honestly? Not entirely," she said feeling embarrassed.

"Really? So maybe it is that you don't know how to ask for what you want," he said with a soft surprise.

"I know I don't act assertively for my sexual needs. I have tried in the past but it always becomes an issue. Just mentioning the topic can make men feel incompetent and defensive. I'm not saying that all of my past relationships have ben sexually unsatisfying. I have had really terrific sex with really beautiful men. But I have also been with men who have wanted to pleasure me but just didn't know how," the girl continued.

"Could it be that you don't know how to please yourself?" he asked with gentle persistence.

The girl laughed outright, "I don't think I will ever meet a man who can make love to me like I can. I can orgasm without even touching myself. I can wet a whole bed just by making love to the air around me. I even have a spirit who I have been making love to for years."

"Whoa maybe that's it! Maybe you have transcended the physical realm of sex and you need someone who can connect with you on a deeply spiritual level?!'" he said with a crescendo in his voice.

The girl's heart and hip exhaled deeply. This felt like the truth. The space they dug so deeply to get to had been exposed. It was a difficult place to reach both physically and emotionally.

The girl learnt that truth talking is fucking hard. It can feel embarrassing and it requires great courage. She felt exhausted but incredibly grateful. He had taken her as deep as he could. His line of questioning was persistent, raw and skilled.

"Wow," he smiled in the candlelight, "I've never heard of someone orgasming without touch before. I would love to see that."

The girl just laughed. What more could she say? They had come to separate places through their togetherness. They had fully exposed their most naked truths. There was nothing more to say. She rolled into his arms and fell asleep.

◆

Love

Love is bliss
Love is your natural state
It is not the sensual experience
It is not the opposite of pain
It is about being in tune and trusting yourself
Love is your birthright

◆

Story Telling

"Are you in love?" asked her Aussie classmate. They were sipping dandelion tea in the ashram's kitchen.

"Wow that's a good question. Let me think about that one," the girl paused to find the right words, "I guess I am trying to be realistic about this. I don't want to fall into delusions of lust. I share a really genuine connection with the Pomelo and the truth talking is unprecedented for me. His line of questioning reduces me to look at my truest self. I feel super raw and exposed but completely safe and turned on by it all."

As the story goes the girl has fallen back into the arms of the Pomelo. After spending a day apart they met haphazardly while they were both out on a restless walk. Their timing and their paths lead them directly to each other. She smiled the instant she saw him. They instantly fell into the dance of their dialogue.

"How is your heart?" she asked him.

"Yeah a bit sad today," he replied, "What about you?"

"Oh I've been restless all day thinking about you," she answered.

They continued talking all the way back to his bed. Instead of making love she read him the stories she has been writing about their romance. She was nervous at first, but his enthusiastic giggles and comments made her feel confident to continue.

"Wow I've never had that before!" he smiled. "It's a really neat experience to hear you write about our experience. It's really good! I was hanging on the edge of my seat to see what was going to happen next and I have already lived it!"

The girl was delighted. He smothered her in positive feedback and she felt charged.

"Are these edited pages?" the Pomelo asked.

"No no," she replied honestly, "this is just my journal in the third person. It is me just hammering out my life into words."

"Wow that's really amazing that you can just do that," he said impressed.

"Well I am sure it has something to do with travelling with a typewriter for seven years. You simply can't edit when you type so you have no choice but to get it right the first time," the girl replied.

"Do you ever get writers block?" he asked.

"No I don't really believe in it. I just write the truth and the truth is everywhere. I can never run out of the truth. I believe if someone gets stuck writing they should simply begin by describing the scene around them," she replied.

To demonstrate this the girl will begin to colour this page with her current surroundings...

She is sitting in her favourite resort on the beach. It is decorated with zebra print pillows, black sofas and soft fabrics. They serve creamy thick cold yogurt (her favourite breakfast food) and they even sprinkle roasted nuts and muesli on it. She can hear lazy hammers in the background getting ready for the busy season. She can also hear a light jazz soundtrack playing softly in the back ground. It is melting into the sounds of the waves that are lazily rolling into shore.

Everything in this moment feels peaceful and dream like. Even the breeze feels like it is on holidays, just gently brushing her skin.

◆

Existence

You already have a valid purpose to be here.
Relax and enjoy.

◆

The Dyno

"You are what we call a dyno," laughed the Pomelo.

"A dyno?" the girl asked sounding confused.

"Yeah you're like dynamite. You keep exploding, but in the most positive way. How many was that anyways? 10? 20?" He is referring to the number of orgasms she just had.

She started giggling hysterically. She has no clue how many times she exploded.

"In all my years..." he continued, "I've never seen that! That was definitely worth breaking my celibacy."

In all her years the girl has never had such incredible sex! She was so amazed that as she was walking home this morning she caught herself speaking out loud, "I have never experienced this phenomenon before. The sex is done when I am! It's a whole new playing field. A whole new world."

Without breaking into the Aladdin theme song the girl grounded herself into reality. This genie in a bottle wish come true is going to burst in three days. He is leaving for his homeland. They will be saying goodbye. Maybe forever...maybe not?

She is utterly conscious of her attachment to the Pomelo. The two are happy to be craving one another. It is a mutual connection. They have been comfortable to get naked on every possible level. She has exposed more of her true self to this man than anyone has seen of her in...maybe ever? There is nothing that she is hiding from him. He has peeled her open on every level imaginable. Her favourite part is their eye contact.

"What do you see?" she asked him as they were locked in eye contact.

"I see a lot of life," he started. "Your eyes are really joyful looking. You are really balanced. I don't see any sadness. Your eyes almost look doe'e.'"

"Like a baby dear?" she giggled.

"Yes it's sweet," he replied. "I also see something devilish. It is not devilish so much as it is curious. Like a little kid who is peering out playfully. What do you see?"

"Hmmm," she smiled and looked into his clear blue eyes, "well your right eye is razor sharp. It is ultra clear and alive. It is almost piercing. I think the right eye holds our intelligence, our knowledge. You have so much confidence in your right eye. Your left eye is sweet. It is where your love lives. It is a little sad and afraid, but it is mostly gentle and sweet. It feels humbled."

He admits to feeling sadness in this area. It is an honest indication of where he is at. When she looked into his left eye she felt like crawling inside of it and cradling it. She wants to hug this man's soul and let him exhale into utter peace. She also knows that he has to be able to let her in.

◆

Pure Gold

"Wow your eyes are full of prana," smiled the Pomelo.

"What is prana? Life force?" she asked half knowing.

"Yeah it is shakti," he said. "It is the life force that makes you shiny and bright. It's like the glow you get after a good yoga class."

"Shakti," she smirked, "yer full of shakti."

They both laughed and settled in for breakfast.

The girl pulled out her laptop to capture their scene. They are lounging in her favourite new hang. It is a stylish heaven that is littered with low black sofas and zebra print pillows. It feels as though they could be anywhere. The resort is fancy enough to be in Miami, but the beach is uncluttered and...

"Can you give me a word to describe this beach?" she pauses mid sentence.

"Hmmmm one word?" he asks. "That's a hard question."

The two have moved from their table to the chaise lounges.

"I don't know if I could do it in a word," he responds.

"Do it in three then," she persists.

"Definitely lazy. Peaceful, lazy, beautiful. Is there some sort of word that comprises all three of those?"

"We could make up a word. My friend made a word for exhausted and exhilarated. It was exhilarhausted," she offered.

He just shrugs, "There is probably a reason that hasn't caught on yet. This beach is kind of lazy like a lake. Even the water feels lake like. It looks lake like too."

"That's how I feel!" she exclaims. "It's kind of like being at the cottage. It's flat like the prairies."

The Pomelo pulls his cap down over his eyes and she sits up to continue writing the moment into a memory. They talked briefly over breakfast about her coming to his home in New Zealand. He sprinkled temptations throughout their meal. Describing his friends and the beauty of the landscape. Inviting her to come and teach yoga with him, maybe even learning Kahuna massage.

She is open to the idea, but feels he needs to go home and get settled before any serious plans are made. It is so easy to dream when you are living in one. She wants him to have his space and his time to heal. She wants to honour his needs. They will make no promises to each other. They will simply scatter seeds and see what grows.

"My whole family is in Disney World right now," the girl says out loud. "My mom really wanted my nieces to see it before they get too old. I am the only one missing out."

"Well you're not missing a thing," he says coyly. "You were on your own wet and wild ride last night."

She breaks into laughter, mostly because it's true! The girl was a puddle of sweat by the time they pulled away from each other.

"See this is the shit I gotta write down," she says as punches these words into her story.

"Yup," he smiles, "this is pure gold."

◆

THE INFINITE
We are the Infinite.
We are not separate from the Universe.
Everything has contributed to our existence.
Everything is connected.

◆

The Wet 'n' Wild Ride

"The woman came to clean my room today," smiled the Pomelo before they entered their nest. "You are going to die when you see the sheets she put on my bed."

When he opened the door the girl exploded with laughter. Her wet and wild ride was covered with images of Walt Disney characters.

"Shut up!" she shouted with wide eyes. "No way. As if! That is way too funny. I'm really not missing out on a thing! Man the universe is brilliant. What a killer sense of humour!!"

They fell into slumber on the Disney parade and it wasn't until morning that she got a ticket for another wild ride. She started off by practicing her walking massage on him. It is a tantra technique that she is learning at school. She was working his body with her toes and feet and when he rolled over from back to front he let out a smile for the scene. She was naked and hanging from the rafters. She was using the bars above the bed to balance her dance on his body.

When she was done her routine she bent down to kiss his feet. She loves kissing this man's body. She can't get enough of it. She worked her way from his toes to his earlobes, then from his earlobes to his wrists. Sucking the whole length of his biceps that are covered in tribal tattoos. She paused to nibble on the soft spots in the belly of his elbows. His skin tastes smooth and sweet. She even likes the way her lips feel around his ankles. She lost herself in the pleasure of pleasing this god.

He is so good at returning the favour. His kisses feel like feathers brushing across her bare skin. His touch is light and sweet and drives her crazy with desire. When he touches her like air it pulls her whole body into focusing on his fingertips. It creates a complete focus of energy that curls her lips and her toes. Once again he released her into a pool of pleasure. Even as she writes this her body feels floppy and fabulous.

"Is there a network of guys like you floating around? Like a Taoist tantric support group?" she asked over lunch.

"No," he laughed, "I don't think so."

"Shit," she muttered honestly. "I am really screwed now aren't I? I thought I had the bar set high before, but you have changed the whole playing field. How am I ever going to find someone to top this? I may just have to take myself out of the game."

The Pomelo laughed and said, "Well maybe now that you know this exists you can start to attract other men who are practicing the same way of life."

"Hmmmm maybe...," she trailed off.

She is hesitant to start hoping for anything. She knows it leads to hopelessness. She has no interest in returning to a self that is seeking. She wonders how easy it will be.

Looking for something is one thing, but longing for something is just as disruptive. She feels that she will miss this man the minute they part ways. They have less than three days together. He will be heading home and she will be sad to see him go.

"My dad makes the best eggnog in the world," she said drifting to thoughts of being home for the holidays. "It takes him two days to make it and it is so delicious. It is famous for knocking you on your ass with one glass."

"Oh my I love egg nog," he replied. "Do you think he would give up the recipe?"

"Oh for sure! No problem," the girl replied.

"Well then maybe that can be my Christmas gift," he suggested.

"Okay! I love the idea of sending you something, but I like the idea of you coming over for dinner even more. My mom makes the best trifle..." she continued to tempt him.

"Oh wow," he smiled, "maybe I will have to marry you."

The girl's heart did a mini backflip, but her lips stayed closed. What she wanted to say was, 'is that a proposal?' but she kept quiet.

The girl wants the Pomelo to go home a free man. She wants to honour everything he has shared with her (the need to spend more time learning to love his mother and the need for more time to heal from his past relationship). He has been very clear and honest with her. She does not want to become an idealistic fool. She has a habit of falling into storybook romance. Perhaps it is because she is writing one.

She has never thought she would have a predictable courting. She is at a place in her life where she could easily make a spontaneous commitment to the right partner. She is also aware that their paths need to be plotting the same course. She doesn't think sacrifice works in the long run. Compromises yes, sacrifices no. She will let this man flow into his natural pace and she will see if they end up walking beside each other.

For now she will simply enjoy what little time they have together. She feels so blessed that she even got a taste of this man. He is so beautiful and sexy. She loves having him as a reflection. He probes her to explore new depths of her being. He is helping her dissolve barriers to her personal truth. He has given her affirmation for her selectiveness in love. She feels validated for being disinterested with mediocre affairs. He has definitely been worth the wait.

◆

True Romance?

"In all the years I have had on this earth," he began, "I have never fallen for someone as quickly as you, never. I could not resist you. You are sexy, intelligent, hilarious, beautiful…it's like check check check," he said crossing off an imaginary list. He was trying to make her feel better. She had fallen into silence since dinner.

They were sitting outside in the warm evening air. The night was clear, but the girl's heart was cloudy. They had a miscommunication that felt like a brick of sadness hitting her in the face. The girl had heard him say that it was easy to be so honest with her because 'this' wasn't a real relationship. She heard that things would be different between them if they were truly laying a foundation for a real future together.

Was this not real? Had she been completely delusional about this whole affair? She was certain she felt complete connections in moments with this man. She knows he has been honest about his recent break up, but did they not share moments of mutual merging? Had she been selfishly unaware? She felt foolish and hurt.

They were now talking about what she heard and what he said.

"No no no," he started, "of course I have felt deep feelings for you. Of course this connection is real. That is why it has been so difficult for me. I was just trying to say that there are things about me that need to change before I can lay a proper path for a future. It has been difficult in moments to give you a hundred percent of myself because I am not a hundred percent myself."

"Hmmmm," she reflected with some clarity beginning to flow, "these are very wise words. I can't ask for more than what you are capable of giving me. So I guess it is up to me to enjoy what I can get."

She crawled across their separateness and curled into his lap. She sighed and held him. She knows the Pomelo is not going to be around much longer and she does not want to dwell in any unnecessary tension. She would rather feel close to him while he is here. Just touching his body makes her body feel warm and alive.

She is grateful they opened their dialogue to let the truth continue to flow. Zahira has a pattern of falling into silence when she is disappointed. It is her way of processing before reacting. She is learning to move through her silence into truth talking. It is hard but always brings her closer to the Pomelo. She imagines it is like this for any relationship.

◆

Alchemical Yoga

"I feel like I just took three caps of ecstasy," the girl said as her legs wobbled her through the dark. She was walking back to the ashram after a three hour yoga class. She had stretched every muscle of her body into a relaxed posture. Deep breathing and relaxation, this is the tantra trick.

The girl flopped onto her Pomelo who was patiently awaiting her return.

"Oh my god!" he said. "Your heart is racing like a little rabbit being chased by a dog. Your skin is on fire! Are you okay?"

The girl could hardly respond. She was beyond okay. She had moved through a full body orgasm while in Shivasana (corpse pose). She had brought her attention to her body one part at a time. It started in her loins and worked it's way outwards and upwards. She felt her arms, wrists, palms and fingertips grow stimulated just by thinking about them. Her earlobes, her cheeks, her teeth, her hair. Everything was humming with Prana, a life force that was tickling her into an aroused state. When her focus finally reached her toes her entire being was humming.

The girl could barely respond to the Pomelo's concern. She had landed on his chest and the contact of their bodies doubled her self-induced euphoria. The tingling sensation that was coursing through her body was now being received and returned by a man. It became cyclical. She sighed deeply into his heartbeat.

"I think you should have a shower," he said more than once, "you are burning up."

He was oddly worried about her. Probably because she could not fully express her bliss. She looked like she was high on drugs; delirious, despondent and blubbering without body control. Her muscles had transformed into pomelo jello.

Her hunger for this man was trumped by her hunger for food. She was beyond starving and she could feel subtle shaking begging for nutrients. She found the strength to roll out of bed and then rolled back in it with a plate of food from the ashram's kitchen. They were in for the evening. Once again the elements were plotting their course. The rain outside was begging them to curl into comfort.

"Will you work on my hip a little bit?" she asked in a blubbery voice.

"Of course," he said without hesitation.

He churned her body into butter. He has the ability to access a part so deeply inside of her it brings her into spastic fits of pain and tears. She was whimpering like a child.

"I noticed in yoga that you cannot put your hands in prayer position behind your back," he said.

"I knew you were going to notice that. I knew it!" she cheered. "Thanks for bringing it up. I was going to ask you about it. What is blocking me?"

"Well the shoulders are connected to the hip," he said as he started to work on her upper body. "You are having difficulties opening up. You are protecting yourself from something. What is it?"

"Hmmm..." she sighed, "I don't know. Let me think."

"It is a vulnerability thing. Are you afraid to be vulnerable? It is also connected to your heart. Your heart isn't fully open," he remarked.

The girl laughed at this. *Impossible,* she thought. She feels she has opened her heart as wide as it will go. "I don't think it could be that. If I have spaces in my heart that are closed then I am completely unaware of them," she said.

"Yes exactly," he replied, "I am not saying you aren't open, I am saying that you are not *completely* open. I can't give you answers. I can only make suggestions. I can only read what your body is telling me. You need to come to your own conclusions."

"I just don't see my heart being closed," she repeated.

"Well it can also be a fear of responsibility. You have a slight slope in your shoulders so things just tend to roll off of you. You do however have the strength to support it," the Pomelo observed.

The girl laughed out loud, "Oh that one is a no brainer. I totally shrug off responsibility. I can own up to that one no problemo! I just can't see where my heart could be closed."

"Well what about blockages you have in love? Are you able to fully express what you want? Are you always finding something wrong in men? Are you always wanting more than they can give you?" he probed.

"Yes," she said, "it's true. I am always wanting more and I also seem to want what I can't have."

Zahira cannot deny this on any level. She has spent many years isolating herself from love. Getting into her space was like trying to get into Fort Knox. Before her last lover she spent half a decade alone. She had a few fleeting romances, but for five years she met no one who could win the key to her heart. She grew exceptionally lonely.

When she did finally open herself up to her last love she knew from the start it was destined to fail. He was eleven years younger than her and she always felt they would eventually grow their separate ways. He tried convincing her otherwise. She had tried more than once to leave him but always fell back into his incredible beauty. He loved her unconditionally, she loved him with all of her heart.

When they did part ways it was her doing. The final push being a pregnancy scare. Her immediate reaction to a condom falling off was joy, his was total fear. It was a clear indication that they would never be able to walk at the same pace. He would always be trying to catch up with her and she would always be waiting.

She spent a long time regretting her choice. She was angry with herself for being so selfish, wishing she could take back her decision, wondering why love wasn't enough. *How could she possibly want more than love?* This is perhaps what her Pomelo is picking up on. She closed her heart on a man she truly loved. She chose motherhood over him. A decision that has left her with neither love nor a child. Even now, a year later, this truth saddens her.

"What does your body say?" she asked when he was finally done.

"I don't know," he laughed, "you tell me."

"Hmmmm," she cooed as she began to smooth her thumb across his forehead, "let me see..."

She paused for a while. It is easier for the girl to hear truths about herself than it is to speak truths about other people, at least her own interpretations of the truth. She feels like this man is full of opportunity to keep pushing past layers of these fears, so she began, "Sometimes I see a rigidity in your being, one that won't let you be fully open and free, one that is playing defence for your heart."

"Mmmm hmmmmm," he said with closed lips and closed eyes.

"I see that these sexy and strong muscles were built as a protective armour, a shield from feeling vulnerable. I think they are shielding a little boy inside who is just wants to be loved," the girl continued.

"Mmmm hmmm," he said in an encouraging tone.

So she continued, "I see the lines on your forehead that won't let you have complete faith in yourself and your dreams. They stop you from following through. Keeping your ideal life at bay."

"Mmmm hmmmm," he hummed again.

"I also see a spirit that needs to be acknowledged. I think you have pursued so many spiritual practices with out even connecting or acknowledging your spirit. Maybe you need to introduce yourself. Maybe you need a daily practice that opens the lines of communication between you and your spirit. Maybe it is a prayer, maybe it is just giving thanks," she concluded.

"Wow you are good at this," he said with his eyes still closed.

He had nestled his head in between her thighs, a position that felt safe and comfortable for them both. He is open to his own truths just as she is. It is a recipe for growth. It is a new way of building a relationship for the girl. It feels true and honest and sometimes scary as hell.

◆

Tantra

Be honest with yourself.
Be honest with the world around you.
When you are in harmony with yourself,
you are in harmony with the cosmos.

◆

Little Girl Blues

The girl lets out an exhausted and contented sigh. Her hair is still wet from her shower and her bare toes are resting in the sand. She is back at the black lounge, the one that serves her ice-cold yogurt with toasted nuts. She pulls her hair up off of the nape of her neck and lets out a little groan. The ocean breeze is perfectly euphoric and she has a lot of news to report. Where to begin? By eating the yogurt that was just delivered.

"Okay," she exhales. She now has a bit more energy to hammer this out. It has been a few days since her last entry and a lot has happened....

Rewind two days:

"So why do you think my heart is not fully open?" the girl asked the Pomelo again over breakfast.

"It is up to you to figure it out," he replied. "I can only suggest things. It is up to you to ask yourself and to listen closely for the answer."

"Oh come on," she pleaded, "I know you know and I really don't. I am really unaware of closures in my heart."

"Well what is it that you really want?" he asked.

"I don't know," she said feeling unsure. "True love I guess. Someone to start a family with."

He smiled encouragingly, "Okay and what is stopping you from getting it?"

"Hmmm...I think I have too high of standards. I suppose I am waiting for the perfect man. I suppose I will be waiting forever," she sighed.

"Where does the idea of a perfect man come from?" he asked.

"Shit I don't know. My ego?" she questioned.

"Well yes that can be part of it, but it is more of an idealistic view point than an egotistical one. Do you idealize your father?" he asked.

"Oh man you hit the nail on the head there. I've always said my dad has ruined all men for me. I am so crazy about my father," she said with surprise in her voice.

The girl has always admired her dad. He is her favourite person on the planet. They share such a special bond, an unspoken and spoken adoration for each other. He has been her rock in this lifetime, an absolute solid foundation for her personal freedom. His love has allowed her to go out and explore the world with out fear.

She never assumed her love for her dad could potentially stop her from falling into a long lasting relationship. She never made the subconscious connection between leaving men for being less than perfect to viewing her father as exactly that.

"So perhaps making that connection is enough to break it?" she asked after long thought.

"Yes. It may also require having a conversation with your dad. Maybe you need to tell him directly that he can't always play the leading role in your life. It would be hard but maybe necessary," he said.

"No no," she laughed, "I could easily talk to my dad about this. He would most likely just laugh and love me more. He really is the best. This is super interesting for me. I am learning so much. What else do you see? What else is stopping me from finding true love?"

"Well what about the role playing that you do?" he challenged.

"Role playing?" she asked. "What are you talking about?"

"Well sometimes in moments of intimacy you slip into the voice of a young child. Your voice changes and so does the connection," he replied. "Don't get me wrong, it is very sweet and playful and innocent, but where does the woman go?"

"Oh," she said feeling hurt.

It hurt because it's true. The girl can be very childlike in romance. She's always enjoyed that side of herself. She loves when she can find a partner who brings out the little girl in her.

"I know," he continued sensing her disappointment, "I used to do the same thing. My ex pointed it out to me. She said that it was unhealthy and was preventing me from connecting from my deepest level of intimacy. It can be a bit of a defence mechanism."

She grew quiet. The little girl inside the girl sat with her arms crossed and a scowl on her face. How dare this man make such wild and unwarranted accusations? How dare he?! She had so much freedom to play with her last lover. He brought out her most hyperactive and playful self. This was one of the reasons she loved him so much.

What she wanted to say was 'Wow! Your last girlfriend sounds like a real bitch,' but she kept her mouth shut. She was not willing to react just yet. She needed more time to process.

"I know it is hard to hear something like this. You think that something about you is good and wonderful and then you hear that it is something that needs to be addressed. It is not easy," he offered kindly.

"Yeah," she said, "but there also has to be a balance there. I can't imagine not being playful and silly with a lover. I don't want to dissolve that completely. I usually gage how close I am with a person by how easily they get to see that side of me. I don't want to lose that side of myself."

"I am not saying you have to lose it. I am saying it is important to acknowledge it and integrate it into your being as a woman. A woman who is not afraid to speak for what she truly desires. A woman who is not hiding behind a child in love. A woman who is able to connect on a deep level of love and intimacy. Don't worry you can still be silly, but maybe you need to start letting the woman in you do the talking in the bedroom," he suggested.

The girl felt the truth in this statement. It made her want to cry. She felt it on a very subtle level of her being. She was slowly letting go of her anger. She was beginning to see that while this may have been her favourite part about her last lover, it was also perhaps the reason she left him.

Her last lover was a delightful and delicious playmate. From the moment they met they laughed. Their time together was always light and easy. The girl fell madly in love with him, but apart from wanting a child there was always *something else* missing for her. It was something she could never quite put her finger on. It was something she couldn't even vocalize and when she tried she would call it an 'immutable essence.' She felt crazy for wanting something she couldn't even describe!

Choosing motherhood was a clear way out of this relationship, but to be transparent it was the nagging sensation of *wanting more* that tortured the girl. The love was there, but *something was missing.* She realizes now that a deeper level of intimacy is what was lacking. She realizes now how much responsibility *she* must take for this.

"Wow," she said out loud. She could not get up from the table. She had her head in in hands. She felt tears coming but nothing surfaced, "Just give me a minute."

The little girl inside of her was feeling sad and hurt. She was wounded and spiteful. She excused herself to the washroom to let the process begin. She knows herself well enough to know that the things she meets with resistance are the things she needs to address. She understands that only the truth can sting like this. She would stay quiet for the moment. She would not speak until she regained a calm and clear understanding of these new changes that were already underway.

Once the truth is spoken, there is no going back.

◆

Truth

Truth resonates in the body.
Sometimes it can feel like a sting.
Sometimes it can feel like flutters.
Sometimes it can feel utterly peaceful,
like a quiet knowing.

◆

Zahira

The two lovers were coiled together after yoga. The girl's tension had melted into gratitude.

"Thank you," she whispered in his ear, "thank you for making my body so happy...oh wait!" She caught herself red handed, she was speaking in her soft cooing voice, "Wait! Let me use my woman voice!"

As soon as she shifted gears she felt a new confidence and satisfaction within herself. It felt hard at first. It was a very subtle feeling of confidence that was lacking, one that she was unaware of. She really had been 'hiding' behind this little girl voice. The woman in her had been taking cover behind the child who was more accustomed to freedom of expression.

"Wow," she smiled, "I can see how this new way of approaching intimacy is going to make me a hell of a lot sexier!"

The girl had been given a new piece of her personal puzzle. She was grateful to be fine tuning her existence.

"Maybe I need to stop writing stories about a girl," she exclaimed over dinner.

She was surprised she said it. She has been writing from the perspective of the girl for almost a decade. She has always liked the attainability of the character, as in '*if the girl can do it anyone can*.'

"Yeah I was thinking the same thing," the Pomelo said. "Maybe your stories need to be about the woman."

"Yeah, but it just doesn't have the same ring," she said.

She paused for a moment and then it was clear. Her new persona will be the one that was gifted to her during her stay at Osho's ashram. During her stay she was given her Sannyasin name. It is a name that echoes deep within her being. It is a name that makes her feel like the desert wind. It is the name she knows as Zahira.

And just like that (in this moment!) sitting in the black lounge with the ocean breeze filtering all around her, the girl makes an executive decision.

The girl becomes the woman known as Zahira.

◆

SANNYASIN

"The Sannyas movement simply means
the movement of the seekers of truth,"
– OSHO

◆

Postcard Dreams

She awoke to a soft hand barely brushing the surface of her skin. It traced its way gently down the length of her body. She opened her eyes and saw his outline standing beside the bed. The room was dark and quiet. His presence was like a dream.

"Is it time?" she asked still dreaming.

"It's time," he whispered.

She sat up and hugged him with all of her heart. It felt as though they were scarcely touching. He was like warm air and she was suspended by their love. They were saying goodbye. It was four in the morning and he was leaving to catch his train to Mumbai. This would be their last hug.

As she writes this Zahira begins to cry. She is surprised by the tears. She has felt nothing but gratitude and joy since he left her in bed this morning. She has been smiling at her amazing fortune, giving thanks for a love affair that has brought new definition to her being. The tears silently rolling down her cheeks are genuine. She will miss the passion and pleasure this man brought her. They are storybook material.

They had spent their last day together at Cola beach. It was a picture perfect secluded beach dotted with white Arabian-style tents. The day felt like a postcard. She found herself inhaling certain moments, as though taking a deep breath of her surroundings would store them in her lungs and heart forever. She was a walking mental camera locking the scene into place.

When the sun began to set they strolled to a deserted corner of the beach. They climbed along the rocks and sat quietly by each other's side. She was giving thanks to the elements for this man and this moment. She was feeling waves of disbelief for her incredible fortune. The whole scene was one that she could never have imagined in a more beautiful light. It was beyond surreal. It felt like the gods had reserved this place and time just for the two of them. It felt like everything surrounding them had been etched in their hearts before the moment existed, as though they placed an order for perfection and it was now being delivered with ideal timing.

They made love to the setting sun, the soothing waves, the warm air, the green jungle and each other. Zahira felt every little cell in her body break into a smile, a smile that turned the girl into a woman. Even her soul was smiling, smiling because she was brave enough to follow her heart to India alone. It was smiling at the Universe for guiding her to such incredible romance. She was brave enough to look deeply at herself and her reward is a man who has taken her further in.

As Zahira sits and recalls this moment she feels every smiling cell has relaxed into exhaustion. Not only did they make love in the morning and on the beach, but they went for round three after dinner. The final round seemed to last forever. This man's ability to honour the Goddess and Zahira's ability to embrace it made for endless waves of hot sweaty sex. Neither one seemed to quit. They just kept rolling into new positions. Her whole body flexed with ecstasy. She has been laid to rest.

"How many was that?!" he laughed.

"I have no idea," she said honestly. They had been making love for hours.

"Oh come one, can you give me a ball park? Just for my personal records?" he asked.

"Hmmm," she thought carefully. She started to count on her fingers. "At least seven," was her final answer.

They both laughed and rolled into each other's arms for their final sleep. Zahira passed out instantly. The smile on her face faded into her dreams. It was her last chance to hear this man's strong and steady heart beat. It was a sound that made her feel comfortable as both a woman and a child.

She wonders where he is in this moment. Is he staring out the window of the train awake with the dream they have shared or is he sleeping soundly? She will always feel thankful for the Pomelo. He has been an amazing catalyst in her personal transformation. She will embrace the woman she has become through his touch and his talents. She will be forever grateful.

She has grown from the girl in to the woman known as Zahira.

It is time.

PART 2

G U R U
(Gee You Are You)

◆

Fossilized Culture

"How have you been?" asked Bhagavan.

"Well that's a big question," sighed Zahira.

She was sitting in Bhagavan's home watching the ceiling fan and sunlight create a strobe-like effect across his face. The result was quite ethereal, as though she were sitting in a super 8mm film strip. She was grateful for a chance to talk with him.

"I have recently experienced some pretty powerful emotions in every direction. There are some incredibly intense energies floating around the ashram right now. I don't want to get into details, but I feel like I am loosing some balance here. I am also feeling confused about some of your teachings. I keep having to remind myself that I am the master of my own existence," Zahira began.

"Ah yes this is one thing I want to talk to you about, the word master. I want to talk to you about these things; one the idea of master and two the fossilized culture I feel you are stuck in," replied Bhagavan.

"Okay," Zahira smiled. She was feeling a bit nervous, wondering if he was going to pull the rug right out from underneath her. She crossed her fingers behind her back.

"A master is not someone who gets to the top of the mountain and then sits there. A master does not reach any end. A master is like two dogs engaged in a fight," he used his hands to create an image of the dogs rolling as a single unit. "They are locked into complete awareness of the moment."

"So the master is one who is engaged for life. One who is locked into a constant state of awareness and can roll without fear through existence," she reiterated.

"Yes. Now I have said before that you have no neurosis," Bhagavan continued. "This is something I never say. You are strong and clear, but I feel you are stuck in an old culture. If we can shift you out of this culture we can move you to the next level. This is what I want to bring to your attention."

"Okay great," Zahira smiled. So far she liked what she heard. She uncrossed her fingers.

"I don't know why you are stuck here, but you are stuck in a culture that is fossilized. It no longer exists. It is the Mother Goddess culture. This culture is a misrepresentation of the truth," he explained.

He was speaking about the culture that the feminists and the hippies had introduced into the West. These cultures brought meditation and yoga into western society as a social response. Yoga was used as a way of expressing freedom and femininity. To express love not war. To express the Goddess in a society that was dominated by one male God. These approaches were beneficial for the time, but according to her teacher were not based on correct translations of the spiritual sciences as written in the Vedas.

"Your interpretations of spirit are misconstrued," Bhagavan continued. "You are not allowing yourself to see more than the subject. Your experience is subjective not analyzed. You are seeing through the senses rather than the higher senses. Before intuition we have to understand the different dimensions. It is important to understand the different dimensions so you can understand where the Goddess is, the true dimension of the goddess rather than the idea of the Goddess."

Zahira has had many moments in her life where she has connected with herself as a divine being, where she has felt the presence of spirit in many forms. Where she has touched, danced and made love with these entities. She hears her teacher saying that her connections with spirit are not being correctly interpreted. He sees them as being bio levels of experience. He was trying to tell her that her experiences with spirit and her spiritual self needed a closer inspection.

"The spectrum of consciousness, what you call spirits, angels, etc, is separated by galactic time and galactic space. The experiences are like the fish and the turtle. The fish cannot leave the ocean to talk to the turtle. Only after we let go of karma can we cross galactic time and space. Only when we die," he continued.

He was saying that she has completely misunderstood her own experiences. That she could not possibly connect with spirits because they exist in a different realm. That there was no way to cross over into that realm in this lifetime.

"So if I understand you correctly there is no way to connect with spirit in this lifetime? That only through fulfilling our karma in death we can pass through the spiritual realm?" Zahira asked.

"The spirit is not an entity. It is a spectrum of consciousness rather than a being. Why do you want to connect to a spirit rather than the spectrum of consciousness itself? Why not aspire to move through the entire spectrum to be united with the Brahman?" he asked

Zahira asked about the work that she has done with her shaman Maestro Flores. He has a healing centre called Mayantuyacu in the Peruvian Amazon. He works directly with the spirits of the plants to learn their healing properties. He works as a healer in both the physical and spiritual realms. He is an Ashaninka Ayahuasquero who has knowledge from the Shipibo tribe. The Shipibo tribe are considered by some to be the Oxford University of shamanism. This is because they have a well-preserved knowledge of the plants.

"The shamans and First Nations people are missing links of information. Their knowledge has not been passed down through a text. It has been transferred through an oral tradition. The real truth has been lost in translation. The shaman is missing links. He is talking to galactic space and time and he is personalizing everything to his immediate environment. Healing is the work of the person not the healer. The healing comes from within. A tantric has to acknowledge this," replied Bhagavan.

Zahira agrees that healing comes from within (this is brilliant truth) but she is hesitant to believe *everything* Bhagavan says. The fact that he was telling her that all shamans and First Nations people are missing links was posting red flags in her ability to trust him.

"So are you saying I have to let go of everything I have experienced up until now?" she asked.

"You can enhance the work you have done until now by changing your perception of it. What I am saying is to look deeper into it and re-organize the perceptions from a deeper inside. Fine tune yourself to get a clear perspective on every level; intellect, intuition, awareness and external. All of these levels are to be taken into perspective," he replied.

"Okay," she said willing to be open, "I will do this, but you have to tell me how."

"Remove the blocks. You are sitting in a fossilized culture and not accepting the higher dimensions. The newer culture is the culture of Brahman. The highest spectrum of consciousness is what I am talking about," he replied

"How do I remove the blocks?" she asked still feeling confused.

"Analyze how you perceive spirit. How do you see it? Why did you see it that way? Could I have produced the feeling of spirit?" was his response.

"Okay I can do that," she said honestly.

Zahira is open to the challenge. She is not afraid to question herself on any level.

◆

BRAHMAN

Heaven

Supreme universal spirit.

Liberation is realizing our true selves as Brahman.

◆

HOW DO YOU SEE SPIRIT?

WHY DO YOU SEE IT THAT WAY?

COULD YOU BE PRODUCING THE FEELING OF SPIRIT?

These questions have been running through Zahira's head all day and night. It is starting to exhaust her. Has her entire experience with spirit been a product of her imagination? She is certain she danced with her grandfather the day he passed away. She is certain her hands have been moved by high spirit in moments of deep healing meditations. She has had many ayahuasca experiences where she has worked as a healer in the spirit realm. And what about the god she has made love to? Is he also just a product of her imagination? Is he just an idea that she created to get her through so many lonely nights?

These questions are filling every level of her being with doubt. It is not an emotion she is used to, not when it comes to trusting others and *especially* not when it comes to trusting herself. To be clear, Zahira is unclear. She is unclear about *everything* in this moment. She has already paid for another month of studies at the ashram, but she is no longer sure she wants to stay. Not only are the teachings creating a cloud of confusion for her, but the new wave of students are also adding a set of challenges.

The population of the yoga school has tripled in size but the small kitchen has not grown. The new students are frustrated. The required reading is not available and the schedule isn't either. There are people who are already complaining about all the things that Zahira has politely overlooked. She is more interested in adapting to her environments than trying to change them. The other students however are upset that the kitchen is so dirty, the food is terrible, the lectures keep getting cancelled and the required readings are not available.

Many of the new students have sought Zahira out as a confidant. There is a lot of confusion and disappointment in the air. Some students have even left in the middle of the night to avoid confrontation. Zahira is trying to stay neutral. She is trying to stick to her original plan.

She would prefer to sink into the background and remain invisible.

◆

Do not follow anyone else.
Relax into self,
this will bring you great harmony.

◆

Ashdrama

"I know you don't want to be involved with the politics of the ashram," said the Occultist, "but there is stuff going on around here and I think you should know about it."

"Alright," replied Zahira. She braced herself for the worst and crossed her fingers behind her back. She is already on shaky ground and was not looking forward to more shifting. She really likes the Occultist, but she also knows he is a bit of a drama king.

"As you know the Dark Wizard is leaving due to family problems. He has paid for a year and he has been here for three weeks. He has asked for a partial refund and it does not look like he is going to get it. The Dark Wizard is seriously pissed and if he doesn't get his money he is going to do something about it. He has very powerful friends in the dark realms of black magic and trust me, you don't want to be around here if he leaves unhappy. I know this for a fact. Shit is going to get really ugly really fast," the Occultist warned her.

Zahira could hardly believe her ears. *What the fuck?* She felt like she was caught in a twisted new age version of Melrose Place. She had already been feeling uncertain about her teacher and his teachings, but now she was dealing with confused communal chaos. She couldn't decide how to respond to this news. Zahira was speechless. She uncrossed her fingers and let out a sigh. She felt tired and ready for a change.

◆

Candy Island

"So um, have you thought about whether you are staying at the ashram or not?" asked the Pomelo over a Skype date.

"Yeah I'm feeling a bit confused. There is a lot of shit going on around here. I have already received my 200 hour teaching certificate, but I've also paid for another month. I was thinking of going for a 500 hour teaching certificate, but I'm not so sure anymore. Part of me wants to bolt and the other part of me is still really enjoying the ocean and the asana series," replied Zahira.

"Yeah right," he said slowly, "because I was going to invite you to come and spend some time with me in New Zealand. Seeing as how you are already half way around the world... maybe you could come and hang out with me?"

"Really?!?" Zahira's toes instantly started to twitch.

"Yeah. It may be my last summer here for a while and it would be great to have you. I've got some friends here who I know you would really love and even if I am working you can spend some time on the beach," he tempted.

Zahira was feeling warm throughout her whole body. Warm, tingly and giddy. She liked this idea a lot.

"So what are you thinking?" she asked. "How long would be a good time to come for?"

"Well I was thinking at least a month would be a good start," he answered.

A whole month?! Wow! Zahira's toes were fluttering like she was swimming to candy island.

"Ooh," she cooed, "I really like this idea."

"When were you heading back to Winnipeg?" he asked.

"I have a plane ticket that gets me back to Winnipeg for Christmas," Zahira replied.

"Well let's start looking for flights," he said sounding pleased.

"Wow... so this means I will have to quit my job," Zahira replied feeling somewhat excited and terrified by this idea.

"Why don't you ask for an extension of absence instead?" suggested the Pomelo.

"Hmmm...I don't know if I can push it any further. I guess I could try," Zahira said pondering this idea.

"Why don't we get you here for New Years Eve? We are having a big dock party and everyone is going to take turns DJ-ing. I know you would really like that," he said tempting her even more.

"Alright! Well then that gives me a bit more time in India!" Zahira said still processing this new opportunity.

"Will you stay at the ashram?" asked the Pomelo.

"I don't know. Let's see what happens!" she said feeling giddy about this new flow.

Zahira was bubbling with excitement. The Pomelo was asking her to come and spend new years with him and his friends. She felt a joyful shock flowing through her body like a warm electrical current.

"It's a big decision. Think about it," he said.

"Think about what?" Zahira laughed, "I'm in!"

◆

Zahira Hearts her Parents

"So I've got some news," Zahira said as casually as she could.

"Oh," replied her mom, "what is it?"

"Well remember the guy that I wrote home about?" Zahira started.

"The one from California or the one from New Zealand?" asked her mom.

"The one from New Zealand. He invited me to come and visit him so...I'm going to New Zealand!!" she shouted with genuine excitement. The news was still hitting her.

"Wow!" both her parents coursed in unison, "When are you going?"

"In the new year. Probably the tenth of January. We have talked about spending a month hanging out and getting to know each other better. He is ready for a career change and is thinking about going back to school. If things work well between us he has talked about moving to Winnipeg to study," Zahira replied.

Her parents both shared and supported her excitement. They chatted for a long time about her options. They talked about her thoughts of leaving the ashram, about quitting her job, about changing her return ticket and about her being alone for Christmas.

"Well why don't you just go to New Zealand for the holidays?" asked her dad.

That's a good question said something deep down inside of her, but out loud she said, "He needs to find us a place to stay because he himself is in transition. We figured it would be easier for him to get as much work as possible throughout the holidays and then he would have more free time in the new year."

As she types this Zahira is aware of a little sadness in her heart. The Pomelo had asked her to join him for New Years Eve and then in a subsequent letter decided he needed more time to prepare for her arrival. If the tables were flipped she would be begging him to come and spend a warm and welcoming holiday with her family. He would be ushered in with red carpet treatment and her family would embrace him with open arms. She is lucky to have such amazingly generous parents.

"I love guys so much," she said before she hung up the phone.

"We love you too," her parents chorused.

◆

Doubt is Good?

"I am sorry to keep you waiting," was the first thing Bhagavan said.

Zahira instantly relaxed. This was the second time he has left her waiting for over an hour. She had watched herself growing tense as she sat quietly on his front steps. She had scheduled an appointment to talk to him about some of her doubts and confusions. She has been struggling with some of the new teachings. The ones that have her re-organizing her entire belief system.

"How can I help you today Zahira?" he asked as he invited her in.

"I feel like I am undergoing some major transformations right now and I am feeling cloudy about my progress. I started this course feeling excited and free, but at the moment I feel quite heavy and confused. I am open to this process, but I am experiencing doubt. This is not an emotion I am familiar with, but I see it spreading throughout my life right now," Zahira confessed.

"Doubt is good," Bhagavan replied. "This is good to question the process. Everything you are experiencing is perfectly natural. It is part of the process of tantra. We are working together on many levels. I am working beyond the conscious mind. I take my students' best interests very seriously. You are doing very well, very well. I am waiting for you to catch up with a few things before I take you to the next level."

He was referring to her reading his book. It is a required reading that Zahira can only compare to eating sawdust and tacks. It is a very dry and extremely painful read for her. It is Bhagavan's personal interpretation of the Vedas. It is just as confusing as his lectures.

"There are many levels of yogis," explains Bhagavan. "You are already at a very high level. It is up to you, but I can see you going to the very top. I can see you being at a very high level where you can begin to teach other teachers. I don't know about Canada, but America is ready for tantra. There is a big door there for you if you choose to open it."

His faith in her wins her over every time, but it also confuses her. He recognizes her potential, but for some reason Zahira is starting to doubt his...

◆

Self Confidence
Above all trust yourself
You are your own greatest teacher
Do not follow,
lead with your heart

◆

Letters to and from Zahira's Boss.

Dear B,
I hope this letter finds you well. Things on my end have been interesting to say the least. An opportunity has knocked on my door. To be completely transparent and honest with you, it is not an opportunity for professional development. It is an opportunity for myself as a woman.

A gentleman I have met on my travels has invited me to visit him in New Zealand. I feel there is something really worth exploring with this man. He really sees me, he is my age, and we are looking for the same things. He is the first man I have been with in a long time and it feels good to feel love again.

I am writing this letter because I am wondering if there is any possible chance to extend my leave of absence?

To be very honest, I feel nervous and hesitant to ask this of you. You have already gone above and beyond being an amazing boss. You have been very open and helpful to assisting me on my personal path, and I feel that this request is pushing the envelope a bit too far. However, I feel better being truthful with you and I am looking forward to your honest response.

If there is one thing this decision making process has shown me, it is a deeper appreciation for my job, for you and the work that we do.

I hope you are keeping warm and feeling peaceful. Thanks for listening and for your consideration, I value your advice and you!
~ Zahira

~~~

Hi Zahira (*a new name?!*)
Well it certainly sounds like your life is taking a turn and I am glad that you have finally found someone who might be in your life. I know that breaking up with your last love was very hard on you and it sounds like there is a chance for a future with this man. Life is too short and happiness can be the same so grab it when you can. You can have the extension, and am I sure your replacement will not mind at all. He is doing a great job for us.

Follow your heart because when your 60 you do not want to be sorry that you did not take the chance when you had it. I will keep
~~~

in mind that you might want to want longer, New Zealand is beautiful. Your job is here. So follow your heart and keep me posted.

Take care and have a merry Christmas and New Year,
~ B.

~~~

Dear B!
Thank you thank you thank you!

I have tears in my eyes from your words.

I even have goose pimples running up and down my body! You blow me away. What a gift to have you in my life. I must have done something right!
Not only did you say yes to my request, but you did so with effortless grace, wisdom and love. You are a great teacher and a wonderful mentor. I am over the moon grateful for you!

I wish you a warm and wonderful Christmas and I hope you are taking time for yourself. Enjoy, indulge and please give my love to everyone at the office. I will be happy to keep you posted on my adventures!

Once again, from the tips of my toes and the bottom of my heart I thank you!
~ Zahira

◆

Green Light Grow

Zahira has a green light to go. Her boss is truly supportive and so are her parents. Her mom and dad are going to help her change her plane ticket. She feels blessed with this great fortune.
~~~

Putting all of this into motion makes Zahira feel giddy with excitement. She loves the idea of zigging her zag from India to New Zealand. It makes for a great story! She also knows she needs to stay rooted in reality. She is making this move with a small budget and a giant leap of faith. She needs to be sure the Pomelo is ready to jump with her.

She wrote him a letter to open the floor for more truth talking. She wanted to be certain he was genuine with his invitation. When he left the golden beach he was clear that he needed time to heal. She wanted to know if he has had enough time to honour this intention.

Dear Pomelo
Well I woke up this morning feeling very giddy and excited. The thought of having another taste of the Pomelo is more than appealing. I do however have a few things that I need you to think about and be honest about.

When you left here you were very clear about needing time to move through the wounds of your last relationship and to work on loving your mother. These were two things you felt you needed to address before moving into a new relationship. Do you feel that this is something you have accomplished? Have you had enough time to honour yourself in these ideals?

Let me know where you are at.
~ Much love, Zahira

~~~

Dear Zahira,
To answer your question is hard. I have talked with my Ex and we have clarified a lot of outstanding feelings and we know that we are over as a couple. I still have feelings for her but this will just take time to clear. I feel ready to move on and this is why I have decided to ask you to come to Nz to spend more time exploring our relationship.
~~~

As for my mother things have been rocky but are getting better. I've asked her to help me make a ginger bread house for X-mas and we are having fun making it. These little things are bringing us closer and this will be a gradual process. I do have love for her and new found respect and think that I'm embracing our relationship in ways that I never have before. So in summary I'm making leaps and bounds but can't say that I'm there yet.

I guess I would like to see you again before I decide on what direction I go in regards to studying. I know I want to go back to school and If I think we have a future together then it will affect my decision as to where. The University of Manitoba has a program that is similar to the one I am looking at in Melbourne.

I do think about you and think that you are so special. Different than anything I've ever experienced. I think you have a lot of the qualities that I have been looking for in a relationship.

So I have laid it all out for you as far as I can. I don't want you do anything you are unsure of. It's very easy for me to ask you to come and risk everything. I know you will have a good time but is it worth it for you to make such a giant leap? That is the question that you will have to figure out on your own. I hope it is a yes but I will understand if it is a no.

So let me know what you think. I hope all the shit around the ashram has cleared and that this isn't making your life more stressful.

Will look forward with baited breath to your reply.
~ xoxo The Pomelo

Zahira knows not to idealize and only hear what she wants to hear. While he is clear that he has 'moved on' from his ex it also is clear that he still has feelings for her. He still needs time to heal. And while leaps and bounds in the direction of healing with his mother is a positive step he has also been honest that 'he is not there yet.'

Zahira goes forth with caution. She has all the freedom to love recklessly and completely, but she also knows that this love needs an equal not opposite reaction. She knows that her Pomelo is crazy about her, but he is also guarded in moments. She doesn't know if he is ready to give 100%. Knowing this gives her a clear view. She will try her best not to have any expectations. There is a good chance New Zealand will be just a fun detour on her Indian vacation.

Taking all of this into consideration she wrote him back. Her letter was one sentence long. It read;

I am coming.

◆

Letters to and from Mom

Oh mom!

I just opened my new flight info from the airline. Did you pay 800 dollars to change my flight?!? Please tell me you didn't pay 800 dollars. Holy shit please tell me you didn't! My stomach just got nauseous. Before I panic I'll wait for your verification. 800 dollars is too much to ask of you. Please tell me I read the transaction incorrectly.

I love you.

I sent you some white light today, surrounding your spirit with a spiral of love. Hope you can feel it.

~ XOX ME

~~~
~~~

Hi Sweet Pea,
Definitely feel the love.

As far as the money goes it's like this: I expected to pay at least $500 then when you think of the overall picture, what's another $300?

It's all in your perspective. I'd rather spend the money now, then leave it in my will...not that I would have it then anyway, but you know what I mean. Sometimes things don't come around again so stop fussing about a few dollars.

It's your Christmas, birthday, Valentines day, Easter, Thanksgiving, St. Patrick's day gift. I once sent a card like that to a guy I had a crush on. When you opened the card it read: Now don't bother me for another year.
You know the stupid shit didn't call me for a year?! I actually went out with him, but by then I had met your dad and it was no contest!
~ Love you lots, mom

~~~

Oh mom!
You are an unbelievable woman, I am so grateful to have you as my mother. I have been in quiet meditation all day giving thanks for all that has supported me on my journey. You and dad are at the top of that list. I am so grateful for you!
~ I love my mom! xoxo your daughter

◆

Waiting for Lightning

Zahira is feeling nauseous from her roller coaster of emotions. She has gone from being confused and full of doubt, to excited and giddy
~~~

and now back to more confusion and doubt. This time her doubt is not only circling around Bhagavan's teachings, but the Pomelo as well. She hasn't heard from him in over a week and now she is left questioning where he is at.

She needs to be honest with herself about this one. She does not want to end this story with a broken heart. She has some sinking feelings about this man and her decision to go and see him. She doesn't want to be foolish about the Pomelo. She knows she fell hard for him, but perhaps it's because he was able to touch and heal her as a sexual being. Maybe the fact that she hadn't shared her body in so long is blurring her reality? Maybe she is confusing sex with love?

She is still fully committed to finding out. Her hopeful heart wants to give them the benefit of the doubt. She is looking forward to seeing him on his home turf. She can't imagine a better way to get to know him. She is prepared to take a leap of faith with this man, but she needs him to jump with her. That being said, does he still want her to come? He said he would be waiting with baited breath…
so why the hell hasn't he responded to her last letter?

Zahira is also still feeling confusion about her time at the ashram. She arrived an open book and now she is watching herself shut. The teachings are not resonating with her truest self. To be fair there are some very clear tantric insights that she values, but the school is filled with mixed messages. There are subtle waves of male dominance mixed with teachings that praise the Goddess. It can be baffling in moments.

Zahira has pushed herself to bite the Bhagavan apple and now she feels slightly poisoned. He has challenged her entire belief system and it has left her on shaky ground. She is having a hard time connecting with her own personal clarity. She feels easily influenced by the last person she talks with.

She would like to get back to the place where she only hears what is best for her highest self, where she does not get so easily swayed. She knows she can be quicker at discerning what information is useful and what is to be disregarded.

Zahira sees herself writing in circles. It is nauseating. She is caught in a hurricane of doubt and discomfort and yet there is a part of her that is standing solid. Her mind is exhausted from running, but her heart is standing tall in the eye of the storm. It is patiently waiting for a lightning bolt of clarity. Her heart knows that when it strikes her path will be lit.

◆

Heart & Mind

The mind can play tricks
The heart is simply playful
The mind can wander astray
The heart is always home

◆

Delusion & Depression

"Would you consider yourself a depressed person?" asked her Aussie classmate.

She had asked Zahira to join her on a walk. It was clear that something heavy was weighing on her mind.

"Oh, um...no," started Zahira quite surprised by the question. "I have definitely been depressed at one point in my life. It was about 8 years ago and it was something that I invited into my life. Up until that point I thought I always had to be happy and positive. I realized I was completely neglecting a part of my being, so I allowed myself to be sad. It was a beautiful experience, but I had a hard time pulling myself out of it. It gave me a strong appreciation and compassion for people who struggle find the power to help themselves."

"So you wouldn't consider yourself to be currently depressed?" she asked in a sweet and oddly nervous tone.

"No not at all," Zahira replied. "I mean I sometimes get sad, but I am okay with that. Sometimes life is hard. To be honest I have been feeling some confusion and doubt lately, but I don't feel depressed.

Why do you ask?"

"Well...if I say something are you okay with hearing it?" she asked hesitantly.

"Yes please tell me what you need to say," encouraged Zahira.

"Well do you want to hear it even if it will affect your time here at the ashram?" she asked again still feeling hesitant to share.

"Yes of course. Tell me," replied Zahira once again. She was growing more intrigued.

"Well," she started very delicately, "Bhagavan told me not to listen to you or spend time with you because you are depressed and you don't know it. He said you are delusional."

Zahira stopped in her tracks. Her first gut reaction was laughter, "What?!"

"Yeah. He said it weeks ago and it has been really confusing for me because I only see you as being a strong person. It is making me question my own judgement about *everything*," she said with a genuine struggle in her voice.

"Wow," smiled Zahira, "*this* is interesting."

"It's not the first time that he has said something negative about you behind your back. Do you remember when we wanted to have a Goddess celebration under the full moon?" asked the Aussie Angel.

"Yeah, I went to the beach alone and lit a fire and had a skinny dip," Zahira smiled at this memory.

"Well it was Bhagavan who told me and the girls not to go with you. He said that you need help and that this type of celebration is delusional," she confessed.

"Wow. Woah." Zahira said with her jaw dropped. "Well this puts a whole new light on things."

"I was just wondering if he has said anything negative about me behind my back. He has done it with several other students and I am just feeling really confused by all of it. I didn't want to say anything, but it had me questioning my own personal judgements which are already in question," she said with brave honesty.

"Well he has been very careful not to say who I can and cannot spend time with because he knows I would never accept that. He has not said anything rude about you, but he did tell me that I was one of his only students who is neuroses free. So how can he say this to my face and then say I am depressed behind my back? What kind of teacher is this?" Zahira said in full power.

"He told me that I was one of his only students who is neurosis free!" replied the Aussie Angel feeling her own shock and disappointment grow.

Zahira grew quiet in contemplation. This was a lot to process.

"Well thank you for telling me," Zahira finally spoke. "I really appreciate your friendship and your honesty."

"I feel scared," said the Aussie Angel. "I don't want to feel like there is a showdown about to happen. I don't want to have to pack my bags in the middle of the night. I don't want to have to say I am going back to Amma's (her hugging guru) and have Bhagavan tell me I am a failure. I can't hear him say anything else negative about Amma. She has just done so much for me. I just cant handle that right now."

Zahira felt a protective anger rise inside of her. Bhagavan had been taking advantage of the Aussie Angel's fragile state. She had recently lost her lover to cancer. It was a wound that was still fresh and throbbing. She came to India looking for a healer, but instead she had found a master manipulator.

"Whoa whoa whoa," said Zahira, "first of all you don't need to worry about a showdown. I am capable of speaking calmly and clearly. Second of all, you are *not* a failure. You are a beautiful and powerful woman. You need to stop focusing on which guru to trust. *This is not about anyone else but you. You are only up against yourself my dear, and therefore you have nothing to worry about."*

◆

Look in the mirror and spell Guru.

◆

Over Minded & Underestimated

The very first time Zahira sat down with Bhagavan she asked him if there was anything she needed to work on. She asked if there was anything about herself that she could not see but needed to change. His response was no. He told her there was nothing on a personal level that she needed to fix. He was more interested in talking to her on a professional level.

Zahira gave this man an open floor to speak honestly and he chose to say she is neurosis free. Now she learns he is calling her depressed behind her back. How is this possible? If he sees this as truth then he should be honest to her face. The basic laws of tantra are honesty and love. How can a tantric master be so deficient in both?

Zahira came to this school an open book. She had romantic ideals about finding an enlightened teacher. She was ready to learn. She has done her best to integrate this man's teachings, but all she has felt is confusion and doubt. She has not complained or challenged Bhagavan in any way. She has been quietly observing herself. She now feels her power is being over minded and underestimated.

She is ready to be heard.

◆

Huh?!

'There are some things I need to talk to you about before you decide to come,' wrote the Pomelo in a letter.

What!?! But she had *already* decided to come....

◆

Sea of Tears

Zahira sat next to the sea trying to stay afloat in her reality. She was struggling with the irrepressible doubt that has been seeping into every pore of her being.

"Could I really be depressed and not know it?" she asked the sky as she sifted sand through her hands. "*What the fuck does that even mean?*"

She sat quietly for some time. She licked the tears that had fallen down her cheeks to her lips. They tasted exactly like the ocean she adores. She felt like she could have cried an entire sea. She felt more confused then sad. Then she felt sadness for her confusion. Then she felt even more confused because she had no real reason to be sad.

There wasn't much she could do. She couldn't connect with the idea of being depressed and not know it because even if it were true she wouldn't know it. Does that even make sense?

Zahira decided that none of this made any sense at all, including The Pomelo's last letter. It was also making her squirm with confusion. She thought she had made it clear that she was coming. Her mom just paid 800 bucks to change her ticket! She asked her boss for an extension of absence! Is he fucking backing out on her!? Or is she just feeling nervous because the rest of her life is so shaky?

Zahira let out a genuine sob. She felt tired and alone. She felt uncomfortable and sad. She wanted to crawl out of her skin and into the sand. She wanted to fall sleep and wake up on a cloud. She wanted to eject out of her existence, but had no choice but to rest with it. She would let this moment exist exactly as it needed to. She gave thanks for her misery and exhaled into the earth.

◆

Sink or Swim

Zahira curls into her laptop to write out her pain. She is genuinely struggling with a mind that is racing with confusing currents. They are pulling her in several directions simultaneously and she is floating with her arms outstretched waiting to reach the shores of clarity. She may never get there, but at the very least she could use a life preserver.

She is treading in the suspense of what the Pomelo could possibly have to say. He has not been available to chat since he dropped the 'before you decide to come' bomb. She also hasn't had a chance to talk to Bhagavan about calling her depressed. Zahira is still so fucking riddled by this. What does it even mean to be depressed and not know it?

Even though she no longer trusts Bhagavan, she remains clouded by his teachings. She is still questioning her relationship to spirit. She has never felt this kind of doubt before. It is challenging the core of her entire existence. She feels like she is starting to sink in her sea of confusion.

Zahira feels trapped in this moment. She was hoping to write herself into some kind of clarity, but instead she is starting to drown in her doubt. She needs some help. She needs a friend. She needs to find a phone.

◆

Nutty Professors and Nut Jobs

Zahira left the ashram to search for a phone to call her Ayahuasquero. Just the sound of his voice can ground her into clarity. She wanted nothing more than to reach out to him. She wasn't having much luck. She managed to find two telephones, but neither one had a dial tone.

The Austrian Wrestler from the ashram found her as she was wondering aimlessly. He could sense her desperation.

"Why don't you come into town with me?" he invited.

She hopped on the back of his motorbike and derailed her mission for a phone to replace it with a mission for ice cream. They sped through the darkness and she closed her eyes. She let the wind sweep through her and she reconnected with her centre.

"Why are you so affected by all of this?" she whispered quietly. "Why is your core so easily shaken right now? This is unlike you. What are you learning from this?"

She realized that she was being tested. The turmoil she was experiencing was an opportunity to dig deep and find faith in herself.

"Are you like the mother of the ashram?" asked the Austrian Wrestler as they ordered their ice cream. "Everyone seems to turn to you when they are upset."

"Oh god no," she replied, "I don't want that title."

"So what's going on?" he asked with a curious grin. "You seem a little out of sorts."

"Look I really don't want to talk about this," she said softly. She had settled into a Nutty Professor sundae that could have fed a family of five. She instantly felt better. "You are new here and you need to formulate your own opinions. I want you to shape your own experience at the ashram."

He was persistent at first, but when she wouldn't budge he grew respectful and quiet with her space. He shared stories of his own experience and he melted her like ice cream into a calm soothing space.

"I am very intuitive you know," he said sort of out of the blue.

"Really?" she inquired. "What does your intuition tell you about me?"

"Well it says you are on thin ice," he responded.

"What do you mean?" asked Zahira.

"I mean your foundation is not solid," he answered.

Zahira looked him dead in the eye, "Well you are wrong. My foundation is solid as a rock."

He winked at her and said, "Well good. I am glad I am wrong."

Something however, was not sitting well with Zahira. It was the same something that has been nagging at her for days. Is her foundation really on thin ice? Could this be possible? Could her relationship with spirit be delusional? Could she *actually* be depressed and not know it? *What the fuck does that even mean?* It seemed ridiculous to her. She has always prided herself on her solid core. How is it possible that she was feeling so fragile?

She grew very quiet in contemplation. The Austrian Wrestler was wonderful and joined her. They sat side by side listening to the ocean that was creeping slowly towards them. She let herself sail into the rhythm of the waves. She let go of everything to be completely honest with herself. She closed her eyes and searched for her most sacred self.

When she got home she uncluttered the shampoo and soap bottles from around her tiny bathroom mirror. She stared herself dead in the eyes.

"Alright missy what is going on right now? What is this? How is it possible that you are letting doubt creep in to these new depths? What are you unsure about? Are you afraid that the Pomelo is retracting his invitation? Hmmm....this feels bigger than a man. Are you worried that everything you have experienced with spirit and self is not valid? Are you worried your connection to spirit is delusional? Could you possibly be depressed and not know it? I don't get it. What is it? Why are you on such shaky ground? On thin ice..."

She could see great power and strength in her eyes. They also seemed playful and sweet. They kind of laughed at her in a warm and loving way. They were not shaken. They were not doubtful. They were calm and clear connected to her divine self. Her conscious mind began to unfurl from its uncertainty into the conviction of her soul. She watched her thoughts scatter and grow weak. She felt a small giggle rising from her belly.

"Go to bed you nut job," she smiled to herself, "When you wake up you will feel calm. Then we will talk."

◆

"Yes, when you see for the first time, a great laughter arises in you—the laughter about the whole ridiculousness of your misery, the laughter about the whole foolishness of your problems, the laughter about the whole absurdity of your suffering."
~ Osho

◆

Thank You

Zahira woke up the next morning giggling and hugging herself. She threw the covers up over her head and starting talking to herself.

"Thank you," she whispered. "Thank you for trusting me. Thank you for trusting me. Thank you for trusting me," she repeated, "Thank you for believing in me and honouring me."

Then she sat up and felt the divine sensation that she would call spirit and her teacher would call an auto suggestion. She felt the presence of divinity hold her hands and tilt her chin towards the sky. She felt pure pulsating love and her tears flowed.

"Thank you," she whispered, "thank you."

If Zahira is making up her encounters with spirit then so be it. No matter what anyone wants to call it, in the end, it is all semantics.
Her experience is real.
And though she cannot prove it, she doesn't have to.

◆

Galactic Love

After breakfast Zahira opened a letter that sent a wave of pure assurance through her being. The bond she shares with her Ayahuasquero is beyond explanation. His intuition must have felt her painful wandering. While she was out looking for a phone to call him, he wrote her this letter:

Hey buddy.
I don't really know why I am wanting to share this with you right now... but...consider that...

A - You are a master, a teacher

B - You have worked with other masters, teachers in your lifetime (people, plants and other spirits) all of them helpful in one way or another in your growth.

Not exactly a completed thesis, but...I love you!!!

Zahira is beyond reassured by this letter. Not only are her friend's words exactly what she needed to hear, but he wrote them in the exact moment that she needed to hear them without even knowing why.

According to Baghavan humans are limited by galactic time and galactic space. He claims the fish cannot leave the sea to talk to the turtle, but according to Zahira…the turtle sure as hell knows how to swim.

◆

Levelling

"So I spoke with my Aussie classmate and she told me that you think I am depressed and I don't know it," Zahira said cutting to the chase. She had been waiting too long for this moment, she was not about to tip toe around the topic.

Bhagavan shifted in his chair and responded with an aggravated tone. "This has got to stop. She is making the situation at the ashram uncomfortable for many students. She is clearly delusional and she is creating confusion and tension."

"So you are saying that she is lying?" challenged Zahira.

Her heart was beating quickly. It always does when faced with confrontation, especially one she initiates, but she was calm and cool on the outside. She was sitting with a poised spine and direct eye contact. She would *not* let this man rattle her.

"She is doing something called levelling," Bhagavan started with an aggravated tone, "She is sinking and in the process she is trying to drag everyone down with her," replied Bhagavan growing more agitated.

Zahira looked at the man in front of her and instantly determined he was doing *exactly* that. Bhagavan was going down and he was levelling the Aussie Angel. He had been caught and confronted for being a liar. He was never going to admit it. Instead he re-routed the focus on the innocent to make them seem guilty.

"If you believe I am depressed you need to talk to me directly, not the other students. The foundation of a tantric school should be based on honesty," Zahira's words were persistent and her tone was clear.

"I have said this already, you have no neurosis. There is nothing you need to work on," Bhagavan replied.

"So you are saying that my Aussie classmate is lying?" she asked again point blank.

Bhagavan looked away and then proceeded to blow smoke in Zahira's direction. He went on and on about the delusions of her classmate and he denied everything. Blah blah blah. His words were unkind and lacking love and compassion. He would never admit that he was lying so Zahira tuned him out. She started to plan her next move. She would waste no more energy being confused by this man and his own delusions.

Zahira is now clear that *she is the way*. She is the first and final word of her experience. She came to India looking for teachers and is once again reminded that she is her own guru.

It doesn't matter what anyone else says
it is up to her to believe in herself.

Even if Bhagavan had the only key to heaven she would rather unlock the divine from within.

"I wish you peace on your path," Zahira said as she excused herself.

◆

"The way is not in the sky. The way is in the heart"
~ BUDDHA

◆

SKYPE CALL

POMELO: Sorry can't hear you

ZAHIRA: Hey we need to write this shit out cuz my Skype is whack! frustrating....are you there?

POMELO: Yep I'm here

ZAHIRA: I think it is weak cuz someone else is using Skype right now

POMELO: Ok we'll have to chat instead

ZAHIRA: Boo, but better than nothing

POMELO: I'm not sure what to do

ZAHIRA: You ok?

POMELO: Well sort of, I got a big trigger on Friday and it sent me back to the old dark depths and I'm working my way out. It's all got to do with rejection and letting people down so it's hard to describe, but basically I didn't handle things well because I'm under a lot of stress. I thought I was different with my yoga experience and it is worrying how easily I can be dismantled

ZAHIRA: I see... I wish I could give you a hug

POMELO: I'm sure your not understanding

ZAHIRA: I am

POMELO: That would be nice

ZAHIRA: I hear what you are saying, the question is, what is best for you right now?

POMELO: There are things about me that have to change and I'm afraid that if you come I won't be able to stick to my changes

ZAHIRA: Well that is most important

POMELO: I need to buckle down and prove to myself that I can do what I've set out to do

Zahira: Ok. I support this. I can't be naive and think I can help when you are clearly asking for time to be alone with this

POMELO: I really want to see you but that is the old me wanting to fall in love to take all the pain away

ZAHIRA: I am impressed with your clarity. This is great work!

POMELO: I've been too reliant on others and I need to stand on my own two feet

ZAHIRA: Then you will. You can do this. I am grateful you have been able to be so honest with me. I am also crying because I was so excited to see you. I have already been telling people I am coming to New Zealand so now I feel a bit foolish and heart broken.

POMELO: I'm sorry I've messed you around

ZAHIRA: It's ok I have faith this is all working out as it should

POMELO: I really wanted you to come, part of me still does. I just don't want you to come and take care of me

ZAHIRA: I'll be ok. This is my journey, I have to trust it

POMELO: The timing is just not right. I'm not as ready as I thought

ZAHIRA: Well maybe some other time then. xo

POMELO: I hope so, Canada is still a strong possibility

ZAHIRA: Shit I'm crying and I have to leave the kitchen, hold on... people are coming

Pomelo: I need more time to heal and I don't think I can do it with you here

Zahira: I hear you and I respect you and I will let you go to do your thing

Pomelo: You were such a positive plug for me in India and you got me believing in myself. Problem is I need to learn to do it for myself

Zahira: It's true

Pomelo: I know that I'll get swept away with you

Zahira: It's true

Pomelo: You are the person that I hope to be with, but I need to feel love for myself before I can truly love another

Zahira: I couldn't agree with you more. Thank you for respecting me enough to tell me so. This is really good work. You are speaking my language!

Pomelo: I don't want to wreck things by relying on your positive nature

Zahira: Nice foresight. I just opened a letter from a girlfriend who is getting her heart bashed around by a guy who isn't ready to reflect her pure love. Thanks for saving me the pain.

Pomelo: Relying on others is what I've done in the past, now I must focus on changing myself

Zahira: Well as the Beastie Boys say 'No time like the present to work shit out.'

Pomelo: Lol. Well I'm sorry but I feel this is the best thing for now

Zahira: Hey don't apologize. This is tantra. This is why I am here. To learn and live this honesty. This is truth talking. You have been one of my greatest teachers in this department.

Pomelo: Thanks for understanding

Zahira: Holy shit, I cant believe I've extended my stay and now I have no clue what my next move is. This is no doubt happening for a reason, I just wonder what that reason is!

Pomelo: God I'm sorry. Did you want to be home for Christmas? I hope you didn't change your flight etc

Zahira: Oh yeah, everything is in motion! My mom extended my ticket home from Mumbai and my boss gave me an extension of absence. I guess I have an extra three months in India!

Pomelo: Shit

Zahira: It's all good! Thank you! I get a longer holiday! Woooo woooo! I have to run now. I'm glad we had a chance to be real about this.

Pomelo: Ok talk later?

Zahira: Take care of you and know that I have love for you in my heart whenever you need it. Be strong. I am sooooo proud of you! xoxoxo

Pomelo: Thanks

Wow. Well...there it is. The crystal clear truth delivered in a perfect act of honesty. Zahira's initial wave of self pity burst almost instantly. She could not argue with his truth. She could not ask for more. He has thrown a stake in the ground and declared a need for self love. He is standing firm for the first time in his life. He can no longer rely on anyone for his own happiness. He has to win it for himself, by himself.

His words echo the mantra of her own heart and she is so proud of him.

With this truth they are both set free.

◆

From Within

"Thank you," she whispered to herself and the Universe. She was floating with her arms outstretched in the sea. Her ears were just below the surface of the water and she could hear her voice as though it were coming from within.

"Thank you for loving me. Thank you for trusting me. Thank you for challenging me. Thank you for an opportunity to grow deeper into my own understanding. Thank you for setting me free," she whispered.

Zahira felt her whole being relax into clarity. She was loose in the waves, letting them sway her like a blade of grass in the wind. The sun was dropping into the sea like a perfectly round ball of fire.

"I wish for peace," she said quietly to herself and the Universe. "I wish for peace for Bhagavan, for the Pomelo, for my family, for myself and for the whole planet."

Zahira is now free to drift without direction. She has no clue where she will end up. She has an extra three months to play and absolutely no responsibilities or commitments. She is grateful for an opportunity to indulge in the luxury of timelessness. She is free to do whatever she wants whenever she wants to.

Zahira decides in this moment that she is not looking to find anything. In fact, now that she thinks about it...she would prefer to get lost.

PART 3

I Now Pronounce You…

◆

Tarot Reading

"It is up to you to think of a question that you want to ask the cards. Perhaps it is about something specific or perhaps something general. Perhaps there is no question at all and that itself is the question. It is a way to get you thinking about things," said the German tarot card reader in his perfectly halted English.

"What do I want to know? Hmmm... good question! I am looking to get lost!" she laughed and then thought a bit longer. "I guess it would be nice to have some insight on what my next move should be. What will help me honour my highest self? What will bring me the most clarity and peace?" Zahira decided out loud.

"Alright!" he smiled. "Sounds like a great place to start. Let's see what the cards have to say."

They took turns shuffling the cards and then Zahira spread them into a fan shape across her sarong. She took her time choosing 10 cards. When she flipped over the last card the tarot reader let out a spontaneous coo of excitement.

"I think maybe I should be following you on this adventure!" he laughed. "This is a very good sign. It is the 10 of discs which is wealth! This card represents the outcome of your journey."

"Ooh I like that," smiled Zahira.

The cards also revealed that Zahira's higher self is being crossed by a rational mind.

"A rational mind can become pre-occupied and prevent clarity from prevailing," explained the tarot reader. "Saturation of a rational mind can create a cloudy state and cause unnecessary worry."

"So how does that relate to my next move?" Zahira asked.

"The rational mind is not useful for the answer to the question you have asked," observed the tarot reader. "You need to rely on your fiery energy. Avoid too much attention on thinking. Go to your energy and you will find clarity."

According to the cards Zahira's energetic self is on the winning side. She drew the six of wands, which represents victory. This victory can be brought about by not letting her rational mind steer her selfhood. This rang like a wave of relief through her heart. It was like getting a permission slip from her spirit to follow her bliss.

Zahira's attention kept being drawn back to the princess of disks. She was beautiful and she was pregnant! She kept asking for more clarification on this card, mostly because she had not made any mention of wanting a child.

"This card is all about procreation and nourishment," said the tarot reader noting her curiosity. "It is a very sensuous card and represents fertility on all levels."

"Because it is in the position of the outside world, how does this relate to me?" asked Zahira.

"Well," he said thoughtfully, "it means fertility is yours for the taking."

Zahira was still confused so she decided to share more information.

"I am mostly curious about this card because she is pregnant and I would love to have a child. So how does this relate to being in the position that represents the influence of the outside world?"

He did another excited cooing sound and then with a very clear voice the tarot reader said, "Well then! The pregnant princess needs the knight or a king to come by!"

"Oh I really like *that* answer," laughed Zahira.

"So to summarize," started the tarot reader, "everything ends in wealth in the material plane. You don't need to worry about anything. By focusing on your energy and cutting down on thinking too much you reach a stage where you are rich."

Wow. This is perfect. A green card to shut off her brain and dial in her energetic intelligence. Doing this will lead her to great wealth and in the process she will meet a king or a knight to make a baby with!

So it is written.

◆

The Belgian Lightworkers

"You are very beautiful," said the woman sitting next to Zahira.

"Thank you," smiled Zahira, "so are you!"

"As soon as you sat down I felt a wave of light," said the woman with an unidentifiable accent.

"I overheard bits of your conversation," Zahira admitted. "It was very interesting. You are a healer yes?"

"Yes," she twinkled, "I work with the light energy."

"Ah me too," responded Zahira.

"Yes I can see this," said the woman who seemed to be glowing. She is here with a group of nine students from Belgium. They have been traveling the globe following the earth's Kundalini energy, beginning in Peru then heading to Egypt, France and now India.

"How do you know where to go next?" asked Zahira fully curious.

The Healer smiled and pointed from her heart to the sky, "I am told. This is the connection we all have. When we stop the mind from distracting us we can live in the moment and be open to ourselves as divine beings. The opening creates a channel of communication."

"Yes this I know," smiled Zahira. The Healer was echoing her own heart's teachings.

"You are very clear," smiled the Healer. "I have been working with these students for the past two weeks. It was told to me that they could grow 300 years in three weeks. They have made tremendous progress. I can see you could enter the group at this stage and be ready without preparation. If you like you can join. It is free. I can see you are ready for great things."

Zahira smiled. This is *exactly* the Mother Goddess culture that Bhagavan warned her about. He would find this woman to be exceptionally delusional, but Zahira found the woman to be endearing and sincere. Zahira's energetic intelligence was open to trusting the moment.

"Your fire is in full power," said the healer, "I can see it. It is bursting from the crown of your head! You are very open."

Zahira laughed and met the Healer's apprentice. They have made a date for sunset so she can learn more about what it is they are doing. It is very appealing in this moment. Zahira is open to seeing if there is something more to explore. The full moon solstice is just around the corner and she is looking for a sacred celebration. Perhaps this group is just what she has been waiting for.

Zahira has moved out of the ashram. She has found a new joyful flow and freedom. It's as though she is back on the road even though she just moved a half a mile down it. She chose her new guest house based on the energy she felt when she stood in the garden. It was not the most affordable option, but it was the most peaceful.

She had a momentary debate between her energetic self and her rational self and then remembered her tarot card reading. She would make this choice based on energetic enhancements rather than financial ones. When she moved her bags into her new room a lovely man and his family greeted her like one of their own.

"Welcome home," he said.

◆

"Are you a Lightworker?"
BY JEANNIE JAVELOSA

"Lightworkers are balanced and have found their centers. They do not judge or make fun of anyone because everyone is where they ought to be. Lightworkers have no drama about them and yet you feel their inner joy. Lightworkers are slow to anger and are able to see the duality in our world and learn to navigate their souls through the dark. Lightworkers are sure of themselves but never full of themselves. When they look at you with eyes of understanding and compassion, it is about you, no matter what you are, what you own, or where you are coming or going."

◆

Manifesting Light

Zahira met with the Belgian Lightworkers first thing this morning. It was a lovely affair, each one so gentle and calm. The group had built a Mandala in the sand. It is an infinity symbol that is crossed with a Star of David in the centre. On one side of the infinity symbol is a representation of the Goddess and on the other side is the God, a balance of the masculine and the feminine. The Star of David represents the macrocosmos as being the same as the microcosmos;

As above, So below.

The group entered the Mandala that was inside an oval of palm leaves. Zahira was taught the directions in which to travel along the infinity symbol and then was left to do her own work. She was now in a supportive environment where she could do her hokey pokey dance and turn herself about. She could tune into her own light energy and work on turning it out.

This all sounds very vague so she will try to be more specific. Zahira has had no formal 'training' in Lightwork. She actually doesn't even know if training exists for this type of thing. She has been working with light for as long as she can remember. For Zahira it is an intuition-based craft.

Lightwork is a feeling of peace that transforms her self into a vessel for healing. Zahira usually begins by acknowledging the elements (earth, air, fire, water and space) and invites their presence. When she feels a grounding and uplifting wave of assurance she can begin.

Zahira always starts with herself, giving thanks and searching for places and spaces in her being that need a little love. She nurtures herself through both visualization and soft touch. She often spreads her arms out to the sky, or in this case the sea, and then she slowly draws this energy into her heart. Once she feels inflated and in harmony she can work with others.

Her parents receive most of her attention. They are easy to work with because she absolutely adores them. The instant she thinks about her mom and dad her entire being swells with extra love and light to share. She visualizes them one at a time in their own bodies. She circles them with a white cocoon of healing light. She wraps them from head to toe and then hums into their hearts. She imagines healing their physical bodies with pure love. She prays to the elements to keep her parents healthy and connected to their spirits.

She then moves to her brother and sister, nieces and nephews, sister-in-law and brother-in-law. She also works on others who appear before her. It is usually friends and relatives in her life who deserve a little extra joy. Today it was her boss and her Aunt Elaine.

Zahira has no proof that this 'work' is effective, but she knows it is better than worrying about her loved ones. Connecting with this healing energy transforms her. When she is finished her body feels uplifted, her spirit feels grounded and her mind feels humbled. It is an experience she can scarcely give credit to through the written word. To her this is the reason she chose with her Sannyasin name.

Zahira means manifesting light.

◆

As above, so below
The macrocosmos mirrors the microcosmos
The universe mirrors us
Acknowledge this reflection and it will become a supreme union

◆

Secret Nog

Hello Little One!
Glad to hear your voice the other day. I am happy that everything

is going well for you. I love you and miss you lots. I keep trying to visualize the place that you are at and from your descriptions of it it certainly sounds beautiful.

We just endured a snowy winter storm with high winds and limited visibility. I know that you are not missing that! Your uncle was in town for three days for some work meetings and we had a good visit with him. Your bro is thinking of getting one of those sleeve tattoos. Yikes! Friday is Mom's Christmas party and it's hard to believe that it is December already.

You say you want my Christmas egg nog recipe. You know that this is a closely regarded secret of mine but for you, anything. Here it is.

Combine in a punch bowl:

12 egg yolks
1 cup sugar

Beat till lemon coloured and thick. Slowly add:

13 oz brandy
26 oz rum or rye
2 cups of light cream

Beat to blend well and chill overnight to allow egg to mellow.
In the morning add:

12 egg whites (beat until stiff)
3 cups whipping cream (beat until creamy)

Fold together and mix with the booze and yolks in the punch bowl.
** side note – As much as this recipe is like a family heirloom, it is in fact from a 1976 copy of The Best of Bridge. The classic book is filled with gems and staind with eggs and booze.*

~ VOILA! TAKE CARE MY DEAR LOTS OF LOVE, DAD.

◆

Pomelo Postcards

To my Pomelo,

I love the shoes you left behind. I walked a mile in them yesterday. It was lovely. I strolled along the jungle path speaking out loud. I was talking to you and me and the trees. I invited myself to cry, to feel sad that I won't see you. I had a few gentle tears touch my cheeks. Mostly I am happy for us. The truth you have expressed is impossible to feel sad for. It is beautiful and it has set me free.

When I made it to the ocean I slipped off your shoes and had a float. With my ears below the water I could hear my voice so clearly. I asked the Universe to help you:

'Please give him strength to be gentle with his healing. Please help him find true love for himself. Please send him warm waves of healing light and let his spirit shine bright.'

I know you can do this. It is what I see in you, a man a breath away from pure self. Don't look too hard. You are closer than you think. Be aware, be gentle, be kind in your mind. Keep your speech impeccable. Keep it congruent with your heart. Speak only the truth at all times, in time yours will be revealed.

I can't imagine you at 100 percent and full of self love, look out universe!

If you need me, look to the moon.

All my love
~ Zahira

Oh! I almost forgot… I have attached an early Christmas present for you. It is my dad's egg nog recipe -just like I said I would! Proceed with caution. You have been warned!

~~~

Dear Z,
Wow. You blow me away with your amazing way of dealing with life. So inventive and creative. I'm sad as well that I won't see you but I feel that speaking truthfully about my feelings and needs is bringing me to my true self. I'm using this time wisely and I don't want to rush or do anything out of desperation. I know that we will meet again, I feel you with me always and I look forward to the next time my eyes meet your lovely open soul. I feel strong in my conviction and know if I follow my heart that only the best things will be the result. I'm so thankful that I have a true example of love (you) in my life and know if I follow your example I can find that love inside of myself. Thanks for being so understanding and wonderful.
~ Love always, P.

Ps. Totally excited to try your dad's famous nog. Thanks for remembering.

◆

Mandalas
Establish a sacred space
Enhance meditation
A spiritual teaching tool
A symbolic representation of the cosmos
and the unconscious self
~~~

◆

Porcelain Heart

Zahira is continuing her work with the Belgians. The shape of the mandala changes with the progress of the group. The process of the physical transformation mirrors the transformation of their unconscious.

Today they changed the shape of the mandala from two interlocking cones to two perfect circles. The teacher observed Zahira closely. She had asked her to move the centre piece to be exactly in the middle of the interlocking circles. Zahira moved it once, stood back and then realized it was not exactly perfect. She started to move it again.

"Ah," smiled the Healer over her shoulder, "now you can see that there is only the slightest adjustment you must make to your own centre. You are doing the work on the outside, but this is also echoing the work of the inside."

Zahira smiled and spontaneously hugged the Healer. It was the first time they had embraced. They held each other for quite some time. It felt like a wordless exchange of respect and recognition. Without letting her go the Healer looked Zahira in the eyes and said, "You are so precious, so beautiful. You must protect this porcelain heart of yours."

Zahira gazed deep into her sparkling reflection and welcomed this woman's intuitive perception, "Thank you. You are very beautiful as well."

"You have a crystal heart. It is beautiful and it knows unconditional love. This needs to be protected. My message to you is discernment. You need to discern more quickly who you give your energy to, who you learn from," the Healer advised.

"Wow," said Zahira quite surprised at this accurate observation. She had made no mention of her recent struggles with Bhagavan and his teachings. "How do I learn to discern?" she asked.

"Do not listen with your ears. Listen with your heart and your eyes. Look people in the eyes and get the truth. Feel what is coming from their hearts. You need to trust these readings," smiled the Healer.

This was a huge piece of information for Zahira. It felt like a direct message from the divine, one she had been seeking without knowing how to ask. The answer came before the question was even clear. Zahira felt a wave of gratitude flowing towards her new teacher. They were still embracing and they were looking straight into each other's eyes.

"You are so precious," she repeated. "You have something that everybody wants. This beautiful love needs to be protected. You can give but only when you are overflowing. When your cup is full you keep it for yourself. When it starts to overflow this is what you share with others. You need to protect this sacred heart. This beautiful porcelain heart with roses painted on it," smiled the Healer who was still holding her close.

Zahira hugged her more tightly and said, "Thank you. Thank you for seeing me."

"You are a beautiful mirror for me," whispered the Healer. "Thank you, thank you."

◆

Some Call it Witchcraft

Zahira plunged into the sea to cleanse her body. She was on her way to the ceremonial site. She was empty handed. She wanted to go forth with no baggage, physical or otherwise. Her work for the day would be to unite the masculine and feminine sides of herself. When she arrived at the mandala her heart spontaneously exhaled. It was a beautiful sight.

It was a figure 8 (infinity symbol) that had two interlocking circles in the centre. It was made of sand, stones, shells, acorns and flowers. The design was both intricate and expansive. The sight of it gave Zahira an instant feeling of peace. She was humbled to be present.

She entered on the side of the Goddess and spiralled her way to the centre. She knelt and sat in quiet stillness. She gave thanks for her abundant Goddess energy and asked for containment. Then Zahira crossed over into the masculine side. Once again she knelt and sat in silence. She quietly prayed for the power of discernment and personal protection.

When it was time Zahira slowly moved to the centre of the mandala. She stood directly above the centrepiece and brought her hands to her heart.

"I ask to find a perfect balance between my God and my Goddess, my masculine and my feminine, my love and my strength, my king and my queen. I ask that this union create an act of pure love in my being so I may give birth to a new self," she whispered.

She stood quietly for a while and then continued, "I wish for this transformation of self to be for the benefit of human kind. I wish to find balance in myself so I may radiate this balance into the world. I ask for your help to help me help others. I wish to learn through this process so I may share your teachings. I wish to thank you for this opportunity to be alive."

She drew her hands into prayer position just as the sun was sinking into the ocean. It was perfect timing. A potent moment to invoke transformation and make a wish. She quietly whispered her personal mantra, "Earth air fire water and space, thank you for this time and thank you for this place. Thank you for letting me be a part of the human race. I love you with all of my heart, in all of my ways, for all of my days. Namaste."

Zahira stood with both feet firmly in place and drew the energy of the earth up and through her legs, waist, chest and arms until it reached her fingertips that were raised above her head pointing like a rocket towards the sky. When she felt her whole body tremble with tension and intention she released it with an outward breath. She pulled the imaginary trigger and everything exploded outwards and upwards.

She let out a giggle, "I now pronounce you husband and wife, you may kiss the bride!"

◆

EARTH AIR FIRE WATER SPACE
Thank you for this time
& Thank you for this place
Thank you for letting me be a part of the human race
I love you with all of my heart
In all of my ways
For all of my days
Namaste

◆

LETTERS WITH DAD

HELLO DAUGHTER
What you have to do my dear is let that little theatre in your mind visualize a white Christmas for at least a little while. This is a hard time of the year to be away from home, family and friends and I miss you more with every passing day. May the Christmas spirit be with you and I shall have an eggnog toast for you on Christmas day. So let me give you a great big hug in the theatre of my mind and as the Christmas carol says, "have yourself a merry little Christmas…"

Love you sooooooo much and wishing you were here.
~ XOX DAD

~~~

OH DAD!
I *don't know how you did it, but you just perfected my holiday. Have Yourself a Merry Little Christmas is my favourite carol! It is the one that I like to slow dance to next to the Christmas tree when I am lucky enough to be in love this time of year. And here you are, my dad, singing it to me over seas. You just made my heart swell*
~~~

and my smile glow. Nice one dad. Perfect! I could not ask for more, well except for a sip of your famous nog!

I am doing just fine over here. I feel so peaceful and grateful. The locals have taken such a warm liking to me and have invited me for midnight mass. I will go with a quiet honour in my heart and I will give thanks that we are all healthy. Even though we are oceans apart we will always be together!

Sending you a BIG hug! Miss you lots too. I am so lucky to have a dad that loves me so much! You are my favourite ever!
~ XOX ME

◆

Spiritual Architects

"Don't look with your eye," said the Healer, "look with your heart. You can see four circles but there is only one. Now is the time to travel to the deepest part of yourself. Now is the time to find harmony between all aspects of self. Now is the time to transcend the duality and become one."

The group joined her and like little architects they transformed the mandala into its final configuration. It was a flower with four petals each one intertwined with the next. One for the child, the adult, the God and the Goddess. They represented the four parts of the self, but are to be seen as one. The Lightworkers had spent the previous weeks working on the balance of these, now it was time to integrate them in to one.

Now is the time for oneness.

The final image in the sand is gorgeous. It is a meticulous pattern made of pinecones and flowers, smooth stones and sea shells. It is only to be entered when ready. There is a clear pathway leading to the centre. The infinity symbol is gone. The dichotomy of the God and the Goddess are gone. There are four circles around the centre piece that represent a unity of self.

Zahira has until tomorrow to complete this work. Tomorrow she will integrate the balancing act into one. On Christmas day she will give birth to a new self. One that is not divided. One that is in full power, love and light. It will be her Christmas gift to herself.

◆

Now is the time for oneness.
One who is with self
is with all.

◆

Pomelo Post Cards Part Deux

Dear Zahira,
The heart opening is happening with full force. I've been meditating on opening my heart and having a truthful conversation with my spirit. I had a major release of sadness regarding my mother's rejection of me and inability to show me the love that I needed. I've been scared of this rejection of love and have been too scared to show love to others. I now realize this cycle has to stop. You have to give love to receive love. I have mentally and emotionally let go of this fear of expressing love to my friends and family. I'm working on feeling love inside of me to be able to express it to others. There have been lots of tears and emotion, but I'm starting to feel something I've never felt before.

Yesterday I was high on love and couldn't stop smiling. I know that this is the only path to happiness and I don't want to turn back. It's still a battle internally every day, but I feel I've made an opening that can't be closed. You have given me insights that have led me to this new realization about myself. I want to thank you from my heart, which is full of love for you and all you have done for me. I'm on the verge of tears just writing this and I don't know why. A lot of sadness yet to release.

I really want to see you, but that is the old me wanting to fall in love to take all the pain away. You were such a positive plug for me in India and you got me believing in myself. Now I need to learn to do it for myself. I've been too reliant on others and it is time for me to stand on my own two feet.

I want you to know my thoughts are always with you.
~ All my love, the Pomelo xo

~~~

Dear Pomelo
Holy shitco! (as my dad would say)

This is great work. I am smiling from my toes right now. This happens when I get excited and feel real love. I am so happy to hear you are inviting the tears and speaking with your spirit. Sadness is not a negative emotion, it can be a beautiful way to heal our deepest selves. Welcome this wave of tears and let it wash you clean. Be gentle in these moments. Support yourself and let yourself know it is all okay.

The words you have shared in this letter are so wise. The forgiveness and awakenings I hear you speak are life altering. You are so right to say that once you make these openings they will never close. You are right to see the patterns and to break the cycle. Break it with tenderness and forgiveness.

You deserve real happiness. You will receive it. I can feel it! You are making leaps and bounds towards a new you. The new you will carry forth all your wisdom but with a new compassion and
~~~

tenderness. This process is vital to your path. This process is a gift. Pay attention and you will be able to teach this path to others.

I have moved out of the ashram and feel a new freedom within. I've made a habit out of wearing your Toms. It's like a double whammy for me, I look down and I see both you and my father Tom. Both of you being as comfortable and familiar as an old pair of slippers.
~ Love you loving you, xo Zahira

Zahira is happy to know the Pomelo taking a stand for himself. It makes her feel good about the romance they shared. It was a catalyst of growth for them both. He has once again clarified his need to be alone. He doesn't want to use her to take all the pain away. She respects this clarity. Zahira has no choice but to release him with love in her heart. It does not make her sad; it liberates her. She is free to remain open to the love she knows she deserves. The love that can reflect her own. The love that is ready to take a leap of faith together.

◆

Family Power

"Did you get to unwrap any presents this morning?" asked her dad on the phone.

He was sweetly concerned she was feeling lonely when in fact she was feeling just the opposite. She was feeling incredibly peaceful and joyous.

"No no dad. That's not what it is about, you know that," she smiled, "but the day is not over yet either. Who knows right?"

Then her sister got on the phone.

"Well I was missing you all day, feeling so sad you aren't coming home for Christmas and then you'll never believe what I found," she started with a brilliant disbelief in her voice.

"What?!" asked Zahira with curiosity.

"I walk into the liquor mart and sitting on the shelf in front of me is a bottle of wine called Middle Sister!" she laughed.

"Shut up!" shouted Zahira, the middle sister.

"Yeah and underneath the label it says 'forever cool' and then it has a picture of a hippy on it!" her older sister half shouted with disbelief. They both started laughing hysterically.

"So we are opening it tonight to toast you!" cheered her sister.

"Oh that's brilliant," chuckled Zahira. "Very synchronistic!"

"Hey sis!" her brother chimed in.

"Yo bro! How goes it?" Zahira asked.

"Ruby got into dad's eggnog. She is absolutely shit faced and walking into walls," he said referring to his dog.

"Oh my god! No! Seriously?" Zahira half shouted.

"Yeah dad left it chillin' on the back porch and she scarfed it down," he confirmed.

"Never a dull moment," Zahira quipped and they both laughed.

She also got to speak with her mom who was handling her absence wonderfully.

"Your sister cried the whole car ride from Lac du Bonnet to La Salle and your brother seriously thought you were going to come home as a surprise. I'm doing better than both of them!" she beamed over the air waves.

"Way to go mom!" smiled Zahira, "I love you so much! I will call you guys later tonight which will be Christmas morning for you!"

"We love you too!" they all chorused.

◆

The thread of life is both eloquent and precise,
enjoy the flow and connect the dots…

◆

Gifts of the Heart

"Do you drink tea?" asked a fellow traveler.

"Yes I love tea," replied Zahira.

"Well I have a special cup that I have been using for a long time and I brought it with me to leave behind. It is special to me, but I would love to gift it to you," she said with kindness.

"Oh thank you," smiled Zahira. "My dad will be so happy to know I received a gift on Christmas day!"

As her new friend revealed the cup it was instantly clear that she had given to the right person. It was a delicate porcelain cup with roses painted on it.

Just like her heart.

◆

Journey to the centre of self
Explore your darkness with a ray of light
Illuminate the space within
And life will illuminate the path with out…

◆

I Don't Exist?

Today being Christmas was the last 'official' day of Lightwork. Almost everyone had crossed through the centrepiece, The Flower of Life. The work was to transcend the elements of self to become one with existence.

Apart from Zahira, there was one other woman who also needed to complete the work. She could sense a childish tension over wanting get into the circle before her. It was a feeling that she was completely conscious of. Zahira had to let go of the idea that she must be the one in the mandala as the sun was sinking.

"It will work out exactly as it should," she whispered to herself.

When Zahira returned to the sacred site the woman was just

entering. Zahira went for a swim and then sat quietly in the sand. She patiently watched the sun sink into the ocean and then she watched the twilight overtake the sky. Her fellow Lightworker was taking the time she needed. Zahira exhaled and took the opportunity to fall into a meditative trance. Her attention started to drift at the emptiness just above the horizon. The void where there was nothing; no colour, no clouds just open space. She felt her insides swell with a similar vastness. It was a clear realization.

"Hmmm," she thought to herself, "the eye always seems to drift to some *thing*, any *thing*. Rarely does it attract itself to space, to emptiness, to *no thing*."

This realization awakened a deep ocean of emptiness within Zahira. She felt like she was floating in this void. The time passed from sunset, to a hollow twilight, to a clear picture of space. The stars surfaced one by one until they were glimmering like Christmas in the sky. She left to get some candles and when she returned it was time. She placed two candles on either side of the entrance and kept one close to her heart.

She knelt at the gate and realized that her timing was perfect. Of course she had to enter her deepest depths in the dark. Of course she had to explore this darkness with a ray of light. She could see no one else. She was utterly alone. This was the freedom she needed for this experience. After quiet contemplation and an offering of thanks she stood.

Zahira took one slow step at a time. She journeyed to the centre as though she were walking down her wedding aisle. Slowly, lovingly and sweetly she made the physical and metaphysical journey to the centre of her selfhood. When she got to the first circle, the circle of the Goddess, she entered gracefully.

It is hard to say at this point what she felt because it was no longer specific. The integration of herself was just like the empty sky. The nothingness was complete. She felt no connection to the Goddess as a separate entity. She was already dancing with the God, the child and the adult. They had already started their infinite waltz and it felt effortless and serene. There was no goodbye, only grace. She honoured each circle without recognizing what it represented. Each circle was simply one with the next.

The one bit of clarity she can report came from a moment she had when she looked up to her stars. The constellation she identifies with is the seven sisters (also known as Pleiades). When she stares straight at it, it fades to a point where it completely vanishes. It is always brighter when her gaze is slightly distracted from it.

"What does this mean?" asked Zahira in a moment of clear contemplation, "Why do you disappear when I stare straight at you? It's like you don't exist."

Don't exist. Don't exist. Don't exist.
Was repeating in her mind.

"I don't exist," she whispered to herself, "I don't exist. I don't exist. I don't exist. I don't exist. I don't exist. I don't exist. I don't exist. I don't exist. I don't exist. I don't exist," she kept repeating this to herself. It made her feel giddy until she felt utterly liberated, "I DON'T EXIST!!" she howled.

With this howl her identity came spilling out around her. She saw the silliness of the profiles she has carefully constructed. Her responsibility to maintain a manicured image began to crumble. She was no longer the pleasing daughter and the loving friend, she detached herself as the teacher, the social light and the ex-girlfriend. She felt these roles and any others liquify into a silly puddle of nonsense soup. She released the 'I' that bound her to anything and felt herself floating freely as one.

She could feel a new realm of awareness stirring deep within, as though she had attained a new piece of her puzzle. She had started this chapter with a desire to get lost, but *this* was next level!,

"Oh, this is a gateway isn't it?" she asked herself. "I don't exist! What a concept!"

She dug her toes into the sand and couldn't help but giggle.

"Thank you," she whispered to herself and the night sky, "thank you."

PART 4

Confusion in the State of Wow

◆

Skinny Dip

She left the sacred mandala feeling energized and alive. Zahira had in fact lost herself. Lost herself beyond anything she could have pre conceived. She relinquished her identity and replaced it with a renewed sense of her existence. So many minor things had disappeared from her being. She would tell you what they are, but they are gone.

She can say that she felt light and bright. She felt loud and soft. She felt contagious and excited. She skipped to the Internet cafe to call home. It would now be Christmas morning and she wanted to be a part of the party.

When Zahira entered the cafe a friend from the ashram was sitting inside of a phone booth. She swung open the door and gave him a smattering of spontaneous kisses on the cheek. She was bubbling with love and it was spilling out all around her. She was happy to see him.

"Perfect!" she smiled. "I'm going to call my family. Do you want to hang out when I'm done?"

"Yeah for sure," he replied with his usual easy tone.

The two had been spending random bits of time together. They met at the ashram over a month ago. They share a very effortless friendship. He is a yogi from New York, but he grew up in a small town. He carries himself with confidence and at the same time has a very humble southern sweetness about him. To be honest he reminds her of her last boyfriend. His looks, his cantor, his confidence, his easygoing nature and his age are spitting replicas. It actually freaked her out when they first met.

After talking to her friends and family, Zahira and the (hmmmm she doesn't know what to call him just yet) went to lounge at a sweet seaside paradise. They nestled into one of the nooks that beg for time; big satin pillows, low-lying tables, candlelight, soft music and the sound of the ocean lapping at the shore.

Zahira even ordered a drink drink! Her first since she arrived in India. She had an Irish Coffee that was 3/4 whiskey and it went straight to her head. The (?) had three drinks that were decorated with a plethora of toys including bendy straws, umbrellas, paper pineapples and strawberries.

Feeling a bit buzzed the two fell into each other's arms. It was very innocent. It felt like a perfect moment to be cuddled. It was Christmas night and she had a pair of comfortable arms around her, arms that echoed a love of her life. These new arms, however, were attached to a man who has his own sweet beauty. He has a nature of confidence that knows true self love. He was so easy to melt into.

As they were walking home the water felt warm against the cool night sky.

"I have to go skinny dipping at least once before I leave here," he said not asking.

"Okay!" Zahira laughed as she stripped. She was wearing a dress with nothing underneath it and she was naked and in the water in under ten seconds.

"Okay rubber arm!" he called after her. They were both laughing.

The water was calm and sobering. She entered the blackness with the same calm confidence that carried her to the deepest depths of herself. The moon was the only ray of light in this moment and it seemed to be shining just for them. The two friends floated quietly beside each other. She wondered if they would kiss but decided it was best if they didn't. He has a girlfriend at home and Zahira didn't want him to do anything he would regret. She got out of the water before anything could happen.

"Nice tan," he laughed behind her.

"Yeah my ass is white!" she laughed back.

They dressed comfortably beside each other and he walked her home. They hugged goodbye and she lingered for a while with her cheek on his chest. They had a hard time separating themselves. She was going to invite him in and then again decided to be the responsible one. She didn't want to complicate his life for one night. She said all of this with a look in her eye and pulled herself from his arms. He pulled her back and kissed her gently on the forehead. It was a perfect way to finish Christmas day.

◆

Typos and Truth

"Hyam began success," Zahira laughed out loud. "Hyam began success!" She said it three more times out loud to herself.

She was laughing in the corner of her new favourite restaurant. The food is so flippin' delicious that she is sacrificing sea front views to indulge her taste buds. The atmosphere is family run and the typos on the menu are so priceless she can't help but repeat them out loud, "Hyam began success." What it really means is ham bacon sausage!

Zahira has a fond affinity for typos. She learnet to love them when she travelled with her typewriter. Her's were never quite as charming as Indian food menus, but a part of her art form none the less. They are also a part of the reason she would be resistant to edit this story into a perfect script. There is something to be said about the nuances of imperfection and Zahira is far from perfect.

She looks up from her laptop to see the...what hell is she gonna call him?

"I don't think my name is very mellifluous," said the (?) after he reads her writing. He just joined her for breakfast. "You can call me the kid," he offered.

"But isn't that something that you are trying to overcome?" Zahira asked.

"What do you mean?" he asked.

"Well we were talking about you assuming more masculinity in your life, being the man not the kid," she said. She was referring to a conversation they had shared last night.

"Well I see that the masculine is needing more attention, but I grew up as an adult. I never really had a childhood. I think the kid in me needs more attention too," he said without thought.

"You're right," replied Zahira. "That makes sense."

"I don't know," he concluded, "you decide. It seems a little weird to pick my own avatar in your story."

She laughed. The woman in her wants to call him the Carpenter. He was told in a past life regression that he has the thumbprint of

Jesus on his heart. Apparently they spent time together. He feels this connection is real. He believes Jesus is simply a man who had solved the equation of existence.

Zahira thinks perhaps he is both Carpenter *and* Kid. He is very humble and gentle like she imagines a carpenter to be. He is also a man wise enough to know he deserves a childhood. With this in mind and a smile on her lips she declares him:

The Carpenter Kid.

◆

Fine Lines

The Carpenter Kid is smart. He has reached a phase of fine tuning. Their attraction seems to be growing instead of fizzling. They have been spending a lot of time together since their Christmas skinny dip. They finally spoke about it yesterday.

"What?" the Carpenter Kid asked as she was staring him in the eyes. She was lying on her bed and he was sitting on its edge.

"What do you think?" she retorted. He had been gently caressing her waist and it was turning her on. "I'm not the one in a relationship," she continued, "and at this point we have not crossed any lines that you can't return from."

"I know, but I have a feeling that there are many more lines I would like to cross," the Carpenter Kid said staring down at her with a smile.

"Well I'm not saying I am not worth it," Zahira said with a giggle, "but is it *really* worth it? You are at the end of your trip. You are almost home free."

"Yeah I've thought about that. It's just that I also feel like this is the reason why I should have ended the relationship before I left. This is exactly why I wanted to be free," he responded.

The Carpenter Kid has been with his girlfriend for less time than he has been away. They dated for two short months and he has been away for almost six. They are also experiencing relationship problems. The Carpenter Kid has talked about his girlfriend's need to learn how to be happy on her own. He understands that being happy on your own is the only true way to be happy with another.

"Well I really like you and I like the way I feel when you touch me. I just don't want you to go home feeling bad about the time we share together. I can't believe I am talking you out of this, but..." Zahira stopped unsure of how to finish this thought. Who was she to make his mind up for him? Who was she to be the morality police?

"Well you can always kick me out," the Carpenter Kid said unable to leave on his own.

"Goodnight," Zahira said with a stern but cheeky glance.

She pulled the covers over her head and he left with out another word.

◆

"We all need to know what it means to be honest.
Honesty is more than not lying.
It is truth telling, truth speaking,
truth living, and truth loving."
~ James E. Faust

◆

Honest Eggs

"So how are you feeling about how we said goodbye last night?" Zahira asked the Carpenter Kid directly.

"Well it's got me thinking about a lot of things," he replied a bit awakened by her willingness to cut to the chase.

"Like what?" she persisted.

"I don't know," he said feeling a bit exposed to the call of truth talking.

"Yes you do," Zahira prodded gently. She was prepared to talk openly and felt now was the time. She felt some hesitation on his behalf, not because he was wanting to hide anything from her, but because sometimes it is hard to speak the truth in broad daylight over breakfast.

The Carpenter Kid is no coward so he spoke clearly and beautifully, "Well I have been thinking about my relationship and I feel that it is not going to last, but I also don't want this to be the reason it doesn't."

"Oh wonderful!" Zahira said in an encouraging tone. "Good for you. That's a great realization."

"Yeah, but that's the only conclusion I have come to," he said wanting to leave the door for romance open.

"Well I really like you," she said honestly. "I care about you and I don't want to be the reason you go home feeling any heaviness or guilt."

"Yeah but maybe there is a way to avoid that feeling," the Carpenter Kid said hopefully.

"Yeah maybe, but would you tell your girlfriend about us?" Zahira asked.

"Well… I don't think I would," he said a bit shy about this truth.

"Hmmm, well that doesn't strike me as resonating with the path you are on," she said feeling he was too genuine to live a lie. "I think you would tell her in the long run."

"Yeah but that's my point," he replied, "I don't think there is a long run."

"Oh…right," replied Zahira feeling alleviated by his statement.

So they left it at that. They chatted easily over a delicious began and egg breakfast together. She is still a bit freaked at how much he resembles her last boyfriend, but at the same time he is a clear and beautiful reminder of how far she has come. She has no more pain in her heart from their breakup. It's as though it has dissolved. It would have gone completely unnoticed, but sitting in front of her was an uncanny reflection.

Her attraction to the Carpenter Kid feels familiar. Especially when he locks his hands behind his head. His arm muscles start to bulge and she wants to fall face first into them. He also has very clear wise eyes and a delightfully easy nature. She feels like she can bullshit with him like a friend and at the same time have the urge to fall into his arms. These are qualities she adored about her last lover; funny, wise, light and delicious.

The Carpenter Kid is trying to convince Zahira to leave the Golden

Beach for New Years. It is something she instantly said no to, but he is slowly persuading her. He insists she won't have to plan a thing. She likes this the best. All she would have to do is pack her bags and let him steer. It is tempting. She doesn't have to decide just yet. She has 48 hours.

◆

Blurred Lines

In true Zahira style she finds herself back in her new hang. It is now nine at night and she finds herself sitting in the same chair at the same table ordering the same thing she has had for dinner for the past two nights. She is a creature of delicious habit. She follows her taste buds and when she finds a winning dish she sticks to it.

"Can I hold on to this?" she asks the server. She was referring to the menu. She wants to scan it for more hilarious typos to type into her story. This is what she finds:

1. Normal cheese tomato onion sandwich.
2. Fish masala severed in a think pickle gravy.
3. Pouched egg

Her day wound into an interesting twist. After she finished her morning story, the plot thinkened like pickled gravy. She met the Carpenter Kid for a beach lounge and when the sun became too intense they sought refuge in her room. They talked casually on her bed for quite some time. It was comfortable and effortless. They seemed like old friends. They ended up entwined but again it was an innocent embrace. No more lines were crossed.

It wasn't until after an early evening yoga session that a new line was drawn in the sand. They went to watch the remains of the sunset and found themselves crumpled together. He was holding her gaze and she knew it was coming. He adjusted his body so their faces were close together. Their foreheads were touching and their breath was too. They lingered here for a while and then he kissed her.

At first Zahira felt like she was kissing a friend. Instead of fireworks it felt like a fireplace on a cold winter night. It felt more like a sail boat than a rocket ship. More like a plum than a pomelo. However the Carpenter Kid is not to be underestimated. There is a strong under current of experience running through his veins.

As they rolled around drawing and crossing new lines in the sand, the intensity of her attraction was growing. She was turned on by his sweetness. He was not groping and lunging; he was soft and attentive. He would pull away from their kisses to chat and hold her kindly. She found herself relaxed and giggling. It was very natural.

"Let me be clear that my first priority tonight is a bottle of liquor and you in the sand," the Carpenter Kid smiled.

This made Zahira laugh and she repeated it back to him moments later.

"Well I didn't say it like that!" he half shouted in laughter.

"What do you mean?" she laughed back

"You sound like a news reporter from the 1920s!" he joked.

Then she really cracked up. It was true.

"Bee bee beep bee bee beep this just in..." she said mocking her own tone.

They fell into a pile of laughter in the sand and he just joined her at the table so now she will stop writing their story to keep living it...

◆

Confusion in the State of Wow

"That's a good look on your face," Zahira said to the Carpenter Kid. They had just finished crossing the final line.

"What does it look like?" asked the Carpenter Kid.

"Totally satisfied," she smiled.

"I think it is satisfaction mixed with confusion and amazement," he said after some reflection.

"Confusion?" Zahira asked.

"Confusion in the sate of wow," the Carpenter Kid explained.

"Confusion in the state of wow?!" she repeated out loud a few times. "It sounds like a Taoist riddle or something."

"It would make a good book title," he said.

"Ooh I like that," she cooed. "I'm gonna have to write that one down. That's a good one. Confusion in the state of wow. It would make a good chapter heading."

They had shared everything. The Carpenter Kid had given her a three and a half hour massage and managed to manipulate her body into availability. It wasn't a sure thing. They stopped before crossing each new line to check in with each other. Zahira was feeling a bit of confusion in regards to his honesty. He was honest that he would not be honest with his girlfriend.

"I just need you to know that I am not going to say anything when I go back," he said before they had stripped away any layers of clothing.

"Well thanks for being honest with me," she said.

"Are you okay with it?" the Carpenter Kid asked.

Zahira thought for a moment, "Yes I am okay with it."

"Are you sure?" he asked again.

It was the way he asked the question that started her thinking that maybe she wasn't. Her concentration slipped from her body to her mind and the mood was lost.

"Hmm, well it is a bit of a conundrum. You are being honest with me about your dishonesty with your girlfriend. In all honesty I don't know how to feel about it," she decided.

"Well I just don't see the point in telling her. I tried to tell her before I left that we should not be monogamous but she didn't want to listen. I told her she could be with other men," he said in his own defence. His tone however was not defensive, it was calm and clear.

"Well if she flat out asks you if you have been with anyone when you get back, what will you say?" asked Zahira.

"Well… I will tell her that I don't want to talk about it," he answered.

"What?!," blurted Zahira in half surprise. "You can't do that. She would never let that go. *That* is a chicken shit answer."

"I don't think it is. I think it is fair," the Carpenter Kid said.

"Fair?!" Zahira laughed in disbelief. "So let's take a look at this; you are in a relationship with a woman who clearly believes that you are sharing a mutual commitment, you left for this trip without being fully assertive about your need for freedom and when you return if you are directly asked about your actions you will tell her you 'don't want to talk about it?!' That my friend is chicken shit. You need to man up and find the balls to speak the truth."

He groaned and rolled over with his back to her, "I don't like your impersonations of me today."

"My impersonations?" Zahira asked.

"Yeah, first it was the 1920s news reporter and now this," he said half joking.

She laughed at him, "Well I am just saying how I see it. I think speaking the truth is the difference between being a man and a kid."

Zahira's tone was not condescending, it was warm and soft. She was not attacking the Carpenter Kid she was talking to him. There was no tension in the room. It was comfortable and real.

The Carpenter Kid rolled back over. He was smiling. He was still hopeful they would keep crossing lines together. "Well you know where I stand so it's up to you to decide what you are comfortable with. We can practice some tantra if you like."

"This *is* tantra," Zahira declared. "Honesty is tantra. This is the first rule. Without this honesty there is nothing to build upon."

They were quiet for a while. He held her with respect and without pressure. She was convinced she would just fall asleep. She was content with her massage and their talk. She did not need more from him. She did however need to get the oil off her back. It was mixed with bits of sand that inevitably follow her everywhere she goes. She got up to get a cold cloth.

"Can you please wipe my back clean for me?" Zahira asked.

"Of course," he said as he got up to hold her from behind.

"Thank you for my massage," she said with a sigh.

"Trust me," he said, "you don't need to thank me. That was strictly selfish on my behalf. I clearly enjoyed it."

"Well feel free to get selfish on my ass anytime you want," she smirked.

The Carpenter Kid was smoothing the cold cloth against her skin and she sighed into his body. He was gentle and attentive with his touch and once again Zahira felt her body responding to his. Her brain had stopped talking and she decided that what he did when he returned home was not her business. As long as she was truthful on her path and he was truthful with her she had no reason to deny herself this pleasure. So she caved and they crossed the finish line with that look on his face. The look of 'confusion in the state of wow.'

Zahira's confusion however, was different. While she felt happy to have shared herself with the Carpenter Kid, she had a feeling of distance surfacing. She was missing the Pomelo. She genuinely cares about him. She was prepared to give up everything for the Pomelo, but he is not ready for her. So what's a girl to do? Or should she say what's a Zahira to do?

Zahira and the Pomelo still write each other with loving support but they are clearly not in a monogamous relationship. In fact they are in no relationship. He has been direct about needing time alone and yet, she wonders how he will take the news. How will the Pomelo feel about the Carpenter Kid? Of course she will tell him. She has balls (jab jab!).

Zahira decides in this moment to spend New Years Eve alone. She will take time to honour her year and herself. She likes the idea of being alone. She would have followed the Pomelo across an ocean, but she will not follow the Carpenter Kid four hours north. She will let him go with a grateful goodbye and he will leave her with a gentle thumb print on her heart.

◆

Taoism

Through effortless action,
become one with all.

◆

Insert Jeopardy Theme Song

"What are you doing out here?" asked the Carpenter Kid. He had just found Zahira outside on his balcony. She was in deep contemplation.

"Well," she said slowly, "I am trying to decide if I want to come with you or not."

She was referring to his trip up north. The taxi would be arriving in ten minutes. She had nothing packed. She had no plans to leave the Golden Beach. She had no plans to follow the Carpenter Kid. She was sure she would be alone and happy for New Years.

Now, after making love again this morning, her tune was changing. She was feeling a spontaneous urge to be next to him.

She closed her eyes to tune out of her mind and into her energy body. When she thought of fleeing with the wind her toes began to twitch with excitement.

The Carpenter Kid just looked at her and patiently smiled. He had done everything to persuade her up to this point and she had resisted. Now it was time for her to decide on her own.

"Da da dummm," she said with a dramatic musical tone.

She has been in this familiar situation before and has sung the same tune. It is a classic 'Zahira move' to push a last minute eject button. By last minute she means the taxi is pulling up and the verdict is still pending. She has stood in the belly of indecision waiting for clarity to prevail and she has thrown caution to the wind to be blown away with it.

"Are you coming or not? The cab is here," the Carpenter Kid asked.

Her time was up.

"Okay, I'll come," Zahira exhaled.

The instant she said it she was glad she did. Zahira felt a peaceful opening appear before her. The road was all of a sudden in view. The Universe was presenting her with a window to jump through and on the other side was the sweet and sexy Carpenter Kid. He was ready to catch her and take her away.

◆

THROWING CAUTION TO THE WIND:
Be still. Breathe Deep.
If the idea makes your toes twitch
& your heart flutter...
then jump.

◆

WELCOME TO THE ARAMBUBBLE

Zahira is floating in bliss. It's the last day of the year and the Carpenter Kid has just worked her body into absolute womanhood. It is amazing to her that she almost didn't give the kid a fair shot. They spent an entire month together with no sexual chemistry. He wasn't even on her radar. So how she ended up running away with him is a mystery of remaining in the moment. A gift of being present.

"Wow," she said in ecstatic laughter, "that was amazing!" She was giddy with release. He had patiently and gently worked her body into an explosive mess. "Holy shit, thank you!"

"Well don't thank me," the Carpenter Kid said. "That was pretty much the hottest thing I could ever possibly imagine."

"I love how you get off on getting me off," Zahira clapped.

The entire morning was focused on Zahira's needs, on working her body into bliss. She hadn't even laid a hand on him. He was totally turned on by his ability to make her orgasm. She was totally turned on by his approach. It felt gentle and genuine. While she had already warned herself not to underestimate the Carpenter Kid, she had *not* anticipated *this*.

"This feels so nice and comfortable," she said with honest reflection.

"Nice, comfortable and impossible to resist, there's that too," he said as he was holding her.

Impossible to resist. This made Zahira smile. She has to be fair and say she gave him every opportunity to run. She is so glad he didn't.

She is so glad she opened herself to him. It is just like the Pomelo had encouraged, finding a starting point and taking it from there. She was not immediately attracted to the Carpenter Kid, but she is so glad she made a conscious choice to share herself with him. It feels healthy.

Now she is walking with a swagger in her hips. She is sauntering around holding hands and getting kissed over breakfast. She is back in the 'one of *those* people category.' The ones who get to have a headrest at sunset and a footrest over dessert.

The Carpenter Kid is so generous with his affection it mirrors her own love of touching and being touched. He gives it effortlessly and easily. That is how she would describe this whole experience:

effortless and easy.

◆

Happy New Year

New Years Eve was a perfect manifestation of Zahira's desire. She wanted a fire with cozy surroundings and she wanted something ceremonial. With pure fortune she stumbled into her vision: a magic garden full of soft cushions, fire pits and sufi music. She even scored a hula hoop! The whole scene was beautiful and her entire night was lovely. She had the ocean, the stars and sand all over her body. She had giggles, a sea breeze and fireworks.

Boy did she ever have fireworks! The Carpenter Kid is never to be underestimated. She says this again because last night he took her to the next level. His skills as a lover are his pure love of it. He gets off on pleasing her.

"That was the fucking hottest thing I've seen," he said in a husky voice. His lips were pressed right in her ear. He let out a satisfied shutter. He had just spent the last hour working Zahira into a frenzy.

"It's your turn," she said smiling from ear to ear, "tell me what you like."

"I like everything that just happened. I *really* liked that. It just happened and just thinking about it…," another shutter.

Zahira felt another stir within her. "No no no, you need to tell me what you want so I can please you," she persisted.

"In all honesty," the Carpenter Kid said, "pleasing you pleases me so much. Trust me on this one. It is not a selfless act. I could do that again and again."

Zahira just laughed. There was absolutely no sarcasm in his voice. He is genuinely into making her rain. It is his sheer pleasure that does it for her. He is so calm and not rushed. He settles in and simply enjoys every moment. It has taken her to new heights of understanding herself as a sexual being. She has mastered the art of making out with herself, but India is delivering her an opportunity to master it with others.

◆

Grown Up Romance

She chatted on line with the Pomelo today. She told him about her new romance. He was not surprised. He guessed something like this might happen. He offered her all the support in the world. He also said that he knows it is important for her to be open in this area (meaning her sex life). The Pomelo was happy for Zahira. It was a very loving chat, very grown up.

Zahira's romance with the Carpenter Kid is refreshingly temporary. He is leaving in two days and they have no plans for the future. They are unattached and they both agree it is healthy. There is something to be said about casual love affairs. If they feel healthy then they are. If both parties are growing, then why not? The Carpenter Kid is teaching Zahira to never underestimate anyone, especially in romance.

◆

Bloated and Tired

Well the holidays have taken their toll. Zahira has allowed herself to indulge and today she wakes feeling full, tired, and bloated. She is ready for a good cleanse. She wants to do an Ayurvedic detox. She is still unclear of when and how, but she is certain it is an absolute must before leaving India. Zahira is also certain not to be so certain about anything. After all, she was certain she wasn't going to follow the Carpenter Kid north and here she is.

Zahira is so glad she took the plunge to be here. She is having so much fun! The Carpenter Kid loves to cuddle. He holds her all through the night. He checks in with her constantly, making sure her needs are met. Even though she is not attached to him she will miss his attentive nature. She likes being held. She likes being kissed in the streets. She likes holding hands on the beach. She likes having a man who can't get enough of pleasing her. Who wouldn't?

The Carpenter Kid leaves tomorrow. Zahira will remain put until the winds of change sweep her to her next destination. The winds and a hot guy seem to be her only motivation for going anywhere. For now she is grateful, content and at peace in her own little beach shack.

◆

Appreciation is the key to everything.
It holds the power of manifestation.

◆

Bee's Knees and Hobbit's Feet

"Thank you," Zahira said as she was straddling the Carpenter Kid on the edge of the bed. They were looking at each other eye to eye. They were about to say their final goodbye.

"You don't have to thank me," he said.

"Thank you for everything," she said from the bottom of her satisfied toes.

"You really don't have to thank me," he smiled and then he joked, "it gives away your personal power you know."

He was referring to a comment Zahira had made about him

apologizing too often. She told him that saying sorry for things that he didn't do wrong were robbing him of his personal power. The Carpenter Kid whole-heartedly disagreed. He said he has enough personal power to share. Zahira believes him. She also believes saying sorry and showing appreciation are two different things.

"No no no," Zahira said with a smile, "if there is one lesson I will leave you with it is appreciation. *Appreciation is the key to everything*. It holds the power of manifestation. It is where magic comes from. It's where your hobbit feet come from."

She laughed out loud and he groaned and flipped her over on her back.

"You know you are not very nice," the Carpenter Kid said jokingly.

"Hey I like your hobbit feet," Zahira mused.

"I can't believe it! My whole life I have been telling people my feet look like hobbit feet. Everyone tells me I am crazy and then along comes Zahira and out of the blue she says 'you know what your feet remind me of? hobbits' feet.' Man! Unbelievable," he shouts.

Zahira just laughs because it's really not that unbelievable. They actually look exactly like hobbits' feet from the Lord of the Rings. What is unbelievable is the make out sessions they have been sharing. The Carpenter Kid is unbelievably hot. She went from thinking he was cute as a plum to a smokin' hot delicious peach. She uses peach because he has this whole Southern thang going for him; ultra polite manners, a slight twang in his speech, a chivalrous nature, a thoughtful disposition and completely selfless love making skills.

"I am so happy for this time we have shared. I am really pleased with us. I feel we have shared something beautiful and yet I don't feel any sadness that we are going to say goodbye," Zahira paused for a minute. "I don't have any attachments to you."

The Carpenter Kid looked at her and grabbed her hand.

"How does that sound?" Zahira asked curiously.

"What do you mean?" he asked back

"Well when you tell someone you are not attached to them it could perhaps be...difficult to hear?" she said in a half question and half comment.

"No no," the Carpenter Kid said in full power, "I think it is great. I mean isn't that the point? Love without attachment?"

This trip has certainly been a new personal voyage for Zahira. She has been in two romances and they have both left her sexually satisfied. She is starting to gain a new appreciation for the casual relationship. Her love for the Carpenter Kid is so easy that she can easily let go of it. She has never felt this kind of non-attachment before. She has always had a hard time separating sex and love.

Zahira said her final goodbye with a smile and a slap on the ass.

"See you around kiddo," she joked as she kissed him one last time.

They both laughed and then before leaving the Carpenter Kid pulled her in close and quietly whispered, "*Thank you.*"

PART 5

"Awakening isn't spectacular but it is real."
~ Unknown

◆

Balanced View

"So what exactly are we going to?" asked Zahira as they were walking through the coconut grove. She was following some new friends. It was ten in the morning.

"Well it is called Balanced View. It's about finding short moments of clarity through out the day. The idea being that these short moments of open intelligence eventually become permanent. I'm not really sure exactly. I know there is a video by the founder and then some teachers who will be on hand to facilitate questions," replied the Flying Yogini from Ottawa.

"Okay," said Zahira without another thought. She was being led to something new and she was open to trying it. A wise man once told her to try everything twice.

Zahira gave her full attention to the open meeting. The program has one very clear message: Short moments of open intelligence, repeated many times, become continuous. There were testimonials from people who have discovered this balanced view and Zahira liked what she heard. She was curious about the workshop that was starting the same afternoon.

She was debating signing up when she had a moment that solidified her choice. She locked eyes with a woman who looked like she is on fire with life. Zahira noticed her as soon as she walked into the room. In fact she could not take her eyes off of her. When the open meeting was done they walked straight into each other.

"Have we met before?" asked the Dutch Dakini taking Zahira's hands into her own.

"No I don't believe we have," smiled Zahira at their mutual connection.

They exchanged names and then Zahira asked, "Have you done this workshop before?"

"Oh yes," smiled the Dakini with eyes like clear warm ice, "I found this years ago."

"And it is working for you," Zahira observed.

"Definitely. Even if you are already happy, this can take you to the next level" the Dakini said singing a playful tune. "Isn't that what everyone is looking for? Next level happiness?"

Zahira laughed, "Sign me up!"

She needed no more convincing. The clarity, power and beauty in this woman's eyes were enough.

◆

"Balanced View offers a new and vital education
in the nature of the mind,
allowing us to realize our potential
and be of benefit to all."
Balancedview.org/en/about/introduction

◆

Transmission Testimonials

Zahira attended her first afternoon of classes with an open mind, but she left feeling hesitant. She is unsure about taking time to do another course. She feels like maybe she already knows this information. She is well acquainted with the observer in her mind. She has a clear voice inside her head that watches her squirm through difficult times. She can allow her frustrations to rise but not consume her. She has been diligently watching herself for years now.

Balanced View is an uncomplicated teaching. The program accepts people for who they are. There is no dramatic change of identity, no change of faith, no mantras, no meditations, no pressures. It is more like a simple switch in perception. A lightbulb of clarity that illuminates the tensions and frustrations brought about by living according to points of view (also referred to as streams of data). This illumination teaches students to simply allow points of view to rest as they are. There is no need to become consumed by them.

Zahira thinks it is too early to write about this. She doesn't really know what she is talking about. As she types this a Balanced View teacher strolls into the coffee house with two fellow students. One of them sits down to chat with her.

"Hey! I was just trying to write about the program but I got stuck. I don't really get the technique, but perhaps the problem lies in the question. Perhaps there is nothing to get," says Zahira as she welcomes him to her table.

"Yeah I mean there really is no work to be done. Just show up to the meetings and let the transmission begin. Just being present starts a change deep within your yourself," the student smiles.

"Well that is a sign of a good teaching," Zahira replies while typing their dialogue. "I think I am confused though because maybe I have already found this teaching. I have the ability to observe my thoughts with out reacting to them. When I am sad or angry I can watch myself feel sad or angry. I don't know everything, but perhaps I already know this?"

"That's the beauty," begins the student. "We limit ourselves when we think we already know. We think we have attained happiness and we are only scratching the potential of our ability to understand this."

"Well that's interesting. I know that happiness is fleeting. I am more interested in peace," Zahira says.

"Well I think you are in the right place, but this is something that you can feel for yourself. How long are you in Arambol?" he asks.

"Oh I don't know," is her classic response, "I don't have any plans."

"So you stay for the four days and see if you like it. If you do, I recommend you stay for the Twelve Empowerments course. It will help you to connect with your open intelligence instead of getting caught up in your points of view. It will be the best twelve days of your life," he tempts with conviction.

"Wow! Now that is a testimonial!" Zahira cheers.

Zahira recognized a glimmering light in this man's stare. His truth was clear and calm. She decides in this moment to stick around. She will take it day by day and remain open to the transmission of these teachings. If she has stumbled upon the power of now through the lens of clarity then she is in the right place. Her only job now is to sit back and let her story unfold.

◆

Letters to and from the Carpenter Kid

Hi...
So...

My girlfriend and I broke up.

Just thought you'd be interested to know when (not so much if) that happened.... I also just read over an email from my other ex. It was from years and years ago and it was shocking how easily it could have been an exchange between my most recent girlfriend and I...not sure what that means...well I know a lot about what that means, but not sure I like the implications.

Anyways. Its been a while since we've chatted and I felt like checking in. I'm working on the opening of a new pilates studio in Tribeca this weekend and am super busy but wanted to touch base.
~ Xo the Kid

~~~

Hey Kiddo,
Sorry to hear about your split. I suppose you saw it coming, so it came. Voila! This is the way the universe unfolds, one thought at a time.

If you are recognizing patterns in your love affairs, you can change what makes you uncomfortable and keep the rest. It's really that simple.

Give yourself some time for a deep long slow exhale. Don't think too hard. You deserve the best.

I have loads of love for you in my heart whenever you need it.
~ xox Z
~~~

Zahira is grateful for a check in from the Carpenter Kid. She appreciates knowing that he cares enough to stay in touch. She is not happy that he had to go through a break up, but he knows it was the right thing to do. She decided not to pry into all the details, instead she sends him a smile through the wind. She has a feeling she will see him again. She has no clue when, but life is long…

◆

"When we stop thinking for a moment,
we introduce ourselves to open intelligence,
and before long we begin to notice that
the open intelligence that is present when we are not thinking
is also present when we are thinking."
CLARITY IN EVERYDAY LIFE ~ BALANCED VIEW MEDIA

◆

AH HA! I AM HERE! HERE AM I!

Zahira sits in a cafe on the beach front. She is feeling warm even after her swim. The air is lacking the breeze she needs to refresh her body and mind. She is on a break from her second day of Balanced View training. So far she likes what she hears. She had a moment this morning in yoga where her mind went blank. She was not thinking and yet she was completely alert. A comic strip light bulb came on above her head.

'Ah ha!' she said without speaking.

The light bulb illuminated a wide-open space within her intelligence. All of a sudden Zahira could connect to this empty space that is always present. It is there even when her mind is busy. It is there even when she is being bombarded by noisy thoughts. It is there even when her mood is cloudy. This empty space is what Balanced View refers to as clarity or open intelligence.

This was a great 'ah ha' moment for Zahira! For the first time she could see that this open space is *always* available to her. It is unwavering. It is the space that contains all of her busy points of view. It contains her thoughts, emotions and experiences and yet it is completely unaffected by them! This means that no matter what is happening in her life, Zahira can connect with this clear peaceful space. She doesn't need to learn how to meditate her noisy thoughts away. She can just let them rest as they are.

Wow. What a huge revelation.
What a huge relief!

This is a concept Zahira is just scratching the surface of and yet a part of her feels like she is being reunited with an old friend. There is a comfort and a familiarity with these teachings that can only be described as her truth. She wonders if this is the dawning of a more harmonious relationship with herself.

"Thank you," she smiles to herself, "I am here. Here am I."

◆

Balanced View Terminology

Open intelligence:

"Anyone can stop thinking for a moment,
and when we stop thinking for a moment, all that's present is
alertness, cognizance and a balanced view,
and that's what open intelligence is.
When we look at that alertness,
we can't say it is anything.
It is an intelligence that sees every single datum
that appears within it as it."

Clarity in Everyday Life ~ Balanced View Media

Streams of data:

"Another term for the content of the mind is 'data.' Data (one datum or several data) are anything that occurs in the mind. It can be a thought, emotion, sensation or intuition, and it can relate to inner or outer events; it is anything that can be seen, felt, enacted, intuited or experienced in any other way."

One Simple Change Makes Life Easy

~ Balanced View Media

◆

Delicious Dish

"This is the best thing I've eaten since I've been in India!" Zahira said three times. "I love it so much I don't want it to end!"

The waiter just laughed at her. She was speaking more to the gorgeous man who had made it for her. She couldn't take her eyes off of him. He was busy in the open kitchen; talking on the phone, preparing food, chatting with customers. It was clearly his restaurant. When he spoke he sounded German but overheard that he is Danish. She was so attracted to him he caught her staring. He smiled at her and held her gaze for a moment longer. She felt her entire body flush with excitement.

He asked her how her salad was and she repeated the sentence one more time, "It's the best thing I have eaten since I've been in India."

They exchanged names and small formalities. He has been travelling to India for years and decided to make himself useful while he is here. He opened the coolest spot on the beach. It's called the Cheeky Monkey. It is filled with low-lying sofas, soft pillows, candles and glass table tops. The floor is sandy, the scene is stylish and the soundtrack is sexy. To top it off the food is gourmet and the chef looks delicious.

As she writes all of this Zahira wonders why. It seems like a lot of information for such a brief encounter. Perhaps this is a character that will reappear in her story, perhaps not.

◆

Motorcycle Diaries

Zahira went for a walk to contemplate her next move. She is enjoying her introduction to the Balanced View training, but is feeling a bit of pressure to explore more of India. The pressure is entirely from her. Just another stream of datum really. This thought made her laugh.

"Maybe I could hop on the back of Bonito's bike and go on a mini trip with him," she said out of nowhere to herself out loud.

Bonito is a sexy Spaniard with deep brown eyes, dark skin and a dreamy accent. They met at an open meeting for Balanced View. She sat next to him and they hit it off instantly. He had mentioned taking his motorcycle to Hampi.

Zahira stopped on the white steps of a beautiful old church. She found a perfect little perch to take a short moment of clarity. She pressed her back up against the smooth stone, exhaled and relaxed. A soft sigh escaped from her throat. Things fell silent in her mind and in the same moment Bonito's motorcycle turned onto the road in front of her.

"No way!" she started laughing. "Bonito!"

"Hey!" he said looking super sexy on his royal blue Enfield. "What are you doing there? You look like you are waiting for a picture!"

She climbed down from her perch. "What beautiful timing! I was just thinking of you! Do you have time for lunch?" she asked surprised at this perfect encounter.

"Oh shit, I am so busy. I am leaving tomorrow. I am heading to Hampi," he said as he was pulling out his phone.

"Really? I had thoughts about going to Hampi," she said with a hopeful smile.

"You want come with me?" he asked with his thick spanish accent.

"Yeah why not?! I am looking for something to do," she smiled at how easy and perfect this all was.

"Okay! What is your number?" he asked.

"I don't have a phone," Zahira replied.

"No worries. Write down my number and we can work out a plan.

I was thinking of leaving at 10:30 in the morning," he said seeming equally excited about having her company.

She looked at Bonito with bright glowing eyes and said, "Ooh this could be fun!"

He returned the same simple sparkle and kissed her on both cheeks, "I think yes!"

He pulled away and Zahira giggled with delight. She looked up to the sky and smiled a big wide, "Thank you!"

◆

Seriously?

"This place is like cotton candy quicksand," muttered Zahira under her breath.

She never did get on that motorcycle. Zahira was just plain stood up. She packed her bags, paid her rent, mailed her parcels and said her goodbyes. She waited for three hours this morning. She didn't expect anything but smooth sailing. She waited patiently, plucking her leg hairs and enjoying the morning sun.

Eventually she borrowed a phone and called Bonito. He was already on the road. He had left early in the morning. He said he tried to organize his things to make room for her but there was no way. He had to leave without her. He apologized and said that he had no way to phone her to let her know. Zahira had no choice but to laugh and shake it off.

"Okay *now* what?" she asked herself out loud.

She felt a bit disoriented. Her bags were packed and waiting by the front door. She was ready to hit the road. But where would she go? Would she get on a bus and go to Hampi anyway? Would she take flight to Kerala for an Ayurvedic detox? Would she eject herself from India and go visit her parents who are vacationing in Thailand? Or would she stay and continue her Balanced View trainings? She decided she would start with lunch. Of course she headed to her new favourite spot.

She greeted the Cheeky Monkey with an equally cheeky grin. He seemed to light up at the sight of her.

"How is your day?" he asked.

"Strange so far," she replied.

"How so?" he inquired while mixing pesto in a blender.

"Well I was supposed to get on a motorcycle this morning and head to Hampi, but everything fell through last minute," she said while sampling some toasted almonds.

"What happened?" he asked while working away.

"He left with out me! It turns out there was only room for one on the bike," she said trying not sound embarrassed.

"Oh dear," the Cheeky Monkey said looking amused, "then he did not love you."

"Ha ha," Zahira smirked back, "I don't even know this person. We only just met."

"Yes but sometimes it takes just a moment to fall in love," he said with a definite twinkle in his eye. This twinkle was not to be mistaken for him falling in love with her. It was the twinkle of a gentle tease. It was cheeky and caring.

"Of course," she smiled with her own twinkle and a wink, "but it's all good. The Universe obviously has something else in store for me. I'm excited. It could be anything..."

◆

Heaven A vs. Heaven B

Zahira has narrowed her choices. She is feeling a need to honour her physical self. Her body needs a good cleansing. She is watching her pendulum peacefully swaying between the Twelve Empowerments Balanced View training and an Ayurvedic detox in Kerala.

The Twelve Empowerments are being offered after her introductory training is complete. It is what her fellow student claimed would be 'the best twelve days of her life.' This sounds hard to refuse, but she is also feeling like perhaps she has gotten what she needs from these teachings.

The balance between these two options reminds her of a saying that her Ayahuasquero once chimed in her ear, 'Oh poor Zahira, stuck between Heaven A and Heaven B.'

This makes her laugh. It's funny because it's true, but not only for Zahira. She believes that anyone who lives consciously will find heaven on earth. Shifting to the present moment is always a gift. The gift is one of gratitude for all of life's experiences. The act of giving thanks brings a sacred element to everyday existence.

Appreciation is the key to the gates of heaven on earth.

◆

Appreciation
Is free and always available
It is the most powerful tool we have as humans
It puts us from a state of lack into a state love
Abundance flows to and from a loving state

◆

Grandmother Moon

Zahira spent some time alone this evening. She is still unclear of what her next move should be. She decided a moment with the moon was her wisest bet for peace of mind.

She flopped onto the sand and let the sounds of the sea hypnotize her. She felt a wave of peace wash through her.

"Thank you," she whispered to herself and the moon. "Thank you for this moment in time. Thank you for this beautiful paradise. Thank you for my health and for the health of my loved ones."

Zahira felt her hands spontaneously move to cradle her belly. She closed her eyes and started to hum her effortless melody. It was a clear moment to honour the child she knows is waiting for her. She never feels crazy or clouded when she connects to this spirit, in fact she feels the opposite. She feels a calm clear quiet knowing.

"Thank you," she whispered with a wink. "Thank you for being present and patient." Zahira felt her chest spontaneously lift and her heart swelled into the stars. "I look forward to meeting you one day, and your dad too."

She exhaled and let her body puddle like water. She was humming and smiling and feeling connected to her higher self. She let go of the idea of needing to know her next move and decided to enjoy the current one.

◆

Contact Clarity

"I'm hopeless at planning," Zahira said to the contact dancer over lunch. The clarity she shared with the moon last night vanished with the sunrise. She was back in the epic debate of what her next move should be. "It's all fine and dandy until it comes time to make a decision. Sometimes I have a hard time leaving places."

"Well how did you get here?" he asked

"I hopped in a cab last minute," Zahira smiled. "I was following a hot man who was coming here for new years. He asked me every day for a week if I was coming with him. I kept saying no. It wasn't until the taxi was out front that I finally said yes."

"Well it obviously worked! Staying in the moment works. So why question it now?" he remarked with calm clear wisdom.

"Ooh that's a good one. I'm gonna write that down, 'It obviously works.' Yeah I guess it does. I just thought it would be good to do an Ayurvedic cleanse. I really want to detox my body. I also want to spend time travelling with my parents. They are in Thailand right now and I could easily go and meet them. If this doesn't happen now, it will happen within the year. I have decided with full clarity that travelling anywhere with my parents is number one. That is going to happen. It would make them so happy!"

"Well it sounds like when something is important it is easy for you to decide," the contact dancer said with more great simple wisdom.

"Hmmmm you are right again!" she laughed. "Good one!"

"In my opinion the Twelve Empowerments are more fundamental than a detox," he said before leaving.

"Wow yer good," she grinned up at him. "I've known you for ten minutes and I've already written down three things that you've said. Thank you."

In this moment Zahira decides to stay. She will start the Twelve Empowerments tomorrow. Clarity returns and she feels calm and peaceful with her decision. She is in the right place. She gives thanks for the people who are sharing their own clarity and affirmation. Perhaps she can learn a few things to share herself.

◆

Q: How to make a choice?
A: Choose what will be of greatest benefit to all.

◆

Delusion Equals Oatmeal

Today Zahira begins day one of her Twelve Empowerments course. She is back at the Cheeky Monkey on her break and her crush is not here. Probably better. She should be focusing on her work.

There is a gentleman in her course that she instantly started to fantasize about. When he walked into the room Zahira immediately began creating stories around him. He was a perfect father for her children. A perfect partner to wake up beside. His hands were perfect. His quick wit was perfect. His everything was perfect. Even his girlfriend who he introduced her to after class was perfect.

A great lesson in open intelligence versus delusion. Except open intelligence isn't versus anything. Open intelligence includes delusion. It includes: stories, people, places, things. It includes: thoughts, emotions, sensations and experiences. It includes: memories, events and circumstances. It includes the Universe and the elements she prays to every day. It includes all phenomena whatsoever.

So this is a relief. Her delusions about romance are perfect just as they are. They are welcome to rest in her open intelligence. She doesn't need to: stop them, change them, punish them, avoid them, argue with them or transform them. Her delusional thoughts have no more power than her thoughts about oatmeal. They are all just streams of data drifting through her open intelligence.

The Cheeky Monkey just walked in as she typed this last sentence. They exchanged a wave and a warm smile. Zahira takes this opportunity to let it all be just as it is. If she desires to create stories about this man she will at least recognize them as that. She will not give them any power. She will let her points of view do as they wish. She will simply relax in the clarity of her open intelligence.

She closes her eyes, inhales the salty warm air and exhales a deep sense of peace.

◆

"There are only four means of relating to data streams: indulge them, avoid them, replace them or clarify them."
~ Balanced View Media

◆

Empowerment Four hits the Floor

Zahira is mentally exhausted. She went through some serious psychological gymnastics today and it's not over yet. She has homework. Empowerment Four is all about examining her view points with a thorough set of questions. It is a way of making these teachings extremely personal.

Zahira was invited to comb through her existence and get out all of her resentments onto paper. Nothing was to be overlooked. At first she didn't think she would have much to share, resentment being such a strong word. Then she found a wonderful array of tangles to pick through. She took her comb and got to work. Zahira was excited by this. She allowed herself to be brutally honest. Combing through her family and finding her tensions. Brushing through her friends and finding all the little knots.

Zahira's favourite part was going through herself. She took pleasure in nit picking her self into pieces; breaking down her ways of thinking, dissecting her thought patterns and examining her belief systems. She washed through herself with a gentle scouring pad. She invited herself to get it all out, to get to the bottom of this character she has created.

Zahira admitted to herself that even though she says she is not looking for anything she is secretly always on the look out for *the one*. A part of her is always scanning for the father of her child. Sometimes she can marry a man before she even knows his first name. Sometimes she only sees what she wants to see not what is really in front of her. She is good at creating stories and fantasies around romance. It is a way of avoiding clarity.

Zahira also realized that she has manicured a very particular identity for herself and the world. Sometimes she feels pressure from outsiders to live up to a happy go lucky persona. Other times she feels like she has to defend this persona to people who doubt it. A strange realization. She has painted two sides of the same coin with different realities. She has created her own duality to transcend.

Funny that. She has put so much work into being herself, so much time and effort in to having a profile and an image. She is now on the brink of dissolving it for clarity. She is now sensing something deep within her surfacing. It echoes the realization she had in her mandala. The one that told her she did not exist. The connection of these deep awakenings almost came up in tears today.

Her tears of relief were trumped by her genuine confusion. Zahira was doing her best to answer over eighty questions as honestly as she could. She kept returning to one question in particular:

Who is thinking?

"Who is thinking? Are you kidding me? Who is thinking? Jesus," she repeated over and over.

Zahira sat staring blankly into space with this one. She was completely stumped. She doesn't know how much time passed. Her final answer?

"I have no fucking clue who is thinking."

◆

"When you relax with all the ideas that you have about everything—including your ideas about what awareness, clarity and open intelligence are—then your disposition is completely serene and open. There is no need to get all wrapped up in thinking about all our data streams; there is just the easygoing acknowledgement of everything as it is."
~ Balanced View Media

◆

A Spoonful of Meditation

Zahira is back at the Cheeky Monkey. The chef of her dreams is no longer on her radar. In fact no one is. Just clarity, wide open intelligence. It sounds so simple and it is. She has been taking short moments through out the day. This is nothing new. She has been accustomed to self-induced 'time outs.'

She will often stop and roast her cheeks in the sunshine or to inhale the smell of pine needles. She will pause to watch leaves falling to the ground or to listen to the sound of splashing puddles. It doesn't matter why she stops, the point being she stops.

Stop. Pause. Time out. Clarity break. Open intelligence. Whatever you want to call it, it is just plain healthy. As much as these words all carry their own definitions they are all synonymous in this paragraph. They all represent a way to hit the refresh button. They are all short forms of meditation.

The word meditation comes from the same root as medicine.

◆

All Thoughts are Created Equally

Zahira is learning so much. She is learning that her preference for positive thoughts is unnecessary. Over the years Zahira had trained herself to push negative thoughts aside to make room for positive ones. This habit was so engrained in her being it became second nature.

Balanced View teaches that replacing a negative thought with a positive one will only offer a temporary relief. It is not going to eradicate Zahira's reoccurring thought patterns. The only way to do this is to allow thoughts, emotions and sensations to flow randomly and liberally. Relaxing with all streams of data trusts the natural openness of clarity. When all points of view (negative, positive or neutral) can be identified as equal they will no longer have control over her well being.

This new buffet of thoughts to nibble upon are both delicious and nauseating, but enjoying or not enjoying these thoughts isn't the question. The real question is:

Who the hell is thinking them?

◆

"The very, very important point to make about afflictive states is for us not to reject what is appearing. To not reject afflictive states means that when they come up, we rely on open intelligence rather than acting on them or wanting them to go away."

One Simple Change Makes Life Easy

~ Balanced View Media

◆

Mid Day Monkey Bars

"Well then...that was fun," she said with a smile under her breath.

Zahira rolled into the Cheeky Monkey and ended up rolling into bed with one. It was a complete surprise. She had entirely written him off as a character in her story, but apparently life had a different plot in mind. Man she is so glad she didn't get on that motorcycle!

Zahira settled into her usual spot to edit some photos and chill with the ocean air. She ordered a warm lady finger salad and this time it was delivered by the hands of the man himself. The owner of the restaurant plopped himself beside her and she sank instantly into his company. It was as natural as eating ice cream.

"I'm bad," the Cheeky Monkey said in his Danish accent.

"Why do you say that?" Zahira asked. They were lying next to each other on the raised sofa. Their eyes were permanently locked.

"Because then people have no expectations of me," he said with all seriousness. "I don't think you always have to be good. It's better to be real."

Zahira laughed, "Alright I expect nothing of you."

"At the same time I am always good now," he said referring to his own state of being. "I'm always going to be good because I no longer care if it's bad. I am completely unaffected by my moods. When a good wave comes it's nice, but I don't need to hold on to it."

"Sounds familiar," Zahira said, "This is exactly what I have been learning with Balanced View. There is no need to do anything in life but relax."

He put his arm around her and she exhaled into his shoulder. There was something perfect about this moment. It was entirely consuming. Zahira was not drifting out of time and place. She was completely present. She was floating to the sound of the sea, some Spanish music and his heart beat.

"So this Balanced View stuff has been good for you?" the Cheeky Monkey said half observing half asking.

"Yeah it really has. I've learnt a lot about myself in the last few weeks. Especially about myself in intimacy. I realized my personal stories were stopping me from indulging in men. It was really hard to get in my personal space," she admitted.

"Ah you had a really long list did you?" he smiled knowing the story all too well, "Women have long lists, men have short ones."

He touched the tip of her nose with his finger and she smiled. There was definitely an electric connection. It was their eye contact that had her toes twitching. She was getting shocks of excitement from his stare.

"Such intense eyes," he smiled at her.

"You too," Zahira smiled back.

The Cheeky Monkey grabbed her hand and began to massage her arm and her shoulder. She pulled herself in closer to his body. They were in plain view of everyone in the restaurant. This was surprising to Zahira. She had completely released any thought of being intimate with this man.

"I'm having so much fun," she admitted.

The two didn't move from their spot for hours. He was entirely hers. He was present, open, funny, handsome and he couldn't take his eyes off her. She was so delighted to have him in her space. She had been enjoying this man's food for weeks and now she was about to end up on the menu.

"Will you come with me for five minutes?" he said with a Cheeky Monkey grin.

"Yep," she said with out hesitation.

He grabbed her by the hand and lead her upstairs. He had 4 beach huts on the roof of his restaurant and one of them was empty. They went inside and he closed the door behind them.

"Come here," he said as he pulled her in closely. He titled her chin up to his lips and he cusped her cheeks in the palm of his hands. He kissed her so softly it felt like air. So gentle and sweet. He pulled back to look at her again. They just stared at each other for a while.

The air was warm and the lighting in the hut was a soft bamboo glow. He took her hand and led her to the bed. He sat on the edge and she straddled his waist with her legs and they began to kiss again. It was a very steamy scene.

Zahira didn't know how far this was going to go. The whole thing was taking her by complete surprise and yet at the same time it felt very natural and real. She checked in with herself and felt both comfortable and safe. She also wasn't sure what he was thinking, but in hindsight that's a pretty naive statement.

"I think your five minutes are almost up mister," she said when things started to get more intense.

"I don't really believe in time," he said with a cheeky grin.

"Well how far are we gonna take this?" Zahira asked. She had not anticipated any of this and things were progressing fast.

"Well it's up to you," he said pulling back and speaking honestly, "We don't need to know where this is going. We can just enjoy the moment. It's like when two kids play, we can just flow with it. But it's also okay if one kid doesn't want to play. There is no pressure here."

Zahira liked his analogy. She also liked that she was so comfortable with this man. She definitely wanted to play. Any part of her that was feeling resistance belonged to the old Zahira. The one who would make men ache for her, the one who would play hard to get and the one who would inevitably end up sexually frustrated. The new Zahira didn't have to collapse into this old definition of herself. The new Zahira was open to flow with the moment and in this particular moment she was game to swing on some monkey bars.

So it was on. They explored each other's bodies with playful curiosity. She felt both innocent and sexy with this man. The bamboo hut turned into a playground. His strong muscles and sense of adventure were the perfect complement to Zahira's flexible body. They looked like a synchronized gymnastics routine. They were like two magnets bonded by strength, silliness and spontaneity. They were not exactly graceful, but they would have gained points for their presentation. They were smiling and laughing through the whole show.

"I'm so glad you shortened your list," he said with shortened breath. They were both laying in a pool of sweat and grinning from ear to ear.

"Yeah me too!" she replied teasing him, "That was fun! What a way to spend a Sunday afternoon. That was like eating ice cream."

"That's a great way to see this," he said as he kissed her one last time. He had been avoiding responsibility for too long and the restaurant was surely filling with a dinner rush.

"You better get to work. Thanks for a great afternoon," she said.

Zahira was so surprised at herself. There was nothing clingy about this. She felt totally satisfied and completely confident that she had done the right thing. She had stayed in the moment, she denied herself nothing and she indulged in everything.

She could walk away with a confidant smile. She could walk away without feeling sexually frustrated. She could walk away without guilt and shame. To be clear Zahira wasn't walking at all. She was strutting with a smooth beat and a definite feline swagger in her hips. She was curled into her own cheeky grin.

◆

"Any real ecstasy is a sign you are
moving in the right direction,
don't let any prude tell you otherwise."
St. Teresa of Avila

◆

In the words of her nephew:
"Sizzzzzz it!"
Karate chop.

◆

Oh...I get it.

Today another light bulb came on. A question Zahira has been asking for a half a decade has finally been answered.

How do you let go of something?

Zahira would ask this question to anyone who cared to listen. She never found a satisfying answer. She had tried everything. She even hosted 'letting go' ceremonies with her girlfriends. They all seemed to have something they wanted to dispel. They would gather like Goddesses and invoke the elements to join in celebration. They would burn lists and send the ashes down the river on planks of cedar lit with candles. It was always a beautiful experience, but never exactly effective.

So how do you let go of something? The answer in the Balanced View teaching is – *you don't.*

There is no letting go.
There is only relaxing with whatever keeps arising.

Zahira has learnt that she doesn't need to do anything. She can allow her attachments and aversions be as they are. She doesn't even need to observe and accept them. Observation and acceptance are also points of view. They may have been useful techniques for Zahira in the past, but they are also subtle ways of avoiding a true state of relaxation.

There is nothing to be done. The dynamic energy of Zahira's open intelligence is inseparable from her points of view. Like the colour blue and the sky, her clarity and her thoughts are the same things.

There is no weight to her thoughts. There is no scale in the universe that could measure the weight, the length, the ratio or even the location of her points of view. Like a breeze in the air they are immeasurable and inseparable from her wide open intelligence.

Instead of being frustrated and defeated by her repetitious thoughts and feelings, Zahira can choose to greet them like old friends. She can just let them be as they are. She doesn't have to try and let them go.

Her only job is to relax.

◆

"By relaxing your hold on the way you think everything has to be, you allow for everything equally. You begin to experience everything as it is and you experience yourself as you are."
Balanced View Media ~ Clarity in Everyday Life

◆

What came first: The image or the isolation?

Zahira is at the Relax Inn on the beach. It is a starlit night and the moon is three quarters full. The air is warm to her but chilled for the locals. The music from the bar next door is reggae. She is in a white tank top, ratty old black sweatpants and her white hightop Adidas. She is toying with a gold wing that she wears around her neck. It was a gift from her best friend Coco. It symbolizes her freedom on the road and at the same time keeps her rooted in unconditional love for her family and friends.

She is once again mentally zoinked from a long day of sharing. Her Balanced View crew was divided in two and every participant got a chance to put their hearts on the table.

There were tears, but not from Zahira. She thought they might surface. She invited them to flow, but she was more excited than anything. She actually got a chance to share things that she doesn't even admit to herself. She exposed truths into a microphone that she has never even said out loud before! It was terrifying, beautiful and liberating. It was also extremely touching to listen to the honesty and openness of everyone else. It made for a safe and supportive experience.

This exercise taught Zahira that sharing her points of view in a healthy environment acts like a natural release valve. As she spoke from her darkest depths she noticed that it was like cutting the weight off of a helium balloon. She could feel her private points of view drift from the dark into the light and eventually out of sight. Simply sharing them weakened their hold and released their illusion of power. As they continue to drift away only space remains. This space feels like freedom.

Zahira exposed the way she isolates herself by creating an identity that is always in full power. This limits her ability to share embarrassing truths and moments of weaknesses with others. She has carefully manicured this identity to be her reality. It is real even to her. When she feels vulnerable she grows quiet and when she feels sad she doesn't leave the house.

Zahira has always considered this to be okay. She is always gentle with herself in her sadness. She gives herself whatever she needs, but she rarely reaches out to others. Most people only see her when she is blasting with enthusiasm for life. She can't decide what came first, the isolation or the image?

Did the image spur a need to isolate herself?
Or did the need to isolate herself create the image?

◆

Adult Nursery Rhymes

"Would you like a massage?" asked the Cheeky Monkey as he crawled into her scene. She was back in his lounge writing and relaxing.

"Of course," Zahira smiled, "Where? When? You name it, I am..."

Before she finished her sentence he was once again leading her up the stairs to the roof top beach huts. There was no one in sight, just the two of them. He found an empty room and invited her inside. The wind through the open window was perfectly cooling. The harsh afternoon sun felt gentle as it filtered through the thatched bamboo. He closed the door and instantly started kissing her. His kisses were so gentle, just barely gracing her lips with his own.

"Lie down on your stomach," he said as he stripped her naked.

Zahira giggled and flopped face first on the bed. There were no stories running through her head this time. She didn't even have to give herself permission to play. She just went for it!

The Cheeky Monkey spent generous time working her naked body. He massaged her neck, her shoulders, her hands and feet. The odd sigh escaped her breath and she smiled at her good fortune. As his touch grew more sensual her body started to respond. Her hands gripped the mattress and her back arched spontaneously. Her pulse quickened and he flipped her over to shower her with more kisses.

They paused to look each other deep in the eyes and *it was on*. She would say 'game on', but there were no games being played. Just two consenting adults enjoying some hot sweaty mid afternoon sex. How liberating!

"What are you thinking?" Zahira asked when they were done. They were both drenched in sweat and sex. The Cheeky Monkey was holding her hand staring blankly into space.

"That this is nice. Shanti shanti. It is easy when you don't know someone well. You can just relax and enjoy," he said honestly. "It is always more complicated as time goes by. For me that is not the way. For me it is better not to get too involved."

"Yeah I can see that works for you," said Zahira. "I like to grow deeply intimate with people, but this is good for me. I haven't done a lot of casual in this lifetime. I feel empowered by this experience."

"Yeah it's good you shortened your list for me," he said echoing their previous conversation.

Zahira just laughed. The two were on the same page. No need to grow sticky beyond the flesh. She appreciates having this man to devour. He is handsome and honest, but there is clearly no future. He is brash with his truth and he isn't into long-term relationships.

He makes no excuses for his behaviour and yet he can be tender and attentive. She observes that he is extremely clear and present. He is a perfect tasty tidbit for this tale.

Zahira feels a sly smile spread over her lips as she writes this. Life is good. She is open to the flow and it is leading her to mid-day romance. The motorcycle diaries were never hers to write. Instead she gets to indulge in an adult nursery rhyme. She loves it because there is no one to shake a finger in her face to say 'no more monkeys jumping on the bed.'

Even her own fingers are at rest. They are comfortably and confidently interlocked behind her head. Her feet are floating on an imaginary ottoman that is drifting out to sea. She is sipping life through a straw. There is nowhere to go but now. There is nowhere to be...

but to be.

◆

Slowing with the Flow

Zahira left her home last night to book a ticket to Kerala. She found a flight that leaves the same day she finishes the Twelve Empowerments. She was in the Internet cafe with her finger on the trigger. She was ready to put her indecision dog out of its misery. Part of her got trigger shy. It was the part that decided not to be hasty on an empty stomach. She left to find food with the intention of returning before closing time.

She strolled until she stumbled across a beautiful Slavic man making black Russian coffee with a Turkish sand oven. He was posted in a sleek and stylish cafe.

"What's going on here?" Zahira asked.

"I am making black Russian coffee with ancient Turkish methods. You must try. You get next glass," he insisted with a thick accent.

"Oh no no," resisted Zahira, "then I would be up all night."

"Just a little sip, really you must try," he coaxed with his handsome devilish tone (it reminded her of Count Dracula).

"Yes of course. I must try this. I have never seen this before. It is a beautiful process. Slow and magical," she agreed.

"Yes I must watch very carefully. I have one second, just one second before the liquid comes to a full boil," he said as he embraced the precise moment to remove the coffee canister from the sand.

He poured a little in a cup for her. Zahira had one sip and her tongue felt a new flaming desire. It was lust at first taste.

"Oh my god," she groaned from her groin. "That is amazing. I must have my own cup."

That one little sip of black gold changed the flow of her whole evening. It was like opening floodgates and Zahira was happy to be washed away. When she was handed a joint she didn't even think twice. Tobacco and hash made a perfect accompaniment for her coffee.

With great timing her two new favourite female counterparts strolled in. They always look like they have just strolled off the cover of a magazine. She will call them Flower and Sky. Two stunning beauties who are no strangers to both royalty and silliness. They are the kind of spirits who will start a conga line with the queen of Sri Lanka and walk barefoot through the alleys of India. They are consistently crossing her path and Zahira always lights up when she sees them.

"What is happening here?" purred Flower in her argentine accent. She shares Zahira's curiosity and enthusiasm for life. They are remarkably similar and they both instantly recognized it. Their connection is electric and giggly.

"Oh my you *have* to try this coffee," offered Zahira handing her the heroin.

After one sip Flower said, "Oh my god! You genius! I must have," and she took a seat at the counter. She was also instantly treated to joints and cookies. "My god I have not had coffee and tobacco in six months."

"I know the feeling!" cheered Zahira.

"I think this is ze best coffee I have ever had in my life," she said as she flicked her four fingers underneath her chin. It was a gesture of complete conviction.

"I know right?!?" Zahira cheered again.

Zahira was happy to have some female company. She can feel a great bond forming with Flower. They share an effortless chemistry. They joke that they are like cosmic twins. Not only are they both petite with long dark hair, but their personas are both huge and excitable. They also share the exact same cackle. When Zahira hears Flower laugh, it makes her laugh then she makes Flower laugh and then they get caught in a cyclone of cackles. They could be the only two in the room and it would be endlessly entertaining.

Zahira can't help but wonder if Flower is the reason she is still drifting in the Arambubble. She feels a strong curiosity towards this woman. Even though their connection is just 'flowering' Zahira feels like they have some stories to write together.

Needless to say Zahira didn't make it back to the Internet to pull the trigger. Instead she gratefully sunk into the scene that brought everything to her. She decided not to choose her next adventure; instead she will let it choose her.

◆

Leap of Faith

"You are beautiful woman," said the Swiss pilot in his sexy French accent.

"Thank you. You are a beautiful man," Zahira smiled.

They had met on the beach yesterday and he had made Zahira an offer she couldn't refuse. They were now climbing their way to the top of a mountain. They stopped for a while to admire the view. It was lovely to be hiking higher and higher. The sea appeared more and more endless from such great heights. It created an expansive feeling in her chest.

The wide-open view was a clear reflection of her most relaxed self. She exhaled a grateful sigh. She was about to jump off a two thousand foot cliff with this man, an action that didn't even phase her as anything to fear or doubt. She was completely at peace.

They made it to the top and he unpacked his 20 kilo paragliding bag. He revealed a purple helmet that made Zahira laugh. It looked like it was designed just for her (it was just missing sparkles). She would have preferred to leap without a helmet, she wanted to feel the wind in her hair, but he insisted she wear it.

This was her first chance to fly with the eagles. Zahira's spirit name is Strong Heart Eagle Woman. She has an undeniable affinity and connection with eagles. She feels a natural comfort with the idea of flying. This would be her first physical leap of faith into the wind.

"This is your first flight?" asked a man who was watching them prepare for take off.

"Yes!" clapped Zahira.

"You seem so at ease. You are not worried?" he asked with a curious smile.

"No no no. Nothing but peace," she said in perfect honesty.

"Well it's all good then, I hear if you die you get a refund," he joked.

"Ha ha!," Zahira laughed. "Can you imagine? Hey God, you owe me 1800 rupees!"

Everyone standing around had a good chuckle and then the moment to strike had arrived.

"Are you ready?" hummed the sweet pilot into her ear.

"Let's do this!" she said with out hesitation.

They surged forward until they reached the edge of the cliff and without effort they were picked up by the wind and propelled into the sky. It was enough to make her squeal with delight. She was finally flying! After all these years she was finally drifting around in the sky. It was a dream come true. It was so dreamy she felt like napping. She felt like a small child being cradled and rocked by the wind.

"Look! There you go," said her pilot as he pointed below her, "you get your wish."

Zahira looked down to see three eagles circling the air beneath her.

"Oh my! Unreal! I am higher than the eagles!" she expressed with an exhilarated cheer.

She felt free as a bird and light as a feather.

◆

For the Benefit of All or One?

Zahira felt completely stoned from her flight. Her legs were a bit wobbly and her head was light. She was a breath away from nausea but her spirit was so lifted she couldn't quite connect to her discomfort. They magically landed right in front of her favourite restaurant and went in for a drink.

She was still feeling quite high. She greeted her Cheeky Monkey with a smile. There was a part of her that felt relieved to see him. It felt like coming home after a long journey. He reached out his hand to greet her. She grabbed it and smiled.

"I just jumped off a two thousand foot cliff! I feel super stoned," she blurted with a glassy gaze.

"Ah yes powerful," he replied, "like you are on LSD or something."

Zahira just laughed. She was happy to see his face and out of the blue she told him so, "I like your face," she giggled, "you have a good face."

It was a total stoner thing to say. She felt very open and out of it at the same time. She needed to ground herself with some food. She ordered her usual warm lady finger salad and watched the sun sink into the sea. She and the pilot chatted casually and when he finished his orange juice he left with a friendly kiss on the cheek. She was happy to be left alone. She felt like napping, but instead she ended up working. The Cheeky Monkey needed help so she offered to lend a hand.

She put mosquito coils in beer bottles and placed them around the restaurant, she rolled cutlery and she placed candles on the tables. She felt a sweet sense of relaxed joy doing all of this. Many friends from the Balanced View community came in. They were all surprised to find her behind the counter.

"Are you working here?" asked one of them.

"Yeah for the benefit of all," she joked with the Balanced View catch phrase.

She was happy to be helping this man whom she still crushes on. He is so handsome and powerful. He is also completely oblivious to her unless they are locked in body and mind. It is the way he moves through the world, one present moment at a time. She is certain she doesn't exist in his thoughts unless she is talking directly to him. This is his truth. He speaks it clearly and he makes no exceptions. It is quite magnetic and addictive.

As she was rolling cutlery a sweet Swedish massage therapist came to chat with her.

"You work here?" he asked with a confused look on his face.

"No no," she answered, "I am just helping out."

"Oh I see," he said with a joking tone, "you come on holidays to volunteer at restaurants."

Zahira laughed. She instantly liked this guy. He was very funny and very easy to talk to. A Swedish masseuse with an Italian and Hungarian background. She was surprised to learn that his brother had married a woman from her hometown. Zahira found this to be quite incredible.

"Your brother married a woman from Winnipeg?" she asked in amazement, "Wow. That's incredible! What a strange coincidence. You should travel to Winnipeg sometime. There are ridiculous amounts of gorgeous women who live there," said Zahira as she rolled another set of cutlery.

"Why would I go all the way there when you are standing right in front of me?" he asked.

"Smooth," Zahira laughed.

He must have kept her company for a good twenty minutes. He had her in stitches. His humour was warped and his smile was warm. It was enough to keep Zahira engaged. Perhaps she was the one gaining the most benefit of all?!

"What time do you get off work?" he asked

"Oh it's not like that," Zahira replied. "I can leave whenever I want. I am just helping."

"Well can I cook you dinner?" he asked.

Zahira checked in with herself. Was she really going to let this handsome man pick her up in the Cheeky Monkey's restaurant? The instant she thought it she laughed. The Cheeky Monkey would not care. He really wouldn't. He would most likely encourage it. So with no disrespect Zahira replied, "Sure why not?"

"Great! I shall see you later then," he said as he wrote his phone number on a napkin.

Zahira is *still* giggling under her breath as she writes this. She has never ever ever ever had so many encounters with beautiful men. She is astounded at how easy romance is flowing towards her. Is it because she is open to it like never before? Or is this town just a mecca of delicious dreamy men? Either way her drifting daydream reality has kept her from booking a ticket out of here.

◆

Sweet Dish Chef

"So how long are you in Arambol?" asked the Swedish Host as she made herself comfortable.

"Oh geez," she started with her usual response to this question, "I have no clue. I have tried to leave this place so many times and something keeps sucking me back. I've stopped trying."

"I know the feeling," he replied, "I made it all the way to Pune and I got sucked back."

"This place is great," said Zahira looking around. "How long have you been here?"

"Well I just moved in actually. I was supposed to move into my friend's place, but he left on a motorcycle to go to Hampi and his landlord wouldn't let anyone stay there while he is away," he replied.

Zahira's mind instantly clicked, "His name isn't Bonito is it?"

The Swedish Chef stopped chopping vegetables and looked up to her with wide eyes, "What are you saying? How do you know this? How is it you come into my life like this?!"

"No way!? Seriously? That's bullshit! How crazy it that?!" Zahira shouted with an incredulous tone, "He was one of the ways I tried to leave Arambol. I was supposed to get on the back of his motorcycle but he left without me!"

"What?! So we have both been screwed by Bonito! That jerk!" he said with laughing eyes, "I don't believe this. He left without you?"

"Yeah I had all my bags packed by the door, I paid my rent, I mailed my parcels. It was a done deal. He was supposed to pick me up, but never showed. When I finally got a hold of him he said that he had no room on his bike. He said his bags were taking up more room than he realized," she shared.

"Oh he is a jerk. Let's kill him," he laughed as he took the knife in his hands and held it in a mock menacing way. "I'm not sure if I should say anything, but you are in the story so you may as well know…" he started with hesitation.

"What?" asked Zahira with curiosity.

"It's not that he had too many bags, it was that his girlfriend decided last minute to join him," he said with a slight wince.

"What!? No way! Bonito never mentioned a girlfriend. No wonder he didn't stop by to let me know!" Zahira shouted in surprise.

"I'm sorry," said the Swedish Informer, "I'm not sure what your relationship was like. Are you okay to hear this?"

"Oh yeah," she replied with total honesty, "I don't know Bonito at all. He is pretty much a stranger. Wow! This is soooo bizarre. Talk about a full circle!"

"You know we could really complete the circle by surprising Bonito with a visit. We should show up to his house together!" he joked with a playful tone.

"Can you imagine?! That would be too much! What a synchronistic connection," Zahira laughed still feeling surprised.

"Yeah I don't believe it. Small world," he laughed equally astonished.

"This is a perfect addition to my story. It's too good to be true. Man this life kills me. I don't have to make anything up. I just have to stay on top of it," marvelled Zahira.

He asked her about her story and she told him some details; how she is writing her life in the third person, how her character has changed from the girl to Zahira, how she used to travel with a typewriter. He listened attentively before serving her a plate of stir fry and oatmeal.

"Wow," she smiled feeling unsure about the oatmeal thing, "Oats hey?"

"Yeah I'm Swedish. Don't knock it till you try it. I think you will be coming back for more," he responded with a flirtatious tone. "In fact I know you will."

"Oh really?" Zahira challenged, "Let's see about that!"

She bit into her dinner and was more than surprised, "How did you do that? This tastes amazing." She wasn't lying. It was really good. "This oatmeal is savoury and velvety."

"Yes of course. It isn't breakfast. I don't make it sweet. I tell you I am an amazing Swedish chef. Just like the guy on the Muppets. We could sell this to the Cheeky Monkey. We could put our logo on it and make a percentage. What do you think?" he asked.

Zahira was laughing, "What would we call it?"

"Hmmmm, I hadn't thought about it. What about the Bonito Surprise?" he said with lightning fast wit.

Zahira let out a loud genuine cackle. This guy was good.

"Tell me something you like," he asked out of the blue.

"Anything?" she asked.

"Yeah anything," he replied.

"Oooo that's a good question. Let's see. I like the idea of turning food into clothing, like making dresses out of gelati or cotton candy."

"What?" he laughed, "Have you done this?"

"Well not really. I once made a bed out of pancakes, but what I really want is a cotton candy dress making machine," she admitted with genuine desire.

"What!? A bed out of pancakes? Tell me more!" he asked in surprise.

"Yeah it was at a festival called Burning Man. I made a bed out of pancakes and was drizzled with a warm maple syrup blanket," Zahira reflected with a sweet smile.

"Uhhhh," the Swedish Listener was at a loss for words.

"It was really innocent, I swear! It was all about turning my poetry into motion," Zahira explained.

"It sounds delicious," he said with a wink.

"My new dream is a giant cotton candy machine. It's big enough so I can go inside of it and twirl around. As I spin it drapes me with a cotton candy dress," she explained.

"That's hilarious," he said with a wide smile.

"What do you like?" she asked turning the question back at him.

"Oh I should have been prepared for this," he started. "You can't ask a question like that and not think it's coming back."

"Of course," she smiled.

"Well...okay sometimes I like to wake up when it is still dark out. When everyone is still sleeping and the air is still crisp. I like to wrap myself in a blanket and make a coffee and just relax. I guess I like to be cozy," was his final answer. "What else do you like?"

"Oh back to me? Okay hmmmm... I like to float. I like to spread my arms out in the ocean and float. When my ears are underwater I can hear myself so clearly. I like to make wishes and give thanks. It's like I am talking to the deepest part of my being," Zahira replied.

"That's sweet," he said smiling at her.

"Yeah I really love the ocean," Zahira said with hearts in her eyes.

"Yeah you seem like a real beach girl," said the Swedish Dishwasher.

"Yeah it's amazing to me how much I love the ocean. I come from one of the most landlocked cities on the planet," she said.

"What? What do you mean?" he asked.

"I live in the dead centre of North America. From what I can tell by looking at a world map, there is one place in Kazakhstan that is perhaps farther from the ocean than Winnipeg," Zahira clarified.

"Wow that's crazy! You seem like a total ocean girl," he observed.

"Yeah that's a big reason why I can't leave here," she confessed.

"Okay now tell me something you really want to do," the Swedish Dish Dryer continued with his line of questioning.

"Oooo another good question," Zahira paused for a long time. She was hesitant to speak the first thought that came to her mind. She was searching for another answer. She was drawing complete blanks.

"It's funny, I know it sounds like a copout, but I feel really satisfied in my life. There really isn't a whole lot I want to do," she said with partial honesty.

"Really?" he probed, "You can't think of *anything* you want to do?"

"Well okay... to be totally honest I really want to be a mom," she admitted. She was glad she said it. She had no real reason not to.

"That makes sense," was his easy reaction. "I can see you being a mom."

"Yeah I'm not sure if it's a biological clock thing. It feels more like a deep throbbing knowing. I have been talking to my child's spirit through the moon for years now. I know it sounds crazy, but it's my truth," Zahira said with a soft voice.

"That doesn't sound crazy," he offered with a gentle tone. "I think it's beautiful."

"So what about you?" she asked turning the question back to him. "What do *you* want to do?"

"Well let's see," he began, "I would really like to kiss you right now."

Smooth, thought Zahira. She wondered if this whole line of questioning was leading to this moment. She decided it didn't matter. He was funny and genuine and she was enjoying herself.

"Okay why not?" was her final answer.

As soon as he leaned into to kiss her the power failed. They both laughed. He could not have timed it better. The moment was sweet, but Zahira was exhausted. She was still feeling light headed and a bit loopy from her flight. She didn't really feel like making out with anyone.

"I'm gonna go right away," she said in the dark.

"Really? You can stay if you like," he responded as he kissed her again.

"Thanks anyways, but I am totally wiped. I am happy to go to sleep alone," she said in full confidence. She was not going to waver on this one. She was done for the night.

"Okay I will give you a lift home," he said with perfect gentle grace.

"Thank you," she said with gratitude. She was even too tired to walk.

As they were en route she asked him to stop at the bakery.

"Do you want a muesli cookie?" Zahira asked as she pulled up to the counter.

"I'll tell you what I want later," he said with a smart ass grin.

The Indian man behind the counter started laughing. He found this comment to be utterly hysterical. "This is good answer," he said giving a thumbs up.

"You little shit," said Zahira as they were pulling away.

"What!?" asked the Swedish Joker with an innocent tone.

"*I'll tell you what I want later?* What kind of answer is that?" she teased.

"What!? What are you talking about? Pineapple. I want a pineapple," he laughed.

"Oh right a pineapple," Zahira smiled as they were pulling up to her beach hut. She was half way through her cookie already. "Well I can't kiss you goodnight because I have cookie in my mouth," she said with a playful smile.

"Oh no missy. I am waiting until you are done chewing. I'm not letting you get off that easy. I'll take a crumby kiss thank you very much," he insisted.

"A crumby kiss. You know that has two meanings right?" Zahira asked.

"What do you mean?" he asked confused.

"Well crumby can mean like cookie crumbs but it can also mean like crappy, or not that great," she said giving him an English lesson.

"Oh well then. Let's make it a cookie crumb kiss," he said as he grabbed her by the waist. He pulled her in and planted a full kiss on her lips.

When she pulled away she looked at him and smiled, "Yeah that was totally crumby."

He laughed, "So do you want to be my deep tissue massage model tomorrow?"

"I like the sound of that, deep tissue massage model. Can I put it on my resume? Can I make a career out of it?" Zahira joked.

"Yeah for sure. You can travel around the world as a deep tissue massage model," he quipped back.

"What do you mean exactly?" she asked.

"Well I am teaching someone to do massage tomorrow and we need someone to practice on. It will be a combination of Californian massage, body rebalancing and deep tissue. Mostly deep tissue though," he explained.

"Sounds great! I'm in," Zahira responded without hesitation.

"Okay I will pick you up tomorrow at 2:30. Where should I meet you?" he asked sounding pleased.

"How about the end of the road?" Zahira suggested.

"2:30 end of the road. I like the sound of that," he said with a dramatic tone.

"I like the sound of being a deep tissue model," she smiled.

"I shall see you tomorrow," said the Swedish Taxi driver before he sped off into the night.

◆

Death Equals Cotton Candy

Zahira has just been introduced to the idea that extreme points of view are equal to all other thoughts. She understands first hand that the more extreme the thought the more she clings to the illusion of it's potency.

Today she learned that open intelligence doesn't play favourites. All thoughts are created equally. There are no special thoughts. There is no way to measure our thoughts. They are all weightless. A thought about dying holds just as much power as a thought about cotton candy. This is liberation. This is great freedom.

◆

"Afflictive states and the power of wisdom
are one and the same. Even though that might seem
a little inconceivable at present,
by the power of relying on open intelligence
we prove it to ourselves. "
One Simple Change Makes Life Easy
Balanced View Media

◆

Fit for a King

"Oh my god you're kidding right?" Zahira asked Flower as they got in the SUV with tinted windows. It was the first luxury vehicle she has seen since she has been in India and now she was riding in it.

"I know," cooed Flower, "You're going to die when you see where we are going. You won't believe it."

The two girls were dressed for a day at the Kingfisher Villa. Zahira was wearing over sized sunglasses with a teal head scarf and a leopard print bikini under a backless dress. The Flower was wearing a gorgeous floor length sheer gown with a camouflage bathing suit underneath it. She looked like a super model and in pure super model style she made the driver stop to have her nails quickly manicured. Zahira couldn't help but laugh at her.

"*Seriously?*" Zahira teased when she climbed back in their ride.

"Of course, why not?" smiled Flower with her charming grin. They both laughed.

The cosmic twins and friends were heading for a day of royal decadence. They had been personally invited by a friend of Flowers. She seems to be infinitely connected to power and wealth. Their driver was extremely sweet and seemed amused by their genuine enthusiasm for life.

"We need to do business somehow," Flower purred in her Argentine accent. "You and I would make great partners."

"I know, I feel it too. What does that look like though?" Zahira wondered out loud.

"I believe it will appear. There are so many ways to tap into abundance, for today let's just enjoy it!" Flower chimed with sweet wisdom.

"Sounds good to me!" Zahira said relaxing into the leather seats.

Zahira stared out of the tinted windows feeling grateful for a glimpse of decadence. So far, her Indian vacation has been quite humble. She has been living out of her backpack in a weathered beach hut. She loves the simplicity of her life on the road, but she is also a huge fan of luxury.

"You've got to be kidding me," Zahira said to herself as they pulled through the Villa gates, "This place isn't a villa, it's a palace!" Zahira's jaw was dragging on the ground as she was escorted from the vehicle to a massive marble staircase. The front doors of the palace were built for a giant. They were amazingly high and heavy. There were two men in uniforms waiting to open them.

"Please madame," they said as they ushered her in.

Zahira and Flower looked at each other and started laughing in their signature hysterical cackles. Their enthusiasm was totally contagious.

"I'm so happy you are here," greeted their host enjoying their enthusiasm. "Please make yourself at home."

They strolled through the palace that was filled with ponds and pool tables, ancient furniture and alters, drum kits and dance floors. Then they were picked up by two separate golf carts and whisked through the magnificent gardens to a poolside lounge that was over looking the Arabian sea.

"Champagne ladies?" asked their host.

"Yes!" the twins cheered in unison.

He ordered glasses from the bar staff and they served it on a silver platter.

"Thank you!" smiled Zahira. "I say we toast to this beautiful day and our generous host. Thank you for sharing this supreme decadence."

"It is a pleasure," he replied with a genuine smile.

The group of friends swam and danced and dined. Every time Zahira got out of the pool an attendant was waiting with a fresh white robe. It was completely over the top, but she was eating it up (including the warm chocolate brownies and ice cream served by a man wearing white gloves).

The friends shared stories of love and loss. Their host shared feelings of the invisible bars that money can sometimes impose. He talked about the potential of feeling imprisoned by wealth and power, how it can give the illusion of happiness, but the reality is quite different.

"Money doesn't guarantee a good life," he admitted.

"I can see why that would be true," agreed Zahira observing how empty the giant palace must feel. "Freedom comes from within."

"It's true," agreed their host. "Freedom is free and therefore it is available to anyone at anytime. Money is also a bonus because it allows me to spoil the people I care about. More champagne ladies?"

"Genius," Flower grinned as she held out her glass.

"Absolutely genius," Zahira mirrored.

And they both cackled into the sunset.

◆

Clear to the Core

Zahira has finished The Twelve Empowerments. She is so grateful she decided to stick it out. She is not sure if it was the best twelve days of her life, but it was certainly amongst the most valuable. The lessons she has learned are more like understandings. They are awakenings that can never fall back asleep.

She is genuinely touched by the Balanced View community. They have dedicated their lives to the benefit of all. There isn't even a tremor of disconcertion. The community feels like a healthy well-tuned instrument. It is humming a melody that is natural and welcoming. There is no undercurrent of money or distrust. Everyone is donating time because they have caught a glimpse of the indestructible benefit of open intelligence. It's not even impressive it's simply expressive, a clear honest genuine expression of a healthy balanced view. This community shows that clarity is not exclusive it is *all* inclusive.

◆

"No matter what we are involved in, the basis of human life is the same for everyone and everything: open intelligence. By relying on open intelligence, it's easy to live; by relying on data, it isn't easy to live. It is a totally simple equation."

Clarity in Everyday Life - Balanced View Media

◆

How to implement awakenings?

Welcome them
Give thanks
Rest into being

◆

Boys Just Wanna Have Fun

"You are looking very powerful today," said the Cheeky Monkey as she greeted him at his counter top. "These colours are very powerful," he repeated as he eyed her up and down. He was referring to her bright teal scarf, matching harem pants and her neon pink crochet halter top. He was smiling with his usual cheeky wide grin.

"Thank you," Zahira beamed. For some reason she loves having this man's attention. Perhaps it is his face. His expressions are so childlike and sexy at the same time. He carries himself with an animalistic presence, only seeing what is directly in front of him. He seems to be riding on the cusp of time.

"I just tried to book my ticket to Kerala again," she said with a big smile.

"What?! You have not booked it yet? Then you stay longer and we can spend some time together," he proposed with a smile.

Zahira instantly lit up, "Really? Well that could be interesting!"

"I was already thinking like this," he said in his Danish way.

"Okay!" said Zahira. She noted that her toes were twitching, "Then I stay longer! Decision made."

"Yes, but just for fun yeah?" he said with his classic non-committal tone.

"Yes of course," she beamed, "just for fun."

Within two minutes he was curled up next to her. She was

once again delighted to have him close by. He was cracking her up completely. She couldn't stop laughing. Her enjoyment was mostly coming from a place of surprise. She did not expect to have this man back in her space, over a week had passed since their mid-afternoon make outs.

"You look enlightened today," he repeated with a smile. "This turquoise and the pink looks very enlightened. You just need wings."

"I have wings," she said referring to the butterfly tattoo on her back.

"This music makes me want to roller skate," he said with disco dancing hands.

Zahira roared with laugher. She never expected *that* to come out of his mouth. Roller skating? She was trying to imagine this big muscle man on roller skates. She couldn't stop laughing.

"Why you laugh?" he said with a serious face, "This I can do. It is so smooth, like flying."

Zahira was still laughing. She spent an entire summer listening to Jamiroquai and cruising her city on ruby red roller skates.

"What part of Canada do you come from?" he asked

"Winnipeg," she said.

"Winnipig!?" he laughed.

"No not winni-pig! Winni-peg!" she corrected.

"This is a funny name," he said, "Miss Piggy and Mister Winnipeg were crossing the street. Miss Piggy said I want a croissant and Mister Winnipeg called her a pig and so she hit him with her hand bag."

Zahira's eyes grew wide and she roared with laughter. This guy is totally insane. He is so irregular with his thoughts. It's like spending time with a Plinko game, he is impossible to predict.

"What time is it?" she asked.

He looked as his watch, "Soon."

Zahira just laughed. She had no idea what this meant, but she liked it.

"Maybe I go sun bed," he said. "You come?"

"Yep let's do it," she replied excited to have him outside of the kitchen.

"Yes my bikini is there," he joked, "let's go."

◆

Face Plants

Zahira is spiralling right now. She is rushing on sugar and just ordered more. It's all his fault. She bumped into the Swedish Chef on the beach at sunset. She had just left the Cheeky Monkey and she was going to call him.

"I was just going to call you!" she shouted as he approached. He caught her taking pictures of herself in the supper light.

"Yeah yeah yeah," he smiled, "I don't believe you."

And why should he? She broke plans with him last week to spend all her time with the Cheeky Monkey and she did the same thing today. He had every reason to not believe her.

"No really! I really really was! Do you want to have a seat with me?"

"Of course," he said, "You look absolutely beautiful by the way. I love these colours on you."

"Thank you," she smiled. They started to walk and talk.

"How was your day?" he asked.

"It was really peaceful," she started, "I went for a jog along the beach and did some yoga. Then I went to book a ticket to leave here and once again I didn't finish the transaction. I ended up at the Cheeky Monkey's. It turns out I'm going to stick around a little longer to have a romance with him."

"Oh, well I was hoping to have a romance with you," he said without skipping a beat.

"I know," she smiled and touched his arm. "I know, but I don't think it would be fair for me to start a romance with both of you. So I just wanted to be really honest with you about where I am at."

"Yeah we are actually friends," said the Swedish Listener. "I've known him for a long time."

"Yeah another reason it wouldn't be fair for me to be with you. I have to be honest and say I never find myself in this predicament. I am usually aching for beautiful men and it seems lately I am surrounded by them. I just don't have the experience to know how to manage all of this other than to be completely honest," Zahira confessed.

"I appreciate it," he said.

"Yeah I mean I know that the Cheeky Monkey isn't looking for anything serious. We are just having fun together, but I want to respect what we have started," she smiled warmly.

"Well I think you should know that I really like you. In fact I think I could easily fall in love with you. Who knows, I could even move to Winnipeg," he said with a gentle and sincere look in his eyes.

Zahira just fell over. Completely. She was kneeling next to him and she literally face planted into the sand. That was her reaction to this man's comment.

"But maybe we should start by eating a shit load of ice cream," he said.

◆

Ping Ponging

Zahira is sitting in between the Cheeky Monkey and the Swedish Masseuse. She is watching them both. They are friends and she is comfortable being in this position. One on her left and one on her right, both with such different energies.

She has a date with the Cheeky Monkey, plans to play ping pong. The Swedish Masseuse stopped into to ask if she would be a deep tissue model again. He is offering her another full day of massage. Of course she said yes. He held her hands in his before he left and then kissed her on both cheeks.

"Great," he smiled, "then I will see you tomorrow."

"See you tomorrow," Zahira smiled.

She is amazed at the fortune that is unfolding in front of her every move. She has not had a chance to stop and look around. Things are flowing her way with warp speed. She is having a hard time keeping up.

"It was so nice to sit on the beach with you yesterday," said the Cheeky Monkey as he rubbed her shoulder.

"Yeah it was nice," she smiled at him.

"This is another nice dress. What is this panda?" he asked

"Panda!?" she laughed, "No it's a leopard!"

"Leopard? Nooooo dis dis is a bird," he started in his thick accent, "dis is the bird with the big yellow eyes," he said putting his fingers in wide round circles around his eyes.

"An owl?" she asked.

"You know the child's story about the boy and the teddy bear?" he asked.

"No, what are you talking about?"

"You know the story with the boy and the pig and the tiger and the yellow bear," he persisted.

"I have no clue what you are talking about," she said genuinely confused. "Is this a Danish fairytale?"

"No no, you know what I am saying. He lives in a tree house with the yellow bear," he insisted.

"Oh! Winnie the Pooh?" she asked finally getting the picture.

"Yes dis is it, Winnie the Pooh," he smiled smugly.

"Winnie the Pooh is from Winnipeg!" she said with great pride.

"No no, this is not possible," he said with a cocky tone.

"Yes it is! Winnie the Pooh, Winnipeg. It's true," she said trying to convince him.

"Okay well the big bird in dis, dis is what dis is," he said pointing to her leopard print dress.

"An owl," Zahira jested, "I guessed that five minutes ago."

"Yes yes the owl," he replied with a smug smile.

Zahira just laughed, "This is *not* owl. It's leopard."

"Yes you are wearing like an owl and looking like a mouse," he said making a funny face. It was his interpretation of a mouse.

"A mouse!?" she scoffed while crinkling her nose.

"Yes I see you sitting on this side of the counter looking like a little mouse with your big brown eyes," he teased.

"That is *not* a compliment," insisted Zahira. "Most women don't want to be called a mouse. Do *you* like mice?"

"No no, not in the real life, but on the TV they are very cute," he said in his adorable Danish way.

"Yer totally nuts," she remarked in amazement.

They left to go and play ping pong. It was entirely comical. They were both in it to win it. She kicked his ass the first two games and then he ended up winning best out of five. The whole time she giggled.

"You remind me of a ping pong ball," she said to him afterwards. "I never know what direction you are going to go in. You are impossible to follow and predict. Your motions are all over the place. I have tried to write down our conversations and I just get lost. It's like they are impossible to remember because they are so random and then they just disappear."

"Yes this is like what I say the other day. Sometimes when I am singing in the moment I say some really brilliant things and then when I go to say them again they are not so good. They are only for the moment," he replied thoughtfully.

Zahira is hooked on this man. This Cheeky Monkey is not a pomelo or a peach, he is totally bananas. He is so fascinating to her. She hangs on his words because she has no idea what will come next. He really keeps her on her toes. She has to stay awake to follow his thought patterns. They are so surprising and have no particular rhythm.

Tonight is the first time she got to see him outside of his realm. It was a real turn on. He moves through the world like a wild animal and yet he has a gentle attentiveness for the people he passes. It is an exciting combination.

Zahira has to be honest and say that she likes him more than she would like to. She knows he is a fleeting fancy. He has been clear from the start that he is not looking for anything serious. He is open about being elusive and somehow this makes him even more magnetic.

◆

Cosmic Twins

Flower has been weaving in and out of Zahira's days with brilliant timing. She is an Argentine firecracker with a stunning ability to win people over to the point where they simply fall in love. Zahira certainly has.

Zahira can clearly see Flower is a master at manifestation. It is written all over her body language. She is like a wild cat, the queen of her own jungle. She exudes power but in an enlightened feminine way. She sees the world as her playing field. She is not limited to time and space.

They joke about being twins. There is something about their reflection that needs no explanation. They are both equally amazed and astounded by the beauty of this lifetime. They share a quality of excitement for life that could only be described as electric. Zahira compares spending time with Flower to eating lightening bolts for breakfast.

The new friends have been sharing big dreams as of late. Zahira feels she has met her match in this woman. They both see life as pure potential and Zahira is certain if they put their minds together they could sell light to the sun.

Zahira has a hunch that these two have more stories to write. With all the men who have drifted in and out of her story, Flower feels like the one character she will grow roots with. For all the times she has tried to leave this seductive coastal paradise, she believes Flower is the real reason she is still here.

◆

Permission to be Present

The past two days have been nothing but a blissful treat. Zahira resumed her budding career as a deep tissue massage model. The Swedish Masseuse spoiled her with his touch. He is genuine, clear and gentle. Zahira knows he is craving a commitment from her, even if it just means dinner, but she has not been able to give him this. Even though he has spoken the words she has been waiting to hear (I could easily fall in love with you and move to Winnipeg) Zahira is not feeling a reciprocal reaction.

She has been checking in with herself. She notes that she has given herself completely to the badass non-committal super fun Cheeky Monkey over the gentle compassionate handsome healer. She is okay with this. She doesn't have to fall in love with the Swedish Admirer just because he is falling in love with her. She just has to be honest with herself and him.

Zahira has made it clear to him that they will be just friends. She hasn't been avoiding him, but she isn't keen on spending time with him. Her energy is naturally flowing towards the Cheeky Monkey. To be honest, she doesn't have much more to say about the Swedish Sweetheart. She will give thanks and let him quietly slide out of her story.

Zahira's short moments of clarity are giving her permission to simply enjoy the present and relax into life. She is choosing the path of least resistance and it keeps leading her back into the Monkey's arms. He let out the sweetest giggle when they were lying in bed yesterday morning.

"What's so funny?" she asked with curiosity.

"Oh I was thinking about the day that I came and laid next to you at the restaurant. It was so easy, like two kids," he said with a childish grin.

"Like two kids?" she asked.

"Yes, like two kids when they play they don't think about anything. They just meet and they start to play. It is like this," he said.

Zahira loves to play with this man. He reminds her of wind. Sometimes he envelopes her like a soft warm breeze and sometimes he knocks her off her guard and rips her being into awareness. He is too spontaneous to be captured.

This is what makes him so alluring. She will never capture him. He is impossible to pin. He is so full of life that he makes her feel blushingly alive. She is grateful to have him as a playmate. She will continue to swing on his monkey bars until she leaves Goa.

◆

Live What You Speak

Zahira woke up next to the Cheeky Monkey this morning wondering if she was growing too fond of him. He pulled her on top of him for a long warm gentle cuddle. He pressed her naked body against his own and massaged her back while she melted into his chest. She felt herself sighing into the morning. He started to giggle.

"What's so funny?" she asked.

"I laughing about winning the lotto," he said with his classic boyish grin.

"The lotto?" she asked still holding him close.

"Yes, yesterday when we ordered everything on the menu and then started to dance. It looked like we won the lotto!" he said still laughing.

Zahira let out a belt of laughter. It was so true. They rocked up to the fanciest restaurant on the beach and ordered six dishes plus dessert. He spoiled her rotten and their mood was delightful and excited. She got to sample some of the best French cuisine with her Danish chef while watching an Indian sunset.

"Good morning," he sighed.

"Good morning," she said and then smattered him with kisses. She enjoys being close to this mans lips. They are so often curled into a mischievous grin. She will miss this monkey man. He is so much fun.

Zahira could waste days and weeks doing nothing but this man. She knows that he is not looking for anything more than a playmate, but his attentive affection has been so genuine and surprising. He has such a soft way to adore her. She has grown on him. She knows it. He even made a small protest when she told him she was leaving in two days.

"No no, you not go. In three weeks you still be here," he said as he pulled her closer.

"No no, I go. I must," she said mocking his accent. "For sure, not possible."

"I also think you should go. You said that you are happy everywhere you go. You should live what you speak, but of course you are welcome to stay," he said with truthful wisdom.

He was setting her free and welcoming her to stay.

◆

Girl Talk

"There is no long term. Everyday I choose to fall in love with you. Everyday I choose to be with you. This is a wise man," said the beautiful Flower. "I think that is the best exercise, to have someone who is present. This is self-realization. To be next to these people brings us to the next level. It is so powerful. These people can make us more silent. More peaceful."

"I've got to write that down," said Zahira as she starts typing these wise words.

"I have never seen what I've said written down!" laughs Flower over Zahira's shoulder.

The two girls burst out laughing. Their cackles echo through the restaurant and into the night sky. They are curled in the Cheeky Monkey's lounge. The scene is: low-lying tables, candles, music, pillows, glass table tops, soft lighting, international guests, ocean front view. They are nestled into the best spot on the whole beach.

"The man can show you the way," Flower continued. "They can show you a new level of love, a type of unattached love. It is powerful. It is the most healing thing. The mind is calm when you are beside them. There is nothing else going on. Total presence is there. Sharing is there. If we don't have a man to learn from then why do we need them?"

Again the girls burst into hysterics, but the message for Zahira was calm and clear; her mind does not feel calm and clear around the Cheeky Monkey. She doesn't feel more peaceful either. She does feel enamoured and in awe, but she also feels confusion and desire.

Zahira appreciates his wisdom and freedom, but she also feels that humans need other humans to grow close with. Perhaps it is wiser just to speak for herself. Zahira will admit that she would like another to grow close with. She is ready to share all of herself with another. She doesn't fear growing deep. She is ready for roots, calm silent present roots.

◆

True love grows together and apart.
It grows roots and gives wings.
It reflects your deepest sense of self.

◆

Body Mind Soul Self

Zahira and the Cheeky Monkey were lounging on his deluxe sun beds enjoying the luxury of time and indulging in his delicious cuisine. Zahira was sharing the internal dialogue she has been having. The voices that tell her to get moving and the ones that beg her to stay seem to be in constant communication.

"Well maybe you should stay for a few more days and kiss me. Then you can discover that I'm not worth sticking around for and you can go and do your detox," he said with his classic grin. "Just please leave me while it's still good."

Please leave me while it is still good? What the fuck!? Who says this sort of thing? This makes Zahira want to stay. This man is so curious to her. He clearly enjoys her company, but clearly doesn't want things to grow serious.

He started to tell knock knock jokes while they were making love today. She cracked into absolute hysterics because he doesn't even get the concept. He always forgets the order and flow of them.

"Knock knock," he said

"Who is there?" asks Zahira

"Mr Winnipig," he smiled.

"Mr Winnipeg who?" she said going along with it.

"Mr Winnipig knock knock," he giggled.

She roared with laughter because he messed it up again.

"Pig means cock in Danish," he smirked.

Now as she writes this she finally gets the joke!

As much as this man can entertain her and make her laugh she knows that he is not reason enough to stay in the Arambubble. She knows her physical well-being is more important than a fleeting romance. If the Monkey showed any sign of a future she would consider it, but he has given her nothing but wings. This she must be clear about. There is no point in creating stories or delusions.

So she will go. She will leave the Cheeky Monkey. She will pop the Arambubble and she will head to Kerala to detox her body. She knows she must honour her temple. She has cleansed her emotional and mental self and now her physical health deserves some attention. Her plane ticket back to Winnipeg leaves in less than three weeks. This is just enough time to give her body the love it deserves.

◆

200%

"So it's finally time," said Zahira to her beloved Flower.

"Oh my love," purred Flower with her hands on her heart, "My twin! My cosmic twin! I will miss you."

"I will miss you too," Zahira said with all sincerity. "You have been such a beautiful charm for me! I have a feeling I will see you sooner than later!"

"200 hundred percent!" smiled Flower, "You are like my higher self. Of course we will meet again..."

◆

"Knock knock," Zahira says.

"Knock knock," the Cheeky Monkey repeats.

"No no no, you are supposed to say who's there," Zahira corrected.

"There is who?" he laughs.

"Goodbye," she said with a smile.

"Good bye you?" he asks squeezing her hands.

"Good bye you," she said with a kiss.

◆

Free to be She

Zahira leaves this chapter with a clear heart. It is time to honour her body. Even though she felt herself sinking into the Cheeky Monkey, she was able to confidently pull herself away. He has been clear from the start and she is ready for a fresh one.

She is grateful to know she doesn't have to try to let go of him. She can just relax with things exactly as they are. Her new balanced view can invite any squirming attachments to fizzle and fade. They have no more power over her.

Zahira can sense a subtle yet significant shift in her being. Her new awakening is far from spectacular. It is almost nonchalant. It feels so neutral it is difficult to express. What she can express is her gratitude for taking the time to explore herself, to be truly honest with herself. She has been patient and forgiving towards herself. It has left her feeling nurtured and whole.

"Thank you Zahira," she whispered as she boarded her plane, "Thank you for letting me slip into a more relaxed existence. Thank you for allowing my ego and my image to loosen their grip on me. Thank you for being open to new kinds romance. Thank you for loving me. Thank you for helping me. Thank you for being my best friend. Thank you for knowing when it is time to make a move."

With those words Zahira flew into the next chapter of her existence.

PART 6

Ayurvedaaaah

◆

Checking In & Checking Out

Zahira has arrived in the Ayurvedic world capital, Kerala India. She was picked up at the airport and brought to her temporary home, a traditional Ayurvedic hospital. She has officially checked herself in. As she was walking up the stairs to her room she whispered to herself, "This is going to be really humbling."

The hospital is modest to say the least. It is old, but it is clean. This is a huge relief. Zahira rubbed her finger across every shelf in her room. They looked filthy, but it is only their desperate need for a new paint job. The facility is actually spotless, despite all of the spots!

Zahira instantly passed out. She fled the last chapter of her story in the early evening and didn't arrive in this one until morning. It was an overnight haul, a long exhausting transition from one tale to the next. She checked in to the hospital and checked out instantly. The first time she woke up it was to a team of female doctors.

"What the problem is madame?" asked the head doctor.

"My digestive system," said Zahira, "not healthy, always bloated. I also have these white spots that are appearing on my skin. Oh also my right hip has pain."

"Let us look," said the doctor.

The team of female med students in their gorgeous saris crowded around and looked over Zahira with a fine-tooth comb. They took her pulse, they checked her blood pressure and they looked at her eyes, ears and tongue. They asked her a series of questions and she told them about her right hip causing her pain. They listened attentively and with out giving her any answers they all left.

Zahira passed out again. She woke to an assistant nurse asking her to come for an X-ray. An X-ray?! Wow these guys don't mess around. Zahira was half asleep as she followed the assistant into a tuk tuk and they sped off to a neighbouring hospital.

Zahira was whisked past an incredibly long line of locals who were crowding the hospital corridors. They all stared at her white face as she apologized for being pushed to the front. It looked like a scene out of a movie and because she was half asleep she felt like she was dreaming. Was she really going for an X-ray in an Indian hospital?

Yep, they took pictures of her hips. The assistant brought her back to her room and once again Zahira passed out cold.

Knock knock. She wished it was the Cheeky Monkey but instead it was some bitter medicine. Back to sleep.

Knock knock. It was a man with a gold bucket of burning incense. He came through her room to smoke out the mosquitoes with the setting sun. Back to dreamland.

Knock knock. It was the lovely man who met her at the airport this morning. He answered her question before she asked it, "Tomorrow I will have a list for you of how much everything should cost."

"Oh perfect," she said.

Dinner is in five minutes. Zahira will stop writing to go and eat and then hopefully sleep without interruptions until morning. She believes she has enough Zs in her to do so.

She is grateful she is here. Most foreigners who travel to India choose to do these types of Ayurvedic treatments in fancy spa-like atmospheres. Zahira chose this hospital because of its highly reputed legacy for knowledge and tradition. She wanted the real deal, not some watered-down version. She has thanked herself for putting her body first. It has been calling for her attention and she is listening.

◆

Self love

Self love includes caring for your body.
Give yourself what you need to be happy and healthy.
Caring for yourself leads to complete appreciation of all that is.
Through this appreciation all that is, becomes...

◆

Healher

Knock knock.

"Sleep okay?" asked the nurse in the white robe as she took Zahira's blood pressure and pulse.

"I think I still am sleeping," Zahira responded with her eyes still closed. It must have been five in the morning. It was still dark outside her window.

"Medicine after blood work," said the doctor. She put a glass of dark brown liquid on the table and left. Zahira fell back in to a full sleep.

Knock knock.

"Treatment madame," said the woman who was waiting for her with fresh towels.

"Treatment? Oh, I thought I had blood work," said Zahira feeling groggy. She could tell that the woman did not understand her. She pointed her finger into her arm, "Needle? Blood work now?"

"Blood work after treatment madame," said the woman who got the picture.

"Okay treatment," smiled Zahira.

The treatment was not exactly relaxing but it was invigorating. She climbed on top of a wooden massage table and two women preformed a synchronized massage routine. Their touch was powerful and their timing was impeccable. Zahira got the impression they have been working as a team for a long time.

She is now back in her room with medicated oil on her body and some sort of seaweed mudpack on her face. She is in a lilac coloured robe and the sky is a nice grey. She is admiring her good fortune. She is getting such thorough treatment, such hands-on attention. She feels she is in the right place.

◆

THERE IS A SIGN ON THE HOSPITAL WALL THAT READS:
'Health is the state of; the balanced bodily elements, digestive power, body components and proper excretion of waste materials which leads to physical, mental and spiritual well being.'

◆

Ancient Trust

While Ayurveda is new to Zahira it is one of the oldest medical sciences in the world. Some references date it back more than 5000 years. It is a Keralan tradition that has been passed down from father to son through the generations.

Being here requires great faith. Zahira does not speak the language so she must trust that the medicine she is drinking is good for her. It is similar to her experience at her shaman's healing centre in the Peruvian amazon. The healers would knock on her hut and hand her bitter liquids to swallow. She would do so without question.

Without trust there is no healing.

After 24 hours at the hospital, Zahira's personal program has included: an initial consultation, three servings of medicine, an x-ray, blood work, two tag team massages, a gentle yoga class, an ointment for her white spots and some very smelly powder that she applies to her scalp after treatments.

She can already feel the difference in her skin. It is gulping up the medicated oil from her massage treatments. It has been so thirsty. She can see a new glow starting to resurface. She wishes she had three solid weeks of these treatments, but two weeks are better than one. She has nothing on her agenda but rest, rejuvenation and review.

◆

Trust and faith are needed for healing.
Trust comes from within.
Faith comes from within.
Healing comes from within.
Your health is in your hands and heart!

◆

Eye Don't Believe It

"You've got to be fucking kidding me," Zahira muttered to herself.

She was absolutely horrified by her first eye treatment. She is meant to undergo 7 treatments to improve her eyesight. The first one was today and they first words to exit her mouth were a very loud, "Holy fuck lord!"

Her reaction shocked the shit out of the sweet bird-like nurses who were fluttering around her. It was just an honest response to a hit of intense pain.

"Keep blinking madame," said the young nurse. She sounded empathetic.

"How long for this?" Zahira asked as her hands were clenched into fists.

"Treatment ten minutes madame," responded the nurse with a sweet song-like voice.

It was the longest ten minutes of Zahira's trip. She tried to relax and breathe into the pain. She tried not to whimper like a child, but she was having warm medicine poured straight into her open eyeballs. Even the thought of it makes her shutter.

"No reading after this. No TV," said the nurse when the treatment was done.

"What about computer? Can I write on the computer," asked Zahira.

"No computer. No TV for 7 days," said the nurse.

"Seven days!!" Zahira felt a panic sweep through her being. What the fuck was she going to do for the next 7 days if she can't read or write?

"Talk to the doctor. They tell," she said trying to ease the tension Zahira was unable to hide.

"Can I sleep now?" she asked. Her eyes were burning and she wanted to cry.

"No sleep in day time with Ayurveda treatment madame. No good. It makes night sleeping difficult," the nurse explained.

"Really? No sleeping? So wait....no reading, no writing, no computers, no sleeping. What am I supposed to do?" asked Zahira.

She was silently praying this was a communication error.

"Walking madame. Go walking," she smiled and guided Zahira back to her room.

"You've got to be fucking kidding me," she whispered again to herself.

◆

Nothing

Zahira now has two options; do nothing outside or do nothing inside. When she says nothing she literally means nothing. She thought she was good at doing nothing, but this is really something!

Zahira tried sitting outside, but prefers the darkness of her room. So now she sits and sits and sits and sits. She has seven straight days of sitting ahead of her. It's the perfect time to put all of her teachings into practice.

She will patiently let clarity be her guide. She will let all of her bored thoughts squirm through her mind and she will do her best to relax into her peaceful modest surroundings.

◆

The Only Theory is You

"You are illuminating the whole room," said the handsome doctor with silver hair.

She has several visitors a day; nurses, students, doctors, practitioners, cooks and cleaners. They all comment on her gold lights. She has been travelling with them since she left the ashram. She is an atmosphere junkie. She also has a shrine with photographs of her family and friends. Her scene is cozy and welcoming.

"Where are all these places?" asked the same handsome doctor.

He seemed to be more interested in her life than her conditions.

"Oh this is Hawaii, this is Peru, this is an art festival called Burning Man…" she went on to describe each picture.

"Do you do yoga?" he asked quite randomly.

"Yes! And I would love to ask you this question. Is hot yoga good for me?" Zahira asked with her fingers crossed behind her back. She had been told by a student studying at the ashram that hot yoga was messing with the constitution of her body. She loves her practice and wants to continue when she returns home.

"I don't know," he answered. "What is this?"

"It is yoga in a very hot room, almost like a steam room. I go four to five times a week for an hour at a time. I want to know if it is okay," Zahira replied.

"If it feels good than it is okay," he said without hesitation. "If you feel the benefit in your mind, body and spirit then of course it is very good."

"Oh I love that answer," Zahira beamed as she uncrossed her fingers.

"The only theory is you," he smiled with warm glowing eyes. "If you are feeling the benefit than it is good. You only need to listen to your body, your mind, your spirit. This is the truth."

"Oh I love this! You are a wise man," she smiled.

She always knew this, but it felt soooo good to hear a doctor say it.

He looked around the room one more time and he smiled the

most generous smile, "You are illuminating your whole room and you are illuminating your mind."

◆

THE ONLY THEORY IS YOU.
You are the first and final say of your well-being.
Listen to your body mind and spirit.
Trust your inner guidance system.

◆

Eye Can Do It

"And the eye treatment?" asked the head nurse.

"Oh I just hate it," Zahira smiled, "I can be peaceful for the first seven minutes now. I can welcome the healing into my body, but by minute eight I want it done!"

"So I can say to stop this treatment?" the nurse asked.

"No no! It's good. I want," replied Zahira without a moment's hesitation.

Bring on the healing.

◆

Luck is Breathing

"And are you married?" asked Zahira's neighbour in his endearing Indian accent.

"No not yet," smiled Zahira. "Maybe one day...if I'm lucky."

"What is this lucky?" he replied with a sensitive and honest tone. "If you are breathing you are lucky. If you can take a breath by yourself you are lucky."

"You are absolutely right!" cheered Zahira.

"And there is no waiting, everything comes in its right time. When you are pregnant then you wait nine months. The elephant waits 22 months, the alpine salamander waits 36 months. This is waiting. Now—no waiting. Just enjoying," he said with a great twinkle in his eyes.

Zahira laughed and clapped her hands with great delight, "I gotta remember to write that down! That was brilliant!"

She loves this hospital. It is crawling with interesting characters. So many surprising tidbits of wisdom. She went from battling boredom to pure entertainment. All of a sudden her time is passing too quickly...

◆

Not So Hip

Low low low low low low low low. She hit the floor.

Zahira's energy is at zero. She feels like an old lady hobbling around the hospital at a snail's pace. The X-ray results show she has degenerative arthritis in her hips. Arthritis! The doctor says it is from over exertion of a repeated injury.

Zahira can only assume it is from the first few years of her yoga practice. Her original yoga teacher was like a drill sergeant. Zahira was always told to push past her pain. She enjoyed the workout, but she wasn't taught to listen to her body. She put all of her faith into her teacher. She pushed and pushed and pushed and clearly pushed too hard.

She is glad she has solved the mystery of her aching hips. She knows the Pomelo did his best to attach an emotion to her pain, but now she is getting to the physical root of it. It feels good, even though her body is sore.

◆

Listen to your body it knows.
Listen to your body it knows.
Listen to your body it knows.

◆

Patience Patient

Zzzzzzahira is weak and heavy. She feels like lead. She is moving like molasses. Her legs are so heavy she can barely lift them. This weakness has caught her off guard. She has had a few moments of weepy tears.

The staff can see it in her. She is not her usual vibrant self. The sympathy on their faces only makes her feel more weepy. It fuels her pity party. It is easy to play the role of a patient when she is surrounded by nurses.

Zahira is watching herself. Her body may be heavy but her mood is soft. She is allowing her sadness to swallow her with a gentle grace. She is allowing everything to come up as it needs.

"Remember that time we were in the hospital in Kerala and we were sick and tired and staring at the ceiling fan all day? That was my favourite," she said lying on her bed feeling sick and sad and staring at the ceiling fan.

She started laughing. Her little girl voice had come out to entertain her.

Zahira was feeling so lifeless that even her eye treatment took on a whole new experience. She was too exhausted to fight it. Somehow this flicked the pleasure pain switch and she welcomed the burn. She even liked it.

◆

Friendly neighbour's advice of the day:

*"When you have much time to sit and do nothing
many thoughts will come to the mind. You might think about
your mom, your dad, brother sister. You might think about
your country, you might think about what's next.
Don't bother with next, what's next is next.
Just enjoy what is now."*

◆

O MAN!

"You guys are good," she smiled to the plants as she was walking back from the cafeteria.

She was talking to the Universe and its marvellous sense of humour and timing. They have sent her the Arabian Knight, a charming handsome dark eyed prince from the country of Oman. She met him last night over dinner. He is here to help care for his aging father. When she found out he spoke Arabic she asked him if he knew of the name Zahira.

"Yes I know this name," he replied in his thick, rich accent.

"Do you know what it means?" she asked curiously.

"It means flower in my country," he smiled.

"Ooooh flower! I like that!" Zahira cooed, "I was told Zahira meant manifesting light, but I also really like being called a flower. My cosmic twin's name is Flower!"

He smiled and she felt warm. In truth she felt a bit flushed. The last thing she was expecting in the hospital cafeteria was an encounter with a gorgeous man who filled her water glass and cleared her plate.

They met again over lunch today. Just his presence makes her blush.

"The flower is even more beautiful today," he smiled.

It was enough to send her off in disbelief. *Seriously?* Where did this guy come from?

◆

THE UNIVERSE STRIKES AGAIN!

The Arabian Knight tells her that her name means flower and her dear friend Lancelot sent her this poem. She loves her friend dearly and had the honour of being his best man at his wedding!

What a strange and wondrous flower
Its form, unexpected, revealing an inner structure strong, rooted, and reaching.

Its colour stuns, drawing the vibrations out of the white light of the sun, while it embraces the hues and natural radiance of its surroundings.
It is a rare and impossible flower.
To behold it is to be blessed, blessed in a former life in which the seed was planted, and a lifetime to await its revealing.
Its smell…its smell is a rainbow for the senses, indescribable in words, only known through experience itself.
The ground upon which it grows is open, for it finds ways to take root in any soil, any light, any environment.
When it takes root, that place, space, and entire environment is transformed.
The flower simultaneously draws the nectar of its habitat, while at the same time, exuding it right back in a form, more radiant and rich than from which it was originally drawn.
Although it grows before us in this world, it secretly takes root in worlds beyond, evoking the liquid life from places we cannot imagine.
Its secret is that this flower grows and shines most brightly at night, under the stars.
It takes the light of suns from other worlds, other times, and soaks them up with wide eyes, wide mouth, and open arms.
To describe this flower would be like dreaming in a language that one does not yet know.

This flower is known as Zahira.

◆

Kind Mind

Zahira has lived the past four months without a mirror and now she is gorging on one. She has examined every flaw she can find on her body. She has traced every aging line, she has spotted every blemish, she has poked every pocket of fat.

She has nit picked her body to pieces. Her critical glare is starting to bum her out. It is focused only on her flaws and making her feel far from attractive.

"Okay enough," she whispered to her reflection. "Cut me some slack will ya."

She decided instead to focus on appreciating herself with a loving touch. She went to the rooftop of the hospital and sat with the setting sun. She opened her arms to its gentle rays and collected the light in the palm of her hands. She smoothed her whole body with this white light.

"You are growing younger and more beautiful with each passing day," she whispered over and over again.

She can't say if this actually made any difference in her body, but it certainly made her *feel* a whole lot better. Moving from a critical vibration to a state of appreciation had a dramatic effect on her overall mood. She went from feeling flabby and old to lovely and light. Her body didn't shift but her appearance sure did, even if it was just in the way she saw herself. It gave her a genuine understanding of the age old-saying;

beauty really does come from within.

◆

Friendly Neighbour's Advice of the Day

(delivered with perfect timing!)

"Who am I? You must think who am I?
You look in the mirror, you may see spot here, problem there.
I look at your face and I see only cute face is there!
Who am I is more than these little problems.
Think with a bigger picture."

◆

Doing Nothing Changes Everything

Zahira has started to tune into subtle delights, even the air quality in her room has taken on a new level of appreciation. When it is just the right temperature, with a nice soft breeze from her ceiling fan, she sighs into a puddle of contentment.

She has begun to adore the things she has taken for granted like how the colour of the sky changes from morning to night or the way her curtains billow when the slightest breeze pours through her window. They seem to dance in slow motion. Observing these subtleties creates a corresponding response in her body. She is feeling slow, loose and peaceful.

◆

Nothing matters…
it sure does.

◆

King Sundaes

The girls that work on Zahira remind her of birds chirping back and forth. Their native tongue is called Malayalam; it is the language of Kerala. There are over 50 letters and symbols in the alphabet. It sounds like a song when they chit chat. It's not mellow like the songs of the Hawaiians who have only 11 letters in their alphabet. Malayalam is a hyper fast language that sounds like something Zahira would have made up as a child if she were playing India. It is a melodic nattering that feels both gleeful and graceful.

Zahira's favourite treatment is called Pizhichil. Her entire body is drizzled with streams of warm medicated oil accompanied by a soft massage. It takes three women to preform it. It is known as the king of treatments and is supposed to be a powerful immune booster. It is also good for the arthritis in her hips and it helps to arrest the ageing process!

She is on day five of this treatment. When they sit her up she likes to open her eyes to watch the warm oil drizzling over her naked body. She is usually caught in a mental debate over what flavour the oil would be on an ice cream sundae. It looks like butterscotch mixed with caramel, but sometimes she is convinced it's more like chocolate mixed with strawberry. These are things she has the time to think about.

◆

Polygamy?
Pass the pepper please.

Zahira's stay has been been up and down and all around. It has been humbling and it has been healing. She is feeling much better. Her bloating is still present but way less intense. She has not noticed much difference in her eyes and her hips, but she is told that the effects of these treatments will come after some time. The results can take anywhere from one month to six months! She is not worried. She knows that her time here has been a beautiful gift to herself.

She has not seen the Arabian Knight in a few days. They have not spoken since he casually told her about his wife and his right to marry three more. She is still shaking her head at that one. How can she not? Here was a totally modern handsome man talking about polygamy as if he were discussing the weather. 'No no no, I can't have five wives, only four. Pass the pepper please,' like that.

Oddly enough it feels normal when he talks about it. The Arabian Knight is a man who believes in treating a woman with respect. He sees life as the union of man and woman. Woman as the mother, the sister, the wife. These relationships are all incredibly valued in his heart. Zahira can feel this as·his truth.

There is something very solid about this man. Something she does not recognize in her Western friends. Just the fact that he is here to help his aging father is evidence of a different culture. It is not even a question, it is simply his duty. Zahira has a lot of respect for him.

◆

Bullshit

"I'm sorry I didn't call you yesterday, did I tell you what happened to me?" purred the Flower on the other end of the phone.

"No worries," replied Zahira, "What happened?"

Zahira was standing in the hospital corridor on the red phone that is normally reserved for nurses. They had paged her for a much welcomed phone call from her cosmic twin.

"I had the craziest experience. My kundalini woke up," she said.

"What?! What are you talking about? When?!" Zahira said not surprised but totally amazed.

"A few days ago I was smoking a chillum and I felt this electricity starting to spiral up my spine and the next thing I know…I have no words. I was completely gone," she said with her thick and excited accent.

"Holy shit Flower! That's out of control," Zahira said with wide eyes.

"Yes and you will not believe this, everything gets crazier. When you wrote me just now you know who I was sitting with? The Cheeky Monkey!" Flower bubbled.

"No way? He is still in the Arambubble? I thought he escaped," said Zahira feeling intrigued. Just the mention of this man made her own electricity start to bubble.

"Yes and you are not going to believe this," Flower said again. Zahira could hear her smiling over the phone, "Are you sitting down?"

"What? Stop it! Just tell me!" laughed Zahira.

"He's *getting married* tomorrow!" Flower spit out with shock and laughter.

"WHAT?!?" said Zahira equally shocked, "Noooo way. What?!?"

"Yes can you believe it?! He came over to invite me to the wedding," said Flower still laughing.

"Oh my god, seriously? *Married?!* Man that guy is wild! How unpredictable can one human be?!" Zahira half yelled half laughed.

"Yes I know, but it's not like that. He is marrying her for the visa.

She is Indian and he wants to be able to stay and work in India. He is very clear with her that they will someday go their separate ways. This is not something he is doing out of love," explained Flower.

"You've got to be kidding me," Zahira said feeling shocked but not surprised.

"I know I know. Can you believe it? How crazy is that?" Flower gushed with her uncontrollable enthusiasm.

Both girls were laughing.

"Shit I gotta go. I've got three nurses waiting to give me an enema," Zahira said.

"Oh my god I love you," Flower said with her electric and endearing tone.

"As if, your kundalini is rising and I'm having shit sucked out of my ass. This is total bullshit," Zahira joked.

Both girls totally lost it. They were in absolute hysterics, echoing each others cackle.

"I love you," said Zahira through her fits of giggles. They were both still at it when she hung up the phone.

◆

Moonlight Mirrors

"I have you in my head, both of you," said the Arabian Knight. He was speaking to Zahira and her friendly neighbour, "I have thinking about you. You are my best friends here."

Harry beamed at his comment and Zahira blushed. There was still something about this man that made her feel girlish. Perhaps it is because he was such a man. He had been away from the hospital. His father needed to have an MRI scan so they went on an overnight excursion to a different hospital. This explains why she had not seen him.

When she caught his silhouette across the parking lot she found herself lighting up. When he noticed her he did the same. He came straight to her and shook her hand hello. After she let go he was still holding on.

"Do you guys want to hang out in my room for a bit?" Zahira asked them both.

Her neighbour graciously declined for an early rest and the Arabian Knight happily accepted. They walked side by side not speaking until they reached her room.

"Please come in," Zahira said offering him a chair.

She moved to sit on her bed. Her gold lights were twinkling behind her. This was the first time that he had come to her room. They have been alone before, but never in a setting so intimate. His presence filled up the entire space.

"I was surprise when I hear you go day after tomorrow. I ask man and he tell me you go next week. This makes me, how do you say.... bad?" he asked.

"Sad?" she offered.

"Yes sad. After you go this place goes dark. It's like that," he said.

Zahira smiled. In fact she hadn't stopped smiling since he found her in the parking lot. "No no, don't be silly. No sad," she said.

"Yes sad. You make light," he began, "like the moon, how you say... shining. You make light like the moon."

"Oh thank you," Zahira blushed. This guy was too much. His words were so sweet her teeth were aching.

"It's true. I see you beautiful on the outside, but also very beautiful inside," he said as he pointed to his heart.

"You too. You are very beautiful," she returned.

"No no no not like that. It is you. I see you make smile with everyone. You make connections with close to everybody," he said trying to express himself, "Do you understand?"

"Yes, but I see you do the same. You are very bright and beautiful," she insisted.

"This makes my cheeks go, how do you call this?" he asked pointing to his red cheeks.

"Blushing. You make me blush all the time," she said to be perfectly honest. She was happy she could start to even out the score.

"I am very happy to know you. It nice to come here and find shining light like yours."

"Well it is just a reflection of you. What you see in me is what I see in you," she said.

"No no no, it's not like this," he insisted.

"Yes it is. If you see me as unhappy and unfriendly it is because you are unhappy and unfriendly. If you see me as a shining light it is because you are also shining light. I am only a mirror for you," she smiled.

This man had the sweetest glow around him. His honesty and his delivery were delighting her. His English was broken but still so manly and powerful. Even though he was unsure of his words, he spoke with such conviction she had no choice but to believe him. His thick arabian accent and his stature were rock solid. Zahira could feel his personal power coursing through her own body.

He was a perfect gentleman. He didn't imply anything beyond friendship and respect. "I will miss you when you go," he said.

"You are so sweet. I will miss you too," she blushed.

◆

The way you see the world is a reflection of yourself
The Cheeky Monkey is 'powerful'
The Flower is a 'genius'
The handsome Doctor is 'illuminated'
The Arabian Knight is a 'shining light'

◆

You're It

Zahira is in awe of the women who work here. They don't go for beauty treatments and yet they are so beautiful. They don't meditate and yet they are peaceful. They don't do yoga and yet they have beautiful figures. They don't seek therapy and yet they are all smiling. Their way of life is just that; *it is the way*. There is no seeking for something more.

The doctor who gave her an ultrasound was another example of *the way*.

"Why did you come to India?" he asked her.

"I felt a calling to visit your country," she said. "It seemed romantic from afar."

"And what have you done since you've been here?" he asked.

"Well I have spent a lot of time on the beach, but I have also studied yoga and meditation," she said feeling like a bit of a western brat.

"What feeling do you get from yoga and meditation?" the doctor asked

"What feeling? Oh, peacefulness," she replied.

"And why don't you feel peacefulness without yoga and meditation?" he asked.

It was a great question and one that resonated very clearly with her Balanced View teachings. This 'peacefulness' is what she sees in the women who work on her. It is the same quality she sees in the man who posed the question. The man who works twelve hour days six days a week. The same man who has not taken a holiday in 20 years. It's as though they all share the same clarity view except they don't even realize they have it.

They just are it.

◆

"Let your alignment (with Well-Being) be first and foremost, and let everything else be secondary. And not only will you have an eternally joyous journey, but everything you have ever imagined will flow effortlessly into your experience."
~ Esther Hicks

◆

The Camel's Out of the Bag

"Wait here please," said the Arabian Knight, "I have something for you."

"You have something for me? What is it?" she asked with a big little girl grin.

"One minute please," and he disappeared to return with a gift bag. "This is like, how you say subject line in a letter?"

"Title?" asked Zahira back. She was not sure what he was getting at.

"Yes like that, title. This gift is like title. It very small. How I feel inside is very big," he said as he handed her the bag.

Zahira opened it with such appreciation. This Knight was too much! Inside was a teddy bear holding a flower and a glass camel. There was also a card with a rose on it.

Zahira read the card out loud, "We share a very special friendship that's precious and rare. You're a wonderful friend. You add sparkle to my life making each day an occasion to celebrate. I'll always treasure our friendship," she looked up and touched her heart. "Oh my god you are so sweet. I can't believe you did this."

Zahira was genuinely surprised and touched and totally blushing. She felt like she was in high school and it was Valentine's day. A teddy bear holding a flower? Of course, Zahira the flower. Too much.

"Once in a while you meet someone who leaves a..." he did a stamping motion with his hand.

"An impression?" she helped.

"Yes an impression. You leave me with impression. I will remember you for long time. Thank you for everything you give me," his words and his gift were adorable but his presentation was all man.

"You are too much. You're amazing. Thank you for being so wonderful. I love this," she said as she hugged him.

She was totally surprised. The moment was so sweet her taste buds were watering. It has been such an innocent romance they have shared. Nothing but a friendship between two admirers, totally harmless and yet totally enhancing. Zahira feels uplifted by this man. He has gently raised her to sweep beneath her feet. He has been the perfect character for this chapter in her life. She has worked hard to polish her body and he has given her a nice gleaming shine.

"You know I am writing a book," she told him as they started walking. "I have been travelling for a long time and I have been typing my life into a story."

"This is good," he said listening.

"I just wanted you to know that you are now in my story. Your character is called the Arabian Knight," she said feeling like she was letting the camel out of the bag.

"The Arabian Knight? This is good," he smiled.

"Yes, you have been a beautiful and charming character to come into my life. You have made my stay at the hospital so wonderful. It has brought me great pleasure to know you. I want to thank you," she said, "It's like that," she added as a gentle tease. (It's how he finishes most of his sentences...'like that'.)

She could tell he liked his character name because fifty steps later he said it again, "The Arabian Knight?"

"Yes the Arabian Knight," she smiled.

"Maybe one day your story will be a movie," he said with a twinkle in his eye.

"Maybe," she said twinkling back.

◆

The Value of Time

Zahira left the hospital to spend three days next to the ocean. She chose her destination based on it's nickname. The sleepy coastal town is known as the Princess of the Arabian because the sea glitters like jewels at sunset. She rented a sweet little room that floats on the back waters. She has fishermen right outside her window and a giant tree in her bathroom.

She also lucked out with another friendly neighbour. He is a grey haired revolutionary and a fellow Sannyasin. He took her for a vegetarian meal on the back of his pristine Royal Enfield motorcycle.

"I am just reflecting on how luxurious my life has been," she said to Shanti over lunch.

"Luxury?" he asked surprised. "I thought you said you have been in a hospital for the past couple of weeks."

"Oh yeah I have and it was super modest. To me time is luxury and well being is wealth. I haven't worked a day in the last six months.

I have had the freedom to do what I want when I want to. I have had time to invest in my health. This is the greatest decadence I could dream of. This is luxury," she concluded.

◆

"You are beauty and you are life and you are endless."
~ Adam Azimov

◆

You are Heaven!

Zahira went for a stroll on the beach aware that it would be her last night with the ocean. She was not sad, but she wanted to milk it. The breeze was absolutely euphoric. The temperatures felt like they were custom made. With them they brought a very clear message;

You are heaven, you are heaven, you are heaven.

These words danced through her head and she smiled. She wanted to instantly share them with everyone.

You are heaven, you are heaven, you are heaven!

She found a seat in the stones and relaxed into meditation. She closed her eyes and watched her inner dialogue commence.

"You haven't lost touch with yourself as a healer. You have just been playing with new information. Just because you have found clarity doesn't mean you have lost your spirit. You are still connected. You are still the elements. You are still Strong Heart Eagle Woman," instantly her shoulders exhaled and she felt a flood of familiarity flush through her body. It had been a while since she referred to herself as her spirit name.

"You have learnt that you don't need to meditate, do yoga or practice witchcraft to be powerful, but that doesn't mean that you can't enjoy these experiences. You have learnt that you can grow old, get lazy, gain weight and even die and still be connected to consciousness. This is your birthright and your death right, but while you are alive you get to dance with the divine. You are divine. Let's keep you connected with that,' her thoughts continued.

The sun was slowly making its dive into the sea. The Princess was starting to glow a soft golden pink and Zahira was starting to glow from the inside out. She could feel the light from her heart centre growing more radiant. It was a peaceful easy feeling, even the eagles came out to play. They were dancing overhead, playing in the thermals like invisible water slides.

The wind was calling her to spread her arms and embrace it. It was time to say thank you to mother India. She stood with her eyes closed and her arms outstretched. She felt like a willow in the wind and in this moment of effortless existence, Zahira was utterly blindsided by a tsunami of joy.

A wave of peace crashed through her being and streams of tears began to flow down her silent cheeks. The wave seemed endless and uncontrollable. Her entire being was quietly sobbing with pure joy. It felt as though existence had wrapped her in a warm cocoon and she was effortlessly transforming inside.

She thought of the moon and its beauty destroyed her. She thought of the ocean and its endlessness washed through her. And when she thought of the trees she could see the ancestors swaying in their branches welcoming her.

When she finally opened her eyes the sunlight felt as though it were touching her cheeks for the first time. Again the beauty dissolved her into tears. A very clear voice came from the centre of her being. It was not a thought but a message from her source:

'You want for nothing'

And just like that Zahira melted into her truest self; a self who feels ancient and young, a self who feels like a newborn who is pregnant with life, a self whom she had prayed to find at the beginning of this journey.

She had found the peace that asks for nothing.

"In three days you will wake up in your bed and you can remember this moment," she whispered. "You can spread your arms out and float. You can close your eyes and imagine the eagles soaring overhead. You can embrace the breeze from the sea. You can know that you are beauty and you are life and you are endless."

Zahira's entire body exhaled and she lost all limits of her being. She was the water and the wind. She was the eagles and the sand.

She was heaven, she was heaven, she was heaven.

PART 7

Landing into Understanding

◆

Curry Pits

"I feel something has changed on a deep constitutional level for me. Something fundamental has shifted. It is subtle, but it is deep," Zahira expressed to her radiant girlfriend Susu.

She was trying to put her state of being into words. She has had no cravings since she has landed back home. Not for food, not for men, not for plans, not for the past nor the future. She hasn't even been craving chocolate! This is hard to comprehend. Zahira has followed sugar cravings to ridiculous extremes in the past. Now there is ….nothing? She is realizing that cravings come from the feeling of lacking something. At the moment Zahira is…

"It's not even like I am fully satisfied," Zahira continued. "Satisfaction implies that dis-satisfaction is possible…it's something beyond satisfaction. I can't quite put my finger on it."

Zahira has been utterly present since landing. She has been tucked away in her own little world cleaning and nesting. She has carved out time to be alone, not answering her phone, not leaving except to find yoga. She has been perfectly alone in her bubble of contentment. It's not even contentment because this would also imply the opposite. All she can say is that she feels like she is in equilibrium. She feels harmonious with her existence. Apparently it shows.

"Oh my god," beamed the gushing girl, "you are glowing. You look beyond amazing. You are all one colour. Does that sound strange? It's like you are all gold. Solid glowing gold."

"Wow," said sweet girl number two, "I just need to stand next to you. I just need to absorb some of this. Your whole everything is illuminated!"

Zahira giggled and hugged the girls. She was touched but not flattered. She was positively neutral. She was also the only sober being at her party. She hosted close to a 100 people in her home last night. It was a birthday celebration for her brother and girlfriend Susu. It was a perfect way to slide back into the scene. She was on her home turf and she had pointed the spotlight on the birthday crew. It was an effortless evening and it was nice to be appreciated.

"You know you are my spiritual guru," said a tipsy girl at the party.

"No no no you are your own guru," Zahira insisted. "You are your own master. We all are."

Zahira was grateful for their generous words, but she was sober and not swelling. She kept an even keel all night. It was 5am when she turned off the stereo. She was in the kitchen with the final few stragglers. They were all smoking joints and eating cereal.

Zahira was getting ready for sleep. The night was a beautiful success. Everyone had a great time. The dance floor was solid, the kitchen was jammed, the living room was packed. The whole scene was joyful, respectful and light hearted.

"Can I stay with you sometime?" asked the hot Brazilian as Zahira was getting ready to crawl into bed. He had followed her up the stairs and knocked on her bedroom door.

"Oh sure, but I am exhausted. I am seriously just going to sleep," she said with a flat out honest smile.

He was young, totally buff and had that sexy Brazilian thing going for him. He was a tempting and delicious treat, but Zahira was done. He had his hands behind his back in a very polite stance. He leaned in to give her a gentle kiss. She responded. He smelt good.

"I smell like curry though. Are you sure you want to stay here?" she half joked.

"I like this smell," he said as he traced his nose along her neckline. He took a long slow deep inhale.

Zahira giggled. It had been the on going joke all night. Her friend, The Gun, told her that she smelt like the carpets in a Pakistani home. She couldn't help but laugh mostly because it's true. She blames the oils from the Ayurveda hospital along with her spicy Indian diet.

The Brazilian certainly wasn't complaining. He seemed to be enjoying her flesh. He kissed her again and this time his hands came out from behind his back to pull her in by the waist. He had an incredibly firm grip on her. It was confident and his intentions were clear.

"I'm really just going to sleep," Zahira reminded him.

And that's exactly what she did. He struggled a bit laying beside her. He couldn't take his hands off of her. It was the silk pant suit she still had on, it was champagne in colour and sheer like bubbles. It had a deep plunging neck line and she was totally naked underneath it. She wore it like water. She felt sexy and was smiling at this opportunity to share herself, but she was more interested in holding her space and falling asleep with grace. So she did.

◆

Homeostasis

Zahira slips on her faux fur white jacket to warm her cool shoulders. She has been home for almost a month. It is hard to believe, but here she is coasting with the same calm brilliance that she left India with. She has not drifted from her clarity, in fact it feels more engrained.

She has been inescapably breathing with awareness, not a feeling, but a new understanding. She was trying to describe it to herself again. She was walking down the street talking out loud.

"Okay it's kind of like this," she said as she stopped, took one step to the side and then kept walking. "Nothing has changed except everything is seen from a new stance."

It's a new way of seeing all the same old bullshit. The bullshit doesn't go away, it just doesn't have to affect her anymore.

Later that day she was chatting with her roommate. He was asking her about some potential business opportunities. Some of them would require her to get back on the road. Zahira had hesitated when she was trying to explain how she was feeling about it.

"Are you feeling like you are here now? Like you don't want to go anywhere?" he asked her.

"No no, I could leave here tomorrow. I am feeling more like… whatever will be will be," she smiled.

There she is again, trying to explain this new….confidence? Silence? Comfort? *What is this?* She can't quite put her finger on it. Her cravings have remained at bay. She has no desires. For the first time in her life Zahira can *honestly* say she is no longer looking for anything. Her new pace is even and consistent. No ups no downs, just here. It's as though everything has slowly dawned upon her.

"So what epiphanies did you have?" asked an old friend she ran into at the club.

"That there are no epiphanies," she replied.

"No," he said in jest, "What did you learn?"

"That there is nothing to learn, no work to be done. We just need to relax into our natural state of love and well-being," she answered honestly. She also knows it sounds a bit ridiculous. "If I do anything now it's sheerly for the experience, for the joy. There is nothing left to search for. There never was."

Zahira has been having difficulties sharing this new awakening with others. It is so ephemeral and yet so ordinary. She decides it's like spending her whole life trying to see her eyeballs and then one day someone shows her a mirror and she realizes she has been looking through them all along. With this realization comes the most undramatic shift imaginable. It's so natural it's nothing. This nothing is everything. It's everything that is already, that has always been.

As Zahira was settling in for a nap she scooped up a little black book that was sitting next to her sunny sofa. It had only one small passage written inside it:

"Enlightenment is finding that there is nothing to find. Enlightenment is to come to know that there is nowhere to go. Enlightenment is the understanding that this is all. This is perfect, that this is it. Enlightenment is not an achievement, it is an understanding that there is nothing to achieve, nowhere to go. You are already there, you have never been away." ~ Osho.

Zahira must have read it six times. It made her cry. She had found her missing words. Everything about this made sense. While Zahira is hesitant to use the word enlightenment, she certainly resonated with this message.

Instead she will say: she is home now. Not just geographically, but naturally. Her new understanding combined with her Ayurvedic diet has uncovered her optimal life force. The one that she was born with, the one that has been waiting so patiently for her return. Zahira's homecoming has been more than geographical. Her body is home and her being has hit homeostasis.

◆

En-light-en
What brings you levity?
What makes you feel light?
What brightens your day?

◆

Importing Pomelos?

"Sooooo I'm coming to Canada to watch the Stanley Cup," the Pomelo said casually over a Skype date.

They hadn't been in communication for over a month. His call came as quite a surprise.

"Oh yeah?" Zahira replied wondering if he was being serious.

"Yeah the Islanders haven't been in a Stanley Cup for years so I thought it would be cool to be in Vancouver," he confirmed.

"Seriously? When are you coming?" Zahira asked.

"I fly out tomorrow," he said with an excited tone.

"Tomorrow?! Holy shit!" Zahira exclaimed with surprise.

"Should I come and see you in Winnipeg?" he asked with a casual tone.

"You are always welcome here," she said with perfect honesty.

"Has anyone scooped you up yet?" he asked.

"Nope," Zahira replied.

"Well alright then, I better hurry up," the Pomelo said feeling brave and on board.

"So when do you think you will be here?" Zahira asked.

"Well there are some things I need to figure out first," the Pomelo started.

They chatted for a long time about his options. He spoke about everything from starting a business to going back to school to buying a van and cruising the countryside. He seemed generally unclear. He couldn't commit to a time to arrive in Winnipeg. He would have left Zahira hanging except she isn't holding on to anything.

Zahira left their call feeling oddly neutral. She was surprised by her lack of enthusiasm. Wasn't this what she once hoped for? Isn't this the perfect ending to her story? Why wasn't she giddy? Is it because she feels so relaxed about everything? She took a moment to check in with herself. What was the emotion or lack there of it?

To be completely transparent Zahira can't help but wonder if their time as lovers has come and gone. The Pomelo was the perfect match for Zahira at the beginning of this journey. He melted her guard and opened her body. He pleasured her beyond measure and he challenged her to look at herself in new ways. She will be forever grateful for the time they shared together.

But Zahira is not the same girl who fell into the Pomelo's arms. She can now sense the difference between falling in love and rising in love. While the Pomelo has made great progress on his personal journey to clarity, he is still riddled with complications. Sharing a path with him at this time would not be easy and Zahira isn't interested in making her life hard. That being said, he will always be welcome in her world and he is coming her way...

◆

Soups & Poops

Zahira's sleep cycle has finally adjusted to it's new environment. She has found a peaceful rhythm with the season and time difference. She is still void of cravings. She is still clear and grounded. Her new understanding has not abandoned her. It is impossible. It is not a philosophy, it is an understanding. It allows her to move through her old routines within a new framework.

This love for nothing has opened so many doors. It seems every time she leaves the house something magical happens. Her timing is so on it couldn't even be considered time, it just is. Her homeostasis tells her when to move, when to eat, when to be still, when to reach out, when to lay low. In all of these areas she is at rest. Even if Zahira has to rush she is resting.

She has found new joy in the simplicity of life. She is no longer seeking thrills. She is finding pleasure in taking long walks, baking cakes for her neighbours and getting good rest. She likes making soups and taking regular poops. She enjoys sitting on her front porch. She likes going to yoga and she loves this new bakery she is in.

"Is that a cleanse thing?" asked a friend who stopped in for cookies.

"No not really, it's more like a lifestyle. It doesn't feel like I am trying to cut out anything. It's more like a way of life," she said trying to explain her lack of cravings.

"So it's a permanent thing?" he asked

"Oh man, life is long. I would hate to put that kind of pressure on myself. Who knows what the future holds," she smiled with a wise wink.

◆

Everything in life changes…everything.

◆

Deporting Pomelos

Dear Zahira,

You won't believe this, the U.S.A. deported me back to NZ this morning on my way to Vancouver via Seattle. Fucked up country. Anyway don't know what to do at this point. My head and emotions are pretty fucked up. Been flying or waiting in transit for 2 days and got 2 more to go. Will talk to you when I get back home.

~ Ciao bella

Zahira read this letter out loud to herself three or four times. She was trying to wrap her head around it. It was very big news with very little information. *Deported? Seriously? Deported!?*

Zahira knew the proper reaction would have been concern for her dear Pomelo, but instead she broke out into a hysterical laughter.

"Are you kidding me?! Are you f'n kidding me?" she screamed out loud to no one, "Holy shit! Okay then!"

Of course she felt bad that the Pomelo was in distress, but for some reason Zahira felt incredibly liberated. This news brought such a definitive finale to their relationship. She thinks her liberation was coming from having such a big decision made for her. There would be no questioning as to the right path for their relationship. Fate was clearly keeping them apart.

What else can she say? Everything happens for a reason. The Pomelo will be fine. She will send him warm wishes through the winds and pray for peace and clarity on his path. She will always be grateful for the romance they shared. She wrote him back to tell him so. He has been a key player in her story and her life. His return would have made a full circle, but it is clearly not their time.

The Universe has spoken.

◆

Isolation

Zahira packed her parent's car with goodies and headed to the Golden Valley. She was going to spend the weekend alone with the wise old oak tree. The same one that heard her whispers a year ago. The same one that watched her heart-shaped bubbles float into the night sky. The same tree that granted her wish to go to India alone.

She went back to visit her tree friend exactly one year to the day. She wanted to camp beneath its branches that look like black lace against a moonlit sky. As she wound her way down the valley towards the river Zahira stopped dead in her tracks. She stood wearing her backpack and holding two heavy loads of supplies. She was so bewildered that she did not think to drop her bags. She just stood there with her head cocked to one side and her brow furrowed in confusion. Her tree was gone.

"Huh? How is this possible?" she said out loud to no one. She crept to the edge of the bank and looked down into the running waters. There was no sign of any oak tree. "How can there be absolutely no trace of you?" she spoke again to no one.

She knew the old tree was in a delicate spot. Last year its roots were hanging over the river bank. She and her friends were talking about ways to save it. She did not dream it would perish so quickly. She assumed it had years left to live. What was most baffling is that there was absolutely no sign it had ever existed.

The oak was old, maybe a hundred years. Its trunk was thick and branches high. There should have been branches of the giant tree wedged in the bend of the shallow river. Where Zahira stood nothing remained, not even visible roots, just nothing, *absolute nothingness.*

It took Zahira a moment to let all of this sink in. She was genuinely stunned. She finally dropped her bags and stood with her mouth slightly open and her comfort zone shaken. She had come to spend the weekend in her sacred spot. Now she could barely recognize the landscape.

After some time she circled the area. She needed to find a place to pitch camp before night fall. She still had three more loads to trek in from the car. It was a deep valley and the only way in was on foot. She could have packed light, but that would have meant leaving behind her down comforter, her blue taffeta ball gown, her party supplies, her white fur coat and all the other decadent little frills she would spoil herself with. After all, tomorrow is her birthday.

◆

Happy Birthday Suit

Zahira woke up and had breakfast in her birthday suit. She sliced a grapefruit in half and stuck a candle in the centre. Then she sliced a strawberry to slip on the rim of her martini glass that she filled with a green smoothie. She toasted her birthday naked in the sunshine.

"Thank you," she giggled to herself, "thank you".

Zahira loves being alone in the woods with her lap top. She has three nights of nothing but Zahira ahead of her. She loves these isolations. They give her a chance to relax into utter selfhood. No time, no connections to the outside world, just nature's clock and her own appetite to dictate the day.

After lounging on her gold and maroon blanket she decided it was time for a party. She went to the river and found some new friends to invite.

"Would you like to come to my birthday?" she asked the rocks that were sitting by the rushing waters. "There's no cake, but there will be party hats and blow thingies."

She laughed out loud to herself, scooped four large rocks from their beds and brought them to her party. She decorated each one with a party hat and gave them all blow thingies as promised. She organized them into a circle and then she put on her party dress, a royal blue taffeta ball gown covered in blue roses and ruffles. She felt like a cupcake in it.

"Okay!" she laughed and clapped her hands, "let the party begin!"

She put a candle in the other half of the grapefruit and refilled her martini glass with red pomegranate juice. She fluffed up her shiny blue ball gown and she set the timer on her camera. Zahira posed next to all her forest friends for a birthday picture she will keep forever.

"Oh my! Yer totally nuts," she howled when she looked at the picture. She took several more. She was totally cracking up, she was having so much fun.

She came back to camp to light a fire and make some tea. She bought herself a special kind called Three Wishes tea. It was full of roses and lavender. When the water was hot she poured herself a glass and sat back to exhale. She held the glass close to her lips. She could feel the steam rising from her cup into her cheeks.

"Three wishes hey?" she whispered with a sly smile. "I have no more wishes."

◆

Orgasmic Relaxation

She is on day three of her isolation. Her feet are resting on a log next to a fire. She is wearing her decadent white faux fur coat and a pair of ridiculous spandex tights that are completely confused. She can't even describe them. All she can say is that they remind her of Brooklyn but she bought them in Rome.

She is accustomed to being alone in the woods. She doesn't even flinch at the thought, in fact she pants at the idea. Zahira knows how to spoil herself like no other. She adores these isolations. She gets to do what ever she wants whenever she wants to. She naps, she lounges, she sips tea by the fire, she makes love to herself.

Today she found her bare back pressed up against a warm oval stone. She knew her spot as soon as she saw it. She settled in for an afternoon make out session. She had removed her tights and her legs were relaxed apart. She was next to the river and the air was gentle on her body. The sky was painted a dull grey and she felt invisible, at least she hopes she was! She made love to herself in the wide-open valley.

She is good at these make outs. She knows her own triggers. She knows how to tease and coax herself into a fully flexed orgasm. She hardly touched herself today. She let the breeze do most of the work. When she would reach her peaks she would tell each part of her body to relax.

"Relax your hands, relax your jaw, relax your toes," she kept whispering.

Her being would be utterly aroused and yet when she coaxed it to relax it would. It created a new blend of wow. Relax, relax, relax. This is the common thread from all of her teachings in India. Relaxing has been a new key to her existence. She has grown to know the power of relaxing in every moment and now she has discovered the power of relaxing with her self induced orgasms.

Using her breath she took this new discovery to the next level. She would take long slow deep inhales and hold her breath in a relaxed manor. Simply retaining her breath would heighten her bodily sensations. Her exhales were twice as long as her inhales and when they would reach the end so would her containment. She would let out a sigh that felt like a warm kiss from the sun and her body would simultaneously exhale into puddles.

These moments of aloneness are so powerful for Zahira. When no one is watching, when no clock is ticking, when no pressures are pressing, she can be utterly and totally present. This is the best birthday gift she can give herself, the one she celebrates in her birthday suit.

She is grateful for the many lovers she had found in India, but no one will ever come close to the love she makes with herself and the elements. The pleasure she has in pleasing herself is beyond the flesh. When she makes love to her body her whole being is awake. She can push her buttons with out even touching them. She can let the air do all the work. Her only job is to relax

◆

"Remember, to be grateful nothing more is needed.
All that you have is too much, it is too much
to be grateful and thankful for.
Don't ask more from the existence.
Simply enjoy that which is given to you.
And the more you enjoy, the more will be given to you."
~ Osho.

◆

I-so-elated!

The isolation is complete. The lessons are still brewing like the lemon oolong tea that rests in front of her. She is dressed in all grey, a colour that makes her feel cozy and sexy. She can see her reflection in the computer screen and she looks cozy and sexy. Her hair is tousled and clean, her skin is free from makeup and her lips are slightly turned into a contented grin. Where to begin?

Her isolation was different this year because she was not looking for anything. She was not craving solace or nature or the peace that they provide. She has these thing now, they are with her synonymously. They do not escape her even when her head feels troubled. She has a new even flow to her rhythm. This realization brought tears to her eyes this morning.

Before packing her bags Zahira stood along the same river's edge that swallowed her oak tree. She was naked in the mist and the sky was dark. She was standing tall and grateful, her chin titled upwards. She exhaled and felt everything from her neck down relax into a quiet grace.

"Thank you," she whispered, "thank you for everything you have gifted me with in this lifetime. I am so lucky to have a life in this body. I have been spoiled by your beauty and your blessings. I have come so far this year," she said as the tears began to flow, "I have found what cannot be lost. I have uncovered what cannot be discovered. I no longer need to look for that which I cannot see. All I need to do is relax and simply be."

She was crying tears of gratitude for her new understanding. The shifts that have occurred in Zahira are so subtle and yet they are all encompassing. She cannot pinpoint the moment it occurred, but she does know that her new understanding came with out effort. It's as though she bent down to put on some slippers and slid unconsciously into awakening. She has been loafing around in it ever since.

It was such a subtle and gentle transition that she did not even realize she had wafted into this new reality. There were no bells and whistles. The clouds did not part and the trumpets did not sound. There was nothing and is nothing extravagant and astounding about it. There isn't even a need to shout it from the roof tops. Her slippers of awakening are more content to just relax and lounge in the sunless and sun days of her life.

There are still afflictive states that arise, they swell and bubble just like they used to. She allows them to run their course. She doesn't need to do anything about them. She can greet her pain with the same open heart as she greets her joy with. They are equally hers. They are equally beautiful.

This gentle awakening has brought Zahira to the place of nothingness. She needs and desires nothing and yet she gives thanks for everything.

She is no longer looking because she can't figure out what she could possibly be missing. Her life as she knows it is complete.

While she had many beautiful romances on her journey through India, the greatest love she has found is for life itself. Her juicy experiences reminded her what it is like to be a woman, but she has been romanced into a new reality. She no longer needs a fairy tale ending. She no longer needs anything. For the first time in her life she can honestly say that she has found the peace that asks for nothing.

"If this is all my life will ever be...," she said out loud to the sky, "then oh my god thank you, thank you, thank you."

PART 8

King Nereo

◆

Piñatas & Pulses

"What are you laughing at?" she asked him with a smile. He had started to giggle and she didn't know why.

"Your smile," he said with a bit of hesitation. "It's so cute. You look like a little kid."

Zahira laughed out loud. She likes her new friend. His name is Nereo. She feels extremely comfortable around him. Zahira is effortlessly herself in his presence. She gets to be a spastic hyperactive girl and a calm clear wise woman. He naturally reflects both of these qualities.

They have been spending a lot of time together: creating, laughing, imagining, talking and sharing silence. He is an artist of multiple disciplines. He is a painter, a poet, a videographer and a dancer. His talents are rooted in Hip Hop culture but sprawl with out borders.

They recently celebrated their un-birthdays. They turned a regular Wednesday into a party with a cake, party hats and loot bags. They even exchanged un-birthday presents. He gifted her with a beautiful homemade card and a can of gold spray paint. She made him some mixed CDs and a logo for their new partnership. They call themselves the Kindred Klowns.

He showed up to her home tonight with a text saying 'peek-a-boo... come find me'. It made her laugh out loud. He is very good at surprises. She wandered out front to look for him, instead she found a sculpture of his body made out of packing tape! It was propped up next to a tree and he was hiding behind a car watching her reaction. She was clapping her hands and giggling. They were now in her kitchen turning this sculpture into a human size piñata named Hendrix.

"What about your heart?" asked Zahira out of the blue. "Where are you at with romance?"

They had been playing together for weeks and this was the first time either one had brought up the subject.

"Hmmm, well I'm really happy on my own. I have been single for a while and I am totally comfortable with this. I also really like to have company," he said as he looked at her and smiled. "I really like your company."

Zahira smiled and her heart did a little flutter. She was cutting out fortunes to put in their piñata. The air between them was warm and fizzy.

"What about you?" he asked gently, "Where is your heart?"

"Well pretty much the same as yours," she said honestly. In fact she had been quite surprised by his answer. It seemed like something that would fall out of her own mouth. "I'm not really looking for anything. I feel super grateful for my life just as it is, but I also really like company. I like your company too."

The two stopped what they were doing and stared at each other for a long time. Zahira's toes started to twitch. He was not looking away. He held her gaze and their space with confidence and comfort. His presence was filling the entire room. She started to giggle. He moved towards her and spontaneously hugged her.

"I love you," he said with an unabashed super sincere tone.

For some reason Zahira wasn't surprised by his words. They were genuine and perfect for the moment. They echoed her own appreciation, she really does love her new friend.

"You are so..." she was searching for the right words, but all she could come up with was, '...amazing.'

He circled around her back and swallowed her with his arms. The two didn't speak for some time. He just held her gently. Zahira felt warm and sweet and totally at peace.

"I like your wings," he said referring to the butterfly on her back.

"Yeah me too," she said feeling safe and serene.

He began to trace his fingers along her bare skin. He outlined her wings and then he started to write something with the tip of his finger. It was the first time he had touched her in an intimate way.

"I just tagged you," he said.

"What did you write?" she asked. Her toes were still twitching.

"Love life," he said sweetly.

Zahira just laughed. She is constantly being surprised by this man. He is sort of like hanging out with a mythical creature. He is not from this world. He is his own being and yet he can relate, express and engage so naturally with his environment. He sat down beside her.

"I don't know what is happening here," Nereo said with a smile.

"Me neither," she said, "but my toes are twitching so that's a good sign."

They held this moment for a while, neither one in a rush to make a move or say a word. They had been spending an exorbitant amount of time together and yet this was the first time that they had spoken about their relationship. Up until now they had been nothing but playful.

"I just know that I really enjoy spending time with you. I really like this," she said.

She had her cheek resting on the counter top. She was looking up at him with a smile. It was an innocent position to share her feelings from. She didn't feel submissive she felt a little shy.

He came down to her level, "I like spending time with you too."

They sat comfortably in silence for some time. It had been a magical night of creating. The Kindred Klowns had laughed hysterically watching Hendrix come to life. It was late now and they had plans for the morning. He was going to meet her entire family. They were going tubing down a river near her sister's place in Lac du Bonnet.

"I'm going to finish cutting out this stencil and then I'm going to let you get some sleep," he said as he stood to finish his work.

"Okay," she smiled. She got up and started to clean up. She was glad that they didn't push their conversation any further. They were saying more with their energy and eye contact than they were with their words. The room was filled with a peaceful glow.

The two said goodnight with a friendly hug, but this time it felt as though something had shifted. There was less of a question as to what they were both thinking. They had shared their availability and their love of each other's company.

This time their goodbye felt more like a hello.

◆

He's a Poet and He Knows It

On behalf of the smile on my face, I just wanted to say..cheers!
to the Kindred Klowns!
Who love living in the now
Cheers to road trippin' & getting down
Here's to the pretty Gimli light show that was up in the clouds
Here's to the little rascal love you help turn inside out
To the beauty that raises these Frida Kahlo eyebrows
To your whimsical world that fills my mouth with words like "wowWWW"
Eye feel very lucky...
Beyond skin
My dear friend, you have truly touched me
Like you would not believe!
Here is to the big smile on my face
That you can 'picture' but can't quite see
Here is to manifesting extraordinary dreams
that will forever reign supreme over false realities
Here is to the reminder that in life there really is no need to rush
Whatever needs to happen will happen when it happens
Here is to by far one of my most favourite superheroes
Zahira ~ a one of a kind type of feline
that no other cat can copy
If it's okay with you, soon enough I will be knock-knocking
on your door with more non material gifts
Gifts such as this poem
which is the closest I get to feeling rich
So yes. Yes here's to another beautiful day
Here's to the hopes that we get another chance to p l a y
So listen close to the final toast I'm giving
Sweet-sweet woman! Thanks much for existing
Here's to sharing knowledge, wisdom and whimsical visions
Here's to spontaneously driftin'
Here's to living...and loving...LIFE

◆

Upside Down Kisses

Nereo picked up Zahira with perfect timing. They had Hendrix in the back seat, some strawberries, some Yerba mate, the CDs she gave him for his un-birthday present and two huge smiles on their faces. She was happy to be back in his ride, he calls it Paris. It some how feels like home to her.

They made it to her sister's place and spent the day floating down the river on inner tubes. Her whole family was there. Zahira enjoyed watching the jagged rocks and pine trees drift by. It was such a lovely way to travel. The slow river offered a sweet and lazy pace.

They stopped for a picnic along the way and had a rock throwing competition. Nereo was the first to throw his rock clear across the river bank. Zahira cheered. Everything felt friendly and warm, easy and natural.

After a day on the water they went back to her sister's beautiful country home for dinner. They played on the trampoline, took some more portraits of Hendrix and chatted around the patio table. Her dad asked Nereo how he goes about doing his work as an artist.

"When you do a mural do you draw it out first or do you just go for it?" her dad inquired.

"Well it's different," Nereo responded, "sometimes you can draw things out first, but sometimes things just fall naturally into place."

Zahira had been partially napping at this point, but when she heard those words her eyes opened. Nereo was looking directly at her and they shared a spark and a smile. She closed her eyes again and her lips curled.

What was happening here? Every time Zahira allowed her mind to pull her out of the moment she decided she didn't want to know. She was just happy to be sharing time with this man. He loves life just as much as she does.

They drove back to Winnipeg at sunset to go and watch the movie Avatar play under the stars at the park. They brought beanbag chairs and a blanket and settled into a perfect nest. It was the first time that they had puddled together. It was like curling into a cup of tea and a good book.

When the movie was over a soft rain started to drizzle. They pulled the blanket up around themselves and listened to the crowd disappear. They were quiet beside each other. He was lightly touching her finger tips with his own. She could feel an electric current running between them.

"I see you," he said with a funny voice. He was mocking the movie they just watched, but his tone was sincere.

"I see you too," she said in all honesty, "and I really like what I see."

"I like what I see too. I like your energy, I like what's in your head, I like what falls out of your mouth," Nereo shared.

Zahira giggled and squeezed his hand. She didn't say anything. She was feeling peaceful in their puddle.

"There are a lot of things that people take into consideration in relationships like age and culture," he started, "but I just think that when you like someone you like them, that's it."

The two are an unlikely match. She is much older than him. She is short, curvy and Canadian and he is tall, lean and Filipino. That being said, there is also something ageless, race-less, and shapeless about these two characters. They both seem to exist beyond limitations and explanations. They don't subscribe to boundaries and therefore there are not obliged or inclined to stick to them.

Zahira looked up from the ball she was curled into to see his face. "You are insanely beautiful. You remind me of some kind of mythical creature. It's like I'm hanging out with a unicorn or something," she giggled.

Nereo smiled and slowly pulled out of Zahira's arms to quietly gaze at her. After a moment he began to stack the beanbags and blankets on top of her. He created a fort around her whole body and just left a little window around her mouth so she could breathe. She closed her eyes and exhaled. She felt him resting above her head. All of her senses were completely turned on.

She wondered if he would kiss her. Her lips were locked in a smile. She could not see a thing, but all of a sudden she could feel his breath next to hers. He was hovering above her, floating with his face upside down to hers. Then like a gentle breeze he touched his lips to her own. It was so soft and so sweet it felt like mist on a morning lake. She giggled and he kissed her again. This time she responded, her bottom lip was touching the top of his.

"Upside down kisses!" she smiled as he pulled away. She still couldn't see him and was marvelling at how perfect this all was.

Zahira has been borderline shy with this man. She has not had an urge to devour him. She has felt more like crawling into his being and disappearing. She hasn't felt sexy she has felt sweet. In this moment he had found a way to completely turn her on with his innocence and magic.

There is a quality that Zahira shares with Nereo that she does not recognize in any of her previous relationships. It is a quiet quality, it is peaceful. It is perfect just as it is. She doesn't need to know where this is going, in fact she doesn't want to know. She is happy just to take it slow and let it all unfold.

"Hey did you get some flowers?" asks her roommate as she types this last paragraph.

"What?" she asked looking up from her lap top. Her roommate was standing at the front door looking out the window.

Zahira walked over with butterflies already in her belly. She knew it would be some kind of surprise from him. She looked out the window to find beautiful orange and white flowers scattered all over her front porch. Nereo had left them in the middle of the night. She collected them all and put them in water.

This is how she begins her day, grateful and giggling.

◆

A Quiet Knowing

A deep sense of peace arises in Zahira when Nereo is near. Sometimes her stomach flutters and her toes twitch when he holds her gaze, but for the most part she feels like she is in a constant state of exhale. He is really good at surprising and spoiling her. He rarely shows up at her door like the average person. He will knock and run and leave her a gift before revealing himself. Her life has been extra delightful since his arrival.

Zahira is watching herself be amazed by this man. He exists separate of her and yet they seem to be melting into each other. It doesn't feel hectic or nerve racking or scary. It doesn't feel anxious or indecisive. It feels like they already exist together and they are falling into their natural time and space. It's as though their connection has been written in the stars and now they are simply uncovering it on earth. While Nereo is mysterious and mellifluous, he does not leave her guessing. What she feels is more like a knowing.

A quiet knowing.

◆

Sane Love

Zahira and Nereo spent the afternoon doing nothing. It was just as fun as all of the art projects they have been doing together. He strummed a few chords and rapped about the moment. She read him everything she has written about them. She was nervous at first, but he was teary eyed by the time she finished.

"You've been listening," he said as he gave her a strong hug.

The two are officially moonstruck by each other. They are stuck like glue to each other. Nereo even shared a story that made her heart smile.

"I was driving home last night and I felt a wave of emotion crash through me. I had to pull my car over because I started to cry," he said quietly.

"Why?" asked Zahira, "Were they sad tears?"

"No," he said a bit sheepishly.

"Well what was the quality?" she asked.

"The quality?" he asked back.

"Yeah what was the emotion? What were you feeling at the time?" Zahira asked.

"It was a feeling of being in love," he said in a shy whisper. Zahira wondered if she heard him correctly and then he said, "I know I'm strange."

"That's not strange it's beautiful," she said feeling both surprised and elated.

This man is special beyond words. He has a heart that feels deeply and he wears it on his sleeve.

Zahira kissed him and held him. She was so touched by his honesty. She feels a great depth with Nereo. His heart is both wild and rooted. They spoke openly and softly about their pasts. They talked about money and family and love.

"Do you think it's important to have a lot of money?" Nereo asked.

"No not really. I think things can be simple, pleasures can be simple. I don't need a castle, I would be happy with nothing more than a lemon yellow room," Zahira smiled.

"A lemon yellow room?" Nereo asked.

"Yeah, I've always wanted a lemon yellow room, then everyday would feel like sunshine!" Zahira cheered playfully.

"I like that," Nereo said with a twinkle in his eye, "Do you think love is more important than money when it comes to starting a family?"

"Yes of course, it's the love of a unit that counts. A child will only know love, he won't understand money. I think you can simplify your life to make any situation work. I was worried about money when I was your age, but I no longer fear it. I have enough life experience to know that things come when you need them," she replied.

Nereo smiled and seemed to like what she was saying, "So you would choose love over money?"

"I have chosen love over money. I would rather wake up broke next to sunshine than..."

Zahira couldn't even finish her sentence before Nereo jumped into her arms and started kissing her. He held her firmly and she started to giggle, "Hey...I don't think you are always going to be broke either. I think you have an amazingly successful career ahead of you!"

The two stopped talking and started kissing. They kissed and cuddled, kissed and cuddled. It felt fun and sweet and sensuous. She knows it sounds crazy, but this is the most sane she has ever felt with another human. Nereo mirrors her with his own unique spin on life. He moves through the world like water and when he is near she feels like she is floating. She also feels grounded and real and ready.

What ever this is, she is ready for it.

◆

Unicorns Are Real

Nereo text: Doctor Strange would like to pay you and Hendrix a visit this evening around 6 if it's cool with you.

Oh perfect she thought. She was going to ask him if he wanted to play doctor. She was referring more to their poor piñata Hendrix. He is cracked in half from their road trip. Piñatas don't mix well with trampolines. He needs a little love. It turns out poor Hendrix is going to have to wait a little bit longer.

Zahira text: I'm napping upstairs. The back door is open…

She had been in bed all day. It was raining outside and she was feeling lazy and lovely. She even made love to herself this afternoon. It was a powerful reconnection to her sensual self. She found the space that brings her to orgasm without touch. It is such a subtle beautiful place. It transported her into an essence of silence. When she was done loving her body she let time unfold. She was content to just watch her curtains billowing in the wind. It reminded her of her days in the Ayurvedic hospital.

She was perfect in her aloneness until her mythical creature came crawling up the stairs. He was wearing a white lab coat, a pair of black goggles shaped like a super hero mask, and was carrying a silver brief case. He sat on the edge of her bed and just looked at her. Neither one said a word until she started laughing.

"Hello Doctor Strange," she smiled. "Are you wearing a lab coat?"

"Yes I am," he said behind his masked eyes.

"What's in the brief case?" she asked feeling quite marvelled.

"Well…I brought some tools," he said opening it up, "I have some tape to fix our dear friend Hendrix, a red marker to give him a heart because every body needs a heart and a pen to give him a smile. Oh and I brought this for you," he said as he pulled out some massage oil and some music.

"Oh I like the look of that," she said reaching up to take his mask off. She put it on herself.

They talked about their days and then he bent down to give her a kiss. They kissed for a while, softly and sweetly. Nothing hurried, just soft gentle kisses. He slowly laid down next to her.

"You smell good," she said smoothing her nose across his cheeks.

"Thank you," he said, "It's pineapple and coconut. I have it here."

"You have a pineapple and coconut in that briefcase?" she said half joking.

"No no," he laughed softly, "it's a cream."

They laid side by side and she started to trace her hand along his face. She took her index finger and smoothed it over his eyebrows and along his temples. He brought his hand to her face and began to mirror her. She would apply pressure to his temple and he would do the same for her. She would circle around his third eye and he would circle around hers. She would lightly brush his eyelashes and he would lightly sweep across hers. They did this for a while.

They kissed a little more and then she rolled on to her stomach. He got out the pineapple and coconut cream and smoothed it across her bare shoulders. She let out a sigh. Hendrix would just have to wait for now. He worked on her back and Zahira exhaled.

"Is there a danger in massaging someone for too long?" he asked.

"I've never heard of any," she replied.

"Good cause I could do this for hours," Nereo said.

Zahira was feeling so lucky, especially because he seemed to be really enjoying himself.

"Will you write a story on my back?" she asked while fluttering her feet.

"Yes," he said starting at the top of her left shoulder.

His finger tip was firm and felt so good. He wrote the first two words and then whispered them to her, "Butterfly Woman…," then he wrote another line and again he whispered it to her, "came to this life…"

She was melting with this moment. The words he choose, the way he whispered them and his touch were all perfect. Another line and another whisper, "to share love with caterpillars, caterpillars like me."

Zahira was falling in love. He finished his story by saying that the Butterfly Woman is 'a reflection for all to see, a universal model to love life and simply be.'

"Exclamation mark," he whispered in conclusion.

Zahira giggled and rolled over. She pulled him down on top of her and started kissing him.

"You really are special you know that?" she said in between kisses on the cheek.

She grabbed her wing that was already in bed with her and started to smooth it across his cheeks. It's the wing of a snow goose. It's grey and white and black. Zahira has been using it in healing ceremonies for years now. It is one of her most valued possessions.

She brushed the wing softly across the outline of his face. She traced its tip along his nose and lips and then she got to work dusting away all of his worries. She fluttered the wing repeatedly along his forehead sweeping his doubts away. She worked for a while on his third eye. In her mind she was repeating 'you are beauty and you are life and you are endless.'

She was enjoying herself. Watching his exotic face go from smiles into utter peace and then back into a smile. His eyes were closed and he was in a blissful trance. She felt like she could have done this for hours. He was so open and receptive and touched. She finished with a kiss on the ear lobe and whispered, "You are perfect just as you are."

She put her head on his chest and he wrapped her in his arms. She laid there for quite sometime and then she sat up to look at him. His eyes were wide open. He was looking at her with a state of amazement and love. He didn't say a word for a very long time, he didn't have to. He just kept staring at her as though he were seeing her for the first time, as though he were meeting his own mythical creature.

He put his hands on his heart and just held the space between them. He shook his head a few times, he smiled. Zahira could feel that he was open to meeting her in this place. He was ready to meet her as a healer. He was right there with her, connecting with her on the deep level she loves to share, but to find someone to meet her there is so rare.

He put his hands to his mouth and tried to pull some words out. He just shook his head and said, "Nothing."

"It's okay you don't have to say anything," Zahira assured him. She was loving this silence they were sharing. It was filled with emotions beyond words, it felt white and radiant and clear.

"I only have images," he said after some more time had passed.

"Oh can you draw me one sometime?" she asked.

"Yes," he said and kissed her on the top of her head, "It felt like a dream."

"You feel like a dream," Zahira replied as she curled into his peacefulness.

"I love you," he said in a quiet whisper.

"What did you say?" she asked as she raised her head to look him in the eyes.

"I love you," he said looking directly into her.

Zahira broke out into a wide smile and kissed him. She pulled away, giggled and then kissed him again. It was all she could do, giggle and kiss. She could not say it back in this moment, but didn't feel she had to. She wanted to show him instead. So she smattered him with more kisses and hugged him so tightly.

He responded to her and their kisses grew with intensity. He started to move down her torso, kissing her waist and her breast. Zahira was turned on, but not ready. She squeezed him with her thighs and brought his lips back to hers.

"Can we wait a little bit more?" she asked.

"Yes," he said not sounding disappointed, "yes."

"Thank you," she said, "just a little bit longer."

The two have spent so much golden time together building a foundation for a relationship that is not based on sex. They have been playing together with curiosity and innocence. It feels like nothing Zahira has ever known before. She knows this man can turn her on, but she is really enjoying these moments with their clothes on. She wants to move slowly and she wants to savour it all.

"Poor Hendrix," she laughed.

Nereo laughed too.

"I really need to eat something," Zahira said. She had been in bed since two in the afternoon, it was now almost nine, "and you need to get to band practice. I don't want to be the reason you are late."

"It's okay," he said pulling out his phone, "I can tell them I will be late."

"No no," said Zahira, "if I care about you I will keep you on your path. I don't want to be a distraction, I want you to stay on track. Your music is important."

He smiled and they went downstairs to share a quick snack. As they were eating he finally found his words.

"I don't know what that was, all I know is that I left this world," he said. "It felt like nothing I have ever known before. I am not sure what you were doing, but it felt like you were sweeping away bad spirits or thoughts," he said as he brushed his finger tips along his forehead.

"Yes!" she smiled, "I was! I was sweeping away all your worries. Wow you really are amazing. You totally get it."

Zahira was so delighted by this. They chatted about her Lightwork and other things that she rarely speaks out loud. Nereo seems available in this space, available and reciprocal. It was exciting to 'meet' him there. Zahira has not encountered many people who travel to these edges of existence. This man makes her feel like she is dreaming, but she is awake and she is calm and she is clear about him.

They finished their food in perfect silence and then she kicked him out, "Time for band practice."

He collected his things and she hugged him goodbye. He walked out into the rain and she called out, "Hey! You should stop and smell the air. The cedar deck smells so good in the rain."

He stopped, inhaled and came straight back for her. They kissed like new lovers in the rain. They felt like old lovers who will do it again and again.

◆

Beyond Skin

Zahira and Nereo decided to skip town. It was already late in the afternoon, but they were both game to escape into nature. They packed some tea, some snacks, half of Hendrix, a hula hoop, a kite, a blanket and a ghetto blaster. In the end only their blanket got any play time.

They were looking for a hideout on the beach. They found a perfect clearing. It was secluded and soft. The sand mixed in with sweet green plants made for a nice bed and the trees above whispered songs from the wind.

Zahira spread out the blanket and sat down crossed legged. Without saying a word Nereo sat in front of her in the same position. Their knees were touching and he reached for her hands. They gently placed their palms together. Zahira instantly started to hum.

"Keep going," he said after she stopped.

Their eyes were closed and their hearts were open. Zahira began to hum again and this time he joined her. They were making their own music. It was barely audible, but that's what made it so special. They were entirely tuned into each other. They were so still that every subtle touch, sound and motion felt powerful. They had naturally slid into the place where her entire body is turned on by the air around her. He was there breath for breath. Not only did he hold this space with her, he was generating it as well.

"Pick a note and hold it," she said.

Nereo began to hum and Zahira pressed her lips next to his and matched his key. The sound of their voices combined turned into something else all together. Their original note began to shake vibrato style and new notes organically erupted from this base line. It sounded like there were countless voices present.

"Wow!" he said as he pulled back with wide eyes.

"That's transcendental sound," she said. She has always wanted to do this with a lover, but she had never found the right partner. "Again!" she clapped.

The two strange kids got lost in this for quite sometime. They would slide in and out of each other through their voices. Zahira felt herself loosing her own physical awareness. She would escape her body and melt with his energy.

"Who needs mushrooms," she laughed.

The two started cracking up hysterically. They looked like total trippers.

"No kidding," he said as her pulled back to stare at her.

She pulled herself up on his lap to straddle him with her legs. They were hugging so softly. The air between their bodies was totally turning her on. They barely graced each other with touch. Their cheeks were so close that the warmth between them felt like a current of electric grace. Their hands began to move together with out touching. The heat between their bodies was guiding them. When their finger tips met it felt like silk lightening coursing between them.

They were dancing without moving, feeling without touching. They were making love beyond skin. It wasn't sexual it was sensual and her entire body felt orgasmic. She would brush her lips so lightly against his earlobes and let out an inaudible moan. She was so turned on it was not only beyond skin, it was beyond words.

All she can say is that she has been waiting a *lifetime* to find a man to meet her in this space. This is the subtle body that she has been masturbating with for years now. Her ability to orgasm without touch was something that she has never been able to share with another. She didn't even think it was possible until now.

"It's nice to meet you," she said as she opened her eyes.

"It's nice to meet you too," he said with the most beautiful expression on his face. "I know this is going to sound crazy, but I feel like I just made love to your spirit."

Zahira almost creamed herself just hearing those words. They have been a long time coming. "Wow, that's not crazy at all. That's *exactly* what just happened."

"I could see so many colours and animals and shapes around us," he said slowly.

"Really? Like what?" she asked fully curious.

"Well I saw yellows and pinks swirling around you. I saw birds floating between us, I saw a snake and I saw some living creatures that

I have no name for," he replied.

Zahira was feeling peaceful, calm and grateful, "I can't believe how lucky I feel right now."

"I feel it too," Nereo said kissing her.

They kissed for quite sometime, long, slow, sensual kisses. Zahira was still straddling his lap and he picked her up gently and placed her on her back. He was on top of her now kissing her gently. He started to massage the muscles on the front of her neck.

"Wow that feels amazing," she said in a barley audible whisper. "I don't know if I've ever been touched there before."

He worked on the front of her neck while kissing her. It drove Zahira wild. He was on top of her and the whole scene was turning her on. She could hear the wind dancing in the trees and the waves crashing on the beach. His kisses were so soft and his massage was so firm. Zahira was letting her whole body absorb this moment.

When they finally stood to leave they paused to face each other. They were about two feet apart and they both had their hands behind their backs. Zahira was rocking her shoulders from side to side feeling giddy and grateful. They were simply staring at each other from a bit of a distance. Their stance was innocent and open.

"I'll be your clay," Nereo said.

"I love you," Zahira said without thinking.

"I love you too," he smiled.

◆

TANTRA

"Is not technique but prayer. Is not head oriented but a relaxation into the heart. Please remember it. Many books have been written on Tantra, they all talk about technique but the real Tantra has nothing to do with technique. The real Tantra cannot be written about, the real Tantra has to be imbibed. How to imbibe real Tantra? You will have to transform your whole approach."

~ OSHO

◆

Flower Power

"Oh my god I love you so much!" oozed the Flower over the phone.

"I know," beamed Zahira, "I love you too!"

The two girls were giggling and cackling like fireworks. They are so charged by each other. The Atlantic ocean that separates them is no match for the dimension they exist in. They have been in constant communication since they parted ways. They have been planning and scheming their next adventure and it is right around the corner.

The twins are heading to Burning Man! Not only to Burning Man, but they will be reunited in Las Vegas! They are meeting in the city of lights to rent a motorhome, pick up four hundred Acupressure mats, gather supplies and head to the desert.

"Listen," purred the Flower, "send me an invoice of all your expenses. Your flight to Vegas, your Burning Man ticket, the hotel, all of it. The company will pay for it all. I will give you cash when I see you."

Zahira started laughing. The two had talked about becoming business partners when they met in India. Now four months later the Flower has been hired to re-vamp a company that makes unique Acupressure mats. They are a modern day bed of nails that can be used as a tool for self-healing. Her business brilliance has them going to Burning Man to pay it forward. Gifting the mats at Burning Man is a way to tap into the American market.

All of this is so exciting, but Zahira is mostly ecstatic to be going home! Her beloved Burning Man is her favourite place in the galaxy. It resonates with the clearest deepest place in her heart. Just the thought of returning feels like eating fizz candies for breakfast. Her stomach is butterflying and she is giddy with delight.

"What did I do to deserve this!?" she cheered out loud to the morning sky.

She is going to the greatest party on earth, she gets to meet her twin again, her family is healthy, her parents just celebrated their 44th anniversary, and to top it all off Zahira is in love!

Her body has been waking up electrified at 6 in the morning.

Sometimes these currents are warm and peaceful and other times they are thrilling and charged. She wants to yell her fortunes from the roof tops, but also feels like whispering them. When she talks about her Flower she is practically shouting. When she talks about her lover she is barely audible. The combination of the two in her day is orgasmic through experiential contrast; loud and quiet, firm and soft, inhales and exhales.

◆

Set For Take Off

Nereo showed up to the penthouse party as Zahira was digging through her crates of records. She smiled the instant she saw him. He gave her a big hug.

"You're DJing tonight?" he asked with an equally big grin.

"Yeah," she smiled, "but I'm almost done for now. The band is coming on after this song."

His timing was perfect. She finished her track and grabbed him by the hand. He had gifted the party with a bottle of Crystal Skull Vodka and their fabulous hostess was mixing them a drink. Her best friend Coco was hosting another epic event in one of the slickest spaces in the city. A rooftop studio apartment with a skyline view of Winnipeg.

"Will you come with me?" she asked Nereo as she was leading him off stage.

"Yeah," he said giving her hand a squeeze.

She led him to the edge of the roof top. They climbed up on to a little perch and she instantly curled into him. They were like two gargoyles nesting under the stars. The moon was full, the air was warm and the night was just getting started.

When the band was done playing Coco got on the microphone. "Zahira would you like to play some records?" she called into the darkness.

Zahira felt hesitant. She wanted to stay next to Nereo, but she had made a commitment. She looked at him and asked, "Are you cool if I go and spin for an hour or so?"

"Oh yeah yeah," he said encouragingly, "I'm cool. Do your thang."

Zahira hit the decks and within three or four tracks Nereo was by her side.

"Wanna pick a song?!" she asked while bopping around her turn tables.

"Yes!" he said with a massive playful grin.

The two slid into a perfectly matched rhythm. They moved through song after song as though they were the only two dancing under the full moon. It was their first encounter as lovers on the dance floor. Zahira *loves* to dance and Nereo has moves that can melt her own. They were sucked into each other like magnets. He was with her step for step, twirl for twirl, dip for dip.

It was her favourite night with this man to date. Dancing with Nereo was more exciting than any sexual encounter Zahira has *ever* had. She completely lost her sense of being. They teleported to another time and place. They felt invisible to everyone but each other.

Zahira has never had an introduction like this to another human. She feels like she is entering unchartered territories with this man. Their path of playful sensuality over sexuality feels like an evolution. Zahira and Nereo are starting their relationship from a higher place, a place that feels grounded and yet out of this world. She has a feeling they are just getting set for take off...

◆

"Pray with your woman, sing with your woman, play with your woman, dance with your woman, with no idea of sex. Don't go on thinking, 'When are we going to bed?' Forget about it. Do something else and get lost into it. And some day love will arise out of that being lost, suddenly you will see that you are making love and you are not making it. It is happening, you are possessed by it. Then you have your first Tantra experience – possessed by something bigger than you. You were dancing or you were singing together or you were chanting together or you were praying together or meditating together, and suddenly you find you both

have moved into a new space. And you don't know when you have started making love; you don't remember either. Then you are being possessed by Tantra energy. And then for the first time you will see a non-technical experience."

~ Osho

◆

Tutu Tuesdays

Zahira feels like she has met her very own imaginary friend. Sometimes she wonders if anybody else can even see Nereo. He feels too unbelievable to be real. She feels like she is dreaming when they are together. They speak without words and they play like they are in water, floating and drifting with effortless pleasure.

"I really do feel like I am hanging out with a unicorn," she said as they were sitting on a velvety red couch shaped like a pair of lips.

They had turned a regular Tuesday into an evening of costumes and creation. They were drinking French Rose tea that matched the colour of the dusty rose tutu she was wearing. Nereo was drawing.

She was impressed with his talent, but in awe of his being. She decided that Nereo isn't just an artist, he *is* art. He is expression and creation and abstraction. He is ingenuity and inspiration and imagination. Nereo is art, he is *fine fine art.*

"Do you have a best friend?" Zahira asked curiously.

A huge grin spread across his face and stuck like glue.

"What?" she asked grinning back.

"Do you wanna be my best friend?" he asked in the most genuine heart melting tone.

"Yes!" she laughed, "Yes I do."

The two best friends finished their tutu tuesday with a kiss. A slow and sensual kiss.

◆

Superhero & Ayahuasquero

"Do you wanna disappear into a forest together?" asked Zahira as Nereo showed up to play.

"Yes," he said without hesitation.

She loves this about him, he is always ready to go. He doesn't need convincing he just wants to act. It is such a joy for her to have him in her life. He is the ultimate play partner.

The two best friends set out with a blanket and a picnic basket. They went to an urban forest and found a trail head neither one had ever seen before.

"Let's try it!" said Zahira hopping out of Paris.

They ducked through the initial opening and found themselves in a beautiful sea of white poplar trees. They interlaced bodies and Zahira's heart instantly started to hum. They didn't speak. They sat quietly and listened to the sounds around them. The crickets and soft breeze were lulling her into bliss. The sky was fading into dusk and the air was cooling.

"Do you want a cup of tea?" asked Zahira.

"If you're having some," replied Nereo.

Zahira got up to pour some Bengal Spice tea. She placed the mug between her feet to give it a steady balance and then she opened the thermos. The tea was still piping hot and the steam came billowing out into the crisp evening air. As she began to pour it the tea bags plopped out and released a flood of liquid she had not expected. The hot tea poured all over her right foot.

"Ahhhhhhhh!!!!!" she screamed as she ripped off her sock. The skin on her foot had already sizzled and peeled back. It was hanging loosely. "Oh fuck!" she yelled.

Nereo sat up stunned by her reaction and instinctively wanted to help. He put his hands on her foot and she writhed in pain.

"Oh my god! Can you please run to the car and get some water?" she begged.

Her superhero friend was up up and away before she could say thank you. He came back to pour some relief on her burning skin but she knew it would not be enough. This felt serious. She had no choice but to cut their peaceful party short, "I think I'm gonna need to go and get this under a steady stream of running water."

"Of course," replied super Nereo. "Let me carry you."

She giggled in surprise but did not resist. The pain she was experiencing was unprecedented. He scooped her up in his arms like a child and carried her back through the land mines of poison ivy. It was not an easy trail and they had come in quite a ways. He was truly powering through for her. She felt so lucky in this moment. She really could not fathom the pressure of walking.

He placed her gently in the front seat and sprinted back to gather their things. Zahira was breathing to calm herself. She was having intense flashes of pain. They were making her nauseous. She knew this was a bad burn.

They stopped at a drug store and Nereo quickly ran in to get some bottles of water to pour on her foot. He also came out with some antiseptic gel.

"Look it's Pomelo flavoured," he laughed holding up the clear gel.

Zahira couldn't help but laugh, "Oh my god you are the best."

He took her home and put her next to the bath tub. She hung her knee over the edge and let the water run to relieve her pain. Nereo left to go and get her some supplies from the pharmacy. She sat on her bathroom floor and cried. Just then her Ayahuasquero came out of his room and knelt beside her. His presence made Zahira feel better. He is a powerful healer and he instantly started to sing to her.

As her Ayahuasquero sang Zahira's whole body started to tremble. The pain was shooting up her leg and across her torso and out of her left hand. Her left arm was trembling like it was in a paint shaker and her eyes were rolling back in her head. She was sweating profusely and she had an intense feeling of nausea. She was getting ripped apart by pain, but she invited it to come. She was not panicking, she was breathing and doing her best to remain relaxed.

Nereo returned with a movie and medical supplies. He sat beside her and smoothed the damp hair around her face. He looked so concerned and his presence had an extremely soothing effect. He helped her to bed and gave her a massage. She felt involuntary jolts of pain in between resting. She eventually passed out from exhaustion.

When she woke up in the morning she was so glad to see her best friend still laying next to her. He smiled the instant he opened his eyes. She curled down to kiss his toes.

"Good morning funny feet," she teased him.

He curled towards her feet to return the favour. "Good mor… ahhhhh!" he screamed.

Zahira looked down to find a *massive* blister bubbled on her foot. She never imagined a blister like this could exist. It was the size of a mango. It was raw, full of puss and worthy of a special FX award.

"Holy shit! I guess I am going to the hospital," she gasped.

Nereo helped Zahira get dressed, got her in the car, drove her to an emergency medical clinic and drew pictures in the waiting room to keep her entertained. She was so grateful to have him next to her. It wasn't even a question for him. He rearranged his schedule to be there. After the doctor gave her a prescription Nereo took Zahira out for breakfast.

Nereo made the entire experience feel okay. She was not alone. She was not sad. Her emotions for this man and the energy they share was stronger than any pain. She believes it is a strength that could help them overcome just about anything.

◆

Side Note

A long long time ago Zahira lived in the rain forests of Australia with a wise White Witch named Jude. Jude taught her that humans are made up of 4 components: physical, emotional, mental and spiritual. When one of these components experiences injury then all four components suffer.

For example: If someone suffers from emotional abuse, this energy is stored in the body. It can create dis-ease or eventually disease. When a person heals themselves emotionally, the physical must also cleanse to keep up. Accidents are no accidents.

Jude used to call physical illness, purges and injuries 'black sausages.' They are the body's way of purifying old emotional and mental wounds to maintain an overall healthy balance.

Over the years Zahira has been able to connect her mild injuries with some kind of mental or emotional experience. She believes the burn on her foot represents every time she has ever burnt herself in love. Having this physical release is a good sign. It means she is ready for the next level in love.

She is ready for the real thing.

◆

Washing Capes & Polishing Crowns

Zahira text: wanna play?

Nereo text: yes!!! what do you have in mind?

Zahira text: come here and we will let the Universe steer

Nereo picked up Zahira late in the afternoon. He brought her muffins and bliss balls. They sat on her back deck and lounged like lazy lizards. The only plan they had was not to rush.

"So where do you think we should go?" asked Nereo.

"Hmmmm... I know that a beach is out of the question," she said pointing to the massive blister on her foot (it is so big she gave it a name), "I don't think Carl would care for a sandy beach."

Nereo laughed, "I heard there is an eco village out in the Seven Sisters area..."

"Oh that's funny, I was thinking about the Petroforms. They're in that exact direction," Zahira replied.

"Alright," he smiled.

"Alright," she sighed in to his chest.

It was already four o'clock but they stayed true to their plan. They lounged a little longer and then slowly loaded Pairs with blankets, pillows, a mattress, a picnic basket and their cameras. Zahira wrapped Carl in three inches of gauze and they were ready for the road. They had to make one stop before leaving the city limits. They would pick up some supplies for her foot.

"So um," she said as they were pulling out, "I was thinking it would be a good idea to have a conversation about safe sex."

"Okay," he said as he glanced over at her, "Well, um I have been tested since my last experience a couple of years ago and I am clean."

"You were tested for HIV?" she asked.

"Yes," he replied.

"Wait... did you say that your last sexual encounter was two years ago?" she asked with a bit of a surprise.

"Yes," he said in his usual calm tone.

"*You haven't had sex in two years?*" she said with a little more volume in her voice.

"Yeah, there have been women and kisses, but no sex," he replied softly and sweetly.

"Oh my god that is so hot. I can't even tell you how attractive that is," Zahira said feeling astonished.

"What about you?" he said turning the conversation around.

"Well I have *definitely* been sexually active this year, in fact I feel like I just went through a bit of a personal sexual revolution. I had some pretty great romances in India, but I just got tested for all STDs and I am also clean. I am not on the pill just so you know...," Zahira paused and thought about how she would finish, "and I am not afraid of getting pregnant."

"I'm not afraid of it either," he said.

Just those very words made Zahira's heart flutter. A man who wasn't afraid of becoming a dad!! This was even more of a turn on.

"Well I'll get some condoms in case we have sexual intercourse," she said with a silly but serious tone.

She hobbled into the pharmacy and they grabbed some medical supplies for Carl and some condoms. Shortly thereafter they were headed for the highway. The drive was smooth and beautiful.

"I really like this road," he said twice as they wound their way through marsh and forest.

"Yeah it's lovely," she sighed. She was in her own little bubble. The air was warm, the light was golden and she was excited to get lost with this man.

"So um..." he said slowly, "I am trying to get back to the conversation we had earlier. Do you feel you are ready to have a kid?"

"Yeah I'm ready. I know that I am way beyond having an abortion. If I got pregnant I would actually be really excited," she said honestly.

"Yeah I would be too," he said, "Do you think you could afford to have a baby?"

"Yeah I do," said Zahira confidently, "I have had thoughts about getting pregnant and raising a kid on my own. I haven't really thought about it for a while now. I am so content with my life as it is. If I did get pregnant I would be really happy, but there is no pressure for it to happen."

"I don't feel any pressure," he said.

The two continued on in a very comfortable silence. Zahira felt a soft glow humming through her body. It was the first time in her life that a man had brought up the topic of babies. Not only did he bring it up, but he expressed an openness to fatherhood! Her lips were curved and her heart was fluttering.

When they arrived at their destination there was a big barricade across the path. There was a fire ban that would prevent them from going into their sacred destination. They sat for a while pondering their next move.

"I say we go somewhere else. I don't want to be where we are not welcome. Besides every where we go is sacred," she smiled.

"You're sacred," he said with a kiss.

The two best friends got back in the car.

"Let's just see where we end up," said Zahira feeling certain they would find their magic spot.

The two manoeuvred according to feel. They found one cove but it was occupied. They cruised through a campground, but it felt too populated. They stopped to watch the sunset and then continued their search. They were looking for both privacy and freedom. They found it on a smooth open rock right next to the water's edge.

"It looks perfect!" Zahira clapped.

They climbed out of Paris and clamoured down the rocky cliff to the shore line. Zahira hobbled slowly. The air was cool and the wind was strong.

"I think the wind will calm down later, but for now let's check out some of these nooks," Zahira suggested.

They settled into a nest tucked away from the wind and lit their entire box of candles. They exhaled into each other and watched the stars come out.

"Do you think gypsies get grounded through having kids?" asked Nereo steering them back to their conversation.

Zahira was slightly stunned and completely elated that he was bringing up the topic again, "Oh, um... well I used to think that if I had a kid I would just strap it on and keep going."

"Hmmm well I think it's important that you know that I wouldn't want to just be a seed. If I were to have a child I would want to be a part of their life. It would make me sad if I couldn't see my daughter or son. I want to be there to wash his cape and polish his crown," he said with the most beautiful heart warming truth.

Zahira felt a serene explosion sweep through her whole body. *Was this man for real!?* She rolled over and started to hug and kiss him, "Oh of course! Of course! I would never take a child away from their dad. I think that a family is the ideal. I would never dream of taking a kid away from their father."

"So you believe in unity?" he asked.

"Absolutely yes!! That's the dream. That's the ideal," she said still wanting to eat this man with kisses.

Was this conversation *really* happening? She was feeling so calm and clear in the moment, but at the same time she was exploding with joy. *Could this possibly be it?!* Is Nereo genuinely eager to start a family?!

It felt as though the man of her dreams had officially announced his arrival.

◆

Heart of Stones

"The wind has died," she smiled.

"You said it would," he responded.

"Do you wanna go and lay in the moonlight with me?" she asked getting up slowly.

"Yes," he said right behind her.

Zahira tip toed out onto the smooth rock face. The water was black and rolling, the moon was three quarters full and Venus was shining bright.

"Look," she said pointing to her constellation, "there's the Seven Sisters!"

"Where?" Nereo asked.

"If the moon is the centre of the clock the Seven Sisters are at about 8 o'clock," she said tracing a line with her finger, "They're brighter when you don't look straight at them."

Nereo found them and they marvelled at the whole scene. It felt impossible to paint into words. Zahira climbed on to a rock that was just off shore. She stood with her heart humming and bowed her head to the moon and stars. She was offering thanks for this moment.

"Wow! Wow!" Nereo half shouted, "You look, you look....amazing."

She turned to him and smiled, "Will you help me down from here?" she was trying to be mindful of Carl.

He brought her gently back to the flat rock and she laid down. Nereo took his turn on the rocks that were jutting out of the water. This time it was her turn to be amazed. She looked at his silhouette with the black waters flowing around him and she was silenced. She could not even decide what this man was in this moment. A king? A knight? A samurai? A God? Another species all together?

"You look like a queen," he said before she could utter her own compliment.

"I was just trying to figure out what you look like! I can't even decide. Unreal!" she clapped her hands and settled her head back on the earth.

Nereo came to shower her with love and placed a perfectly smooth stone under her head like a pillow.

"Are you comfortable?" he asked tenderly.

"Yes," she said feeling a bit short for words. She couldn't even come close to expressing how she felt about him in this moment.

He stood and started to collect rocks. She watched him as he gathered and placed them at her feet. He began to create a shape around her.

"Hey you are building your own Petroform!" she exclaimed.

"What was your favourite year as a kid?" he asked while working away.

"Nine!" she shouted like a nine year old.

Nereo was standing above her counting the rocks around her body, "What was the toughest year for you?"

"Hmmm, I'm going to say last year. The year before I left for India," she said.

She really didn't know where he was going with all of this but was enjoying watching him. He was moving quickly and kept standing back to survey the scene.

"Not much longer," he said.

"I'm not going anywhere," she sighed, "and you don't have to feel rushed."

He stopped put his hands to his heart and said, "Thank you. Thank you."

His movements became more melodic and Zahira felt herself witnessing something sacred and beautiful. His silhouette in the night was majestic and stoic. He moved like a mysterious creature and Zahira decided that she could live on this very rock with this man for five hundred years. Part of her felt like she already had.

"Okay I'm done," he said.

"What is it?" she asked feeling wonder struck.

"Well," he said as he stood at her feet and started to count the stones around her, "there are; one two three four five six seven eight…" he stopped on nine, "9 is a big rock because it was a big year in your life," he said and continued to count the stones.

Zahira felt the smile fade from her face. She dropped into a state of awe. She couldn't even believe what she was experiencing. *Who was this man?*

He continued counting until he got to the rock right next to her head, "This is a dark rock to represent the dark time in your life and the rock you are resting on is the point of a heart. I surrounded you with a heart! The heart represents love and your body represents life. Love life," he concluded.

Zahira was crying. She was crying tears for every moment in her life where she had dreamt of a feeling like this. And in all of those dreams and all of those fairy tales, she had never imagined such a simply stunning sweet moment. *Was this really happening? Does this man really exist?*

He looked down with a smile and when he saw her tears he knelt beside her. He recognized the look of awe on her face. He took her hand gently into his own, looked her deep in the eyes and said, "Exactly."

Zahira let out a sob and squeezed his hand. *Really?* She thought to herself…*really?*

"Believe it," he said reading her mind with total confidence, "believe it."

◆

Solid as a Rock

He is real! He exists! Zahira is clear and soaring. She is absolutely sold and completely solid with this reality. She does not want to look any further than this man. The stars have aligned and their time has come. The two lovers have found each other. She has never felt more sure about anything in her life. She has no questions with this man, just a deep soulful knowing.

Their Petroform became a sacred temple. They made love until the sun came up. Slow, sensual love. They locked eyes and rocked slowly and sweetly together. His touch was so perfect for her. She did not have to guide or direct him. He already instinctively knew her needs. His body felt like a perfect match for hers and his kisses were like feathers in a breeze. He knew how to trace her line of arousal and how to make her explode again and again. They were both uplifted and exhausted after hours of pleasing one another. They tangled their bodies and napped until almost noon.

"It is real!" Zahira said as she woke to admire his rock solid heart, "That really did happen! This is the proof."

They kissed for a while. The air was crisp, but the sun was warm. He was hovering above her looking her deeply in the eyes.

"I'm yours," sighed Zahira, "if you want me you can have me."

"I do," he said looking her in the eyes, "I do."

◆

Honour and Glee

She met him at the venue and her heart skipped a beat when she saw him. It had only been hours since their last encounter but Zahira was so excited to be back in Nereo's presence. When he saw her at the end of the bar he lit up.

"Hey," he said smiling and walking towards her, "I am so glad you are here."

"Yeah me too," she said with a kiss.

The two ordered some tea and a hookah and found a table at the back. They sat across from each other and he moved their beverages aside to take both of her hands into his own. They sat locked hand in hand and eye to eye. They didn't speak for sometime. Zahira's feet were fluttering under the table. His expression was mirroring her own excitement.

"So um, I know that we had a chat about Burning Man and you gave me all of the freedom to do what I please, but I just want you to know that I don't want to be with anybody else. You are the only person I want to be with," she said referring to a conversation they had weeks ago.

"Wow," he grinned, "Well I don't ever want to pull you away from your path and I want you to love life and be free, but I also know that when I am truly with someone I want to honour that."

"I feel like I could spend the rest of my life learning how to honour you," she said with full confidence.

His eyes seemed to spark and his grip on her hands tightened. "Wow, well this is going to sound crazy, but I just spoke with a friend who has a kid and we were talking about parenthood and out of the blue I told him that I am going to have a kid soon."

Now it was Zahira's turn to spark. Her whole being was radiating with a warm glow and her belly was summersaulting with glee.

"My toes are twitching," she confessed.

"My heart is beating really fast," he replied.

Their eyes did not stray from each other. Zahira was feeling so real about all of this. She really hadn't imagined their night on the rocks. Nereo really was on board! Not only was he on board, but he was eager to take the reigns and share the mapping of their destiny.

Zahira wonders what they looked like to the tables around them. They were physically and energetically locked in the moment. She has never experienced this kind of love before. It feels like it is coming from a higher place. It is everything she has heard whispers of, but nothing she has known before. It feels as ancient as it does present. It feels electric and calm. It feels real and it feels dream like. It is everything and it is effortless.

It is on.

◆

Naked Canvas

"Do you know what I have always wanted to do?" she asked him as they were driving.

"What?" he asked.

"I've always wanted to make love into a painting. I think it would be amazing to paint our bodies and then have sex on a blank canvas," she said.

Nereo jolted his head like he had hit a wall and just looked at her, "Can we do that?"

"Yes please," she said excited he was game.

"Can we do that tomorrow?" he asked.

"Yes please!" she said growing more excited. He was all over the idea.

"Oh my god I'm getting aroused just thinking of that," he said, "Can we do it outside?"

"Wow now I'm getting aroused!" she laughed.

"I have a big piece of vinyl we can use. It's about 4 by 8 feet," he said already planning it out.

"Sweet!" she cheered. She loves this man. He wants to make things happen just like she does. He requires no convincing what so ever, nor does he delay.

The two woke up the next day excited for their plans.

"What do you think about doing our project my studio?" asked Zahira, "I would love to do it in nature, but I also really want to feel perfect privacy. I don't want to have to worry about someone stumbling upon us. I wanna totally relax and enjoy this. We could put on some records, light some candles, make some tea..."

"Yeah alright. I like that idea, let's do it," he said open to the flow.

They went for breakfast and then gathered supplies for their day. They made their way to their private play place and rolled out the vinyl and opened all their paints. They had so many colours to choose from. Zahira was mostly excited by the pinks and greys.

Zahira put on a playlist of love songs assembled by her dear friend DJ Dry Hump. Nereo painted a peach heart on his chest and then did the same to Zahira. They met in the middle of their canvas and sat across from each other. They simply looked at each other not rushing to connect physically. There is nothing hurried about these two. While it seems things are progressing quickly, they move slowly and softly together.

He came closer and began to kiss her. He felt like satin and tasted like raspberries. She let him smooth his lips across her face. She enjoys the space between their touch as much as she enjoys their physical connection. He pulled away and held up his hand. She placed her own inches away. Their palms hovered closely. The vibration linking them was driving her wild. When his fingertip touched hers she almost lost it completely.

They were moving on a different playing field. It felt otherworldly. The air they shared was charged and their eye contact filled Zahira with disbelief and relief all at once. This place beyond skin is where she has prayed to meet another. She has spent time alone in this realm, making love to herself and the air around her, learning to arouse her whole body with out touch, tuning into the subtle frequencies of existence. Now she has found someone who can meet her there.

Nereo needed no directions. It is as though he already knew the map of her body and was honoured to explore it. He made her feel like a queen and she felt like bowing to his godliness. It didn't feel submissive it felt natural. She really does want to spend her life honouring this mythical man.

He spent the entire playlist working her into pleasure. Needless to say they needed no water to mix with their paints. She supplied enough liquid to cover the whole canvas. As he moved her to climax after climax she dipped her hands in the colours and swirled them around her naked body. The feeling of dipping her fingers in the creamy paints was driving her wild. The expression of her passion was oozing all around her. The painting was coming to life.

She sat up to return the favour. She slid her hand into the buckets of paint and smeared maroon and peach across his chest. She dipped her hands in again and wrapped pink around his throat, kissing him and teasing him with her tongue. She smoothed more colours across his back and laid him down before her. She had all the time in the world to return the favour.

The two lovers spent the entire afternoon in the pleasure frequency. They were utterly present and perfectly balanced. They rolled through the colours of their love and the canvas was soon brought to life. When they separated Zahira wrote the lyrics to the song that was playing

'There's a reason for our love.'

She turned to find Nereo writing the exact same message.

Then they took turns lying on the centre of the canvas. She went first and he outlined her body in pink and grey. She was lying on her left side. When it was Nereo's turn he laid on his right side facing her outline. She traced him slowly with black paint. The two lovers were now entwined on canvas. The result looked like their spirits embracing.

Then they each wrote namaste on their bodies, it means *I honour the light within you*. Nereo drew a unicorn next to his outline and then he painted a heart in Zahira's outline. He traced both of their outlines with yellow so it looks like they are glowing and then he drew seven stars between them. Zahira finished by writing:

The stars have aligned.

PART 9

Temples, Tears & Transitions

◆

Burning Man

The two lovers have said goodbye. They will see each other in two weeks time. Zahira is about to board a plane to Las Vegas. She is cruising with her best friends (Coco and the Crow) and she is about to be reunited with her cosmic twin Flower. Zahira is fast approaching her favourite place in the galaxy!

For the past ten years Zahira has made a pilgrimage to Black Rock City for the Burning Man Arts Festival. Black rock is in the blistering hot dusty deserts of Nevada. For Zahira it is both an oasis and a mirage, it feeds and nourishes her soul and then it vanishes without a trace. It is home to fifty thousand people for seven days a year and then it completely disappears.

Black Rock is an ephemeral city with a legitimate infrastructure. There is a Department of Public Works that regulates things like Mutant Vehicle licensing. There are maps and road signs, three local news papers, two radio stations and a post office.

Black Rock City operates on a gift economy. Zahira can cruise around on a motorized bar stool and find service with a smile. Whether it's sangria served on an ice cold water bed, porn and eggs served on a vibrating chair or a margarita mixed with a chain saw, her money is completely useless. It's the most liberating feeling in the world.

Burning Man is a place to run wild and be free, but it is also a place to reconnect with her most sacred self. The Temple is the reason Zahira returns every year. The Temple is the womb of Burning Man. This may sound metaphorical, but it is more experiential.

The Temple is a place to honour the dead and re-birth the living. Every year the Temple is created by a different artist and every year it offers the same service. It is built as a blank slate for expression. Everyone is welcome to share their grief, their gratitude, their greatness.

The souls that visit and colour the Temple walls are asking for relief, for forgiveness, for goodbyes, for hellos, for transition. The scribbles, stories and shrines that grow organically over the week are more poetic and genuine than any gallery. It is a highly conscious and collective work of art.

When the Man burns on Saturday night the entire city erupts into mayhem. When the Temple burns on Sunday night fifty thousand people sit in silence. Zahira sees the Temple as a rocket ship that carries her messages to the stars. It is one of her favourite weapons.

Zahira believes Burning Man is a great gift to humanity. It a part of history she is proud to part of. It is a part of this book that she is excited to write....

◆

Cosmic Reunion

Seeing her twin in the Las Vegas airport was like a giddy dream. Zahira spotted the Flower and instantly got butterflies in her stomach. She snuck up behind her and tapped her on the shoulder. Flower turned around and they both started howling. It was quite the scene. They were hugging and shouting and blasting their signature cackles.

"Check this out!" Zahira said showing off the T-shirt she was wearing.

"Noooo way," the Flower howled.

It was a teal blue T-shirt with gold letters that read 'Have you seen my Argentine twin?'.

"I made one for you," Zahira said as she pulled a T-shirt out of her purse. It read 'Have you seen my Polish twin?'

"Oh my god you genius!" Flower shouted. She instantly put it on and took a picture of them.

Zahira introduced her to Coco and the Crow and it was an effortless connection. The girls were an instant crew. They decided to rent a luxury car to cruise into the city of lights.

"You realize there is a typo on your shirt right?" commented the woman who was ordering their ride.

"Huh?" Zahira said looking down.

"It says have you seen my Argentine tiwn," the woman read.

Zahira and Flower bit the floor. They were laughing so hard.

"Tiwn? Tiwn! I can't even say that word!" sputtered Zahira as they clamoured into their ride.

◆

Shirt Cocking Chicks

"It's socially appropriate boner day," reads Coco from the Playa guide, "Today if you get a boner you get to keep it for as long as it wants to be a boner. You can grow it naturally or strap it on anywhere in Black Rock City! It's also hug a shirt cocker day! We definitely need to get out there with our cocks on ladies!"

The girls laugh. They have homemade boners to strap on along with neon yellow T-shirts that read 'I'M FUN' in giant black letters. There will be a posse of seven babes rocking out with their cocks out.

Zahira loves the freedom she feels here. Burning Man is her annual mind expansion and expression exercise. It's where she can make a bed out of pancakes and be drizzled with a warm maple syrup blanket. It's where she can jump rope on fire and balance topless on a two-storey teeter-totter. It's where she can dance naked under the moon to a giant roaming Robot Heart. It's where she can wear wings on a Wednesday and a nylon penis on shirt cocking Thursday.

"Oh shit we missed the 8th annual White Trash breakfast at the Pancake Playhouse," says Coco as she keeps flipping through the guide.

Just then the Flower yells, "Hey twin! This?"

Zahira looks over to see her twin standing outside in her 'I'M FUN' T-shirt with red sparkly panties, combat boots and a black top hat, "Yeah I love it!"

"We are going to have so much fun in these shirts," adds the Crow', "it's not like we can stand around and be boring!"

"Boooooring," Zahira yells in a playful gesture. The girls all laugh.

"Karma Kids yoga is happening at 10am today. Man that would be so amazing to see them all lined up together. I love seeing kids on the Playa. Shit that's over too. I'll jump ahead at the stuff that is still possible," Coco says, "Hmmmm... from 10 to 12 we can go and get a black and white portrait done…we aren't ready are we?"

The girls rarely look at the guide. Apart from being an entertaining read there is no need. Zahira has learnt over the years that she will never see it all. There is no way and again there is no need. She is happy to be spending silly time with her ladies. It doesn't matter where they go and what they see. The spontaneity of rolling around with no agenda is her favourite thing to do. Living on the cusp of time is where all the magic is, especially in this city.

Burning Man is the ultimate play zone, but it goes deeper than nylon cocks, synchronistic mind fucks and art that warps the imagination. For Zahira it is her life-affirming mirror to the limitless. It is the place that whispers to her wildest dreams and dares them to come true. Burning Man is the ultimate reminder to be silly, to be sacred and to simply love life.

◆

Ashram Galactica Grand Hotel

Zahira rolled out alone last night. It was perfect. She loves to follow her flow to see where it goes. Last night it lead her straight to her favourite spot on the Playa, the Ashram Galactica Grand Hotel. It is the sexiest freshest most styling venue she has ever seen.

She discovered it years ago and has been a regular ever since. For 7 nights a year she finds herself in awe of the production. The staff will valet park her bike, lift the gold rope at the entrance, enter her name to win a themed hotel room and then serve her a mixologist cocktail (on the house of course!). The atmosphere is like an elegant circus with a cosmopolitan twist.

The Grand Hotel is next level fabulous for so many reasons, but mostly because it feels like love at first sight. In a crazy city full of the new and the unknown it also feels like home. It's like finding both an old friend and a new lover. It is instantly heart warming and soul tingling.

Last night Zahira plopped down at a bar stool and didn't move for hours. She met a sexy top hat who was working the bar. Zahira noticed him instantly and he apparently noticed her too. He kept her cup full and the conversation flowing. It turns out they are both writers, both event planners and both advocates for change. He has great awareness, a fast sense of humour and also loves life.

The more they chatted the more their similarities surfaced. Zahira was thoroughly enjoying their conversation. He was sexy and funny and smart and and and....

and then out of the blue a man wearing a glow in the dark frisbee on his head came over and asked, "What is the definition of true love?"

"Oh," Zahira sparked, "true love happens when two people who are truly connected to their own centre come together. When you truly love yourself true love will find you."

"Wow!" shouted the man and his mini entourage, "That was deep. Shit that gives me something to think about."

Zahira laughed and then smiled at his timing. He felt like a messenger from the stars coming with a gentle tap on the shoulder. A soft reminder that her own true love has arrived. While it is only natural to be attracted to attractive men, she does not need to indulge in them.

She told this story to her girls over breakfast and the Crow laughed, "Yeah the Universe has already sent you a unicorn. What more can you want?"

◆

True Love

True love happens when two people
who are truly connected to their own centre come together.
When you truly love yourself
true love will find you.

◆

It Is Lilly (and Nereo)

Zahira rode to the Temple to pay her respect. This year's theme is the Temple of Transition. She stopped about a hundred yards away to admire the sacred architecture. Her jaw dropped as she stood before the largest plywood structure to ever exist. The central tower was a 120 feet high and surrounded by five hexagonal towers. Within each tower a different phase of life was marked and explored. It stirred a deep peaceful reverence in her body that felt other worldly.

Zahira's natural reaction upon entering the central tower was to curl into a fetal position and cry. It was the music being made that crumbled her to tears. The walls were lined with gongs and chimes that were set to automatic timers. The result was a lullaby from the stars. Her body was covered with goosebumps and filled with joy.

Goosebumps, sacred, silent, lullaby, spirit, ethereal, emotional, magical, maternal, womb, wondrous, peaceful, hum, heart, heal, humbling, uplifting, joy, loss, freedom, stars, birth, death, family, interplanetary. The Temple of Transition escapes definition. She doesn't even know if she wants to try and explain it's wonder.

She brought photographs of Nereo to tape to the walls. One is of Nereo jumping off a bail of hay and the other is of Zahira lying naked on their painting. She wrote him a letter on behalf of her spirit guides. It read like this:

Once upon a time, Feather Heart Woman
heard my whispers for a higher love.
She is the spirit who listens to all of my thoughts.
She helps to bring me what I need to fulfill my truest self.
She called upon Yellow Snake Woman
to choose a sensuous mate.
They brought me to you and I am
so grateful our time has come.
Let's dance and fly and play together.

The stars have aligned.

As she was writing this a woman next to her asked to borrow some tape. The two got to talking and the synchronicity of their moment started to unfold. The woman was taping up a photograph of a baby and on it was written 'It is Lilly'.

"What is that all about?" Zahira asked pointing to the picture.

"Oh it's a beautiful story," the woman replied, "My friend met his partner a few weeks before coming to Burning Man last year. He knew right away that he was going to make a life with her and on the Temple walls he wrote 'It is Lilly'. He instantly knew Lilly was the one he had been waiting for. Now they have a baby together!"

Zahira almost started crying, "Wow really? They only knew each other for a few weeks and he already knew? That's amazing. It's giving me goosebumps because I think I have just met the father of my child! I was just writing a dedication to him. I chose to do it under this beautiful carving of a baby."

"Oh my god? Are you serious!?" replied the woman radiating love and enthusiasm, "Amazing! I don't believe it! I am so happy for you! My friends really wanted to give thanks to the Temple. This is a picture of their baby!"

Zahira smiled. She took a black sharpie and wrote 'It is Nereo' on the wall above their pictures. She felt a wave of pure love ripple through her body. She looked over to see the woman holding her hand over her heart.

"Can I take a picture of this for my friends?!" she asked appearing teary eyed.

"Of course," Zahira replied. She was feeling a surge of synchronistic magic in this moment. Many people come to write about people they have lost on the Temple walls, but these two women were writing about people found.

Zahira was wearing beautiful flowing iridescent wings and a long cream coloured satin gown, both were gifts she had received that day. She looked like she was getting married. She felt like it too.

"You do realize this is the Pillar of Birth you are writing on?" asked the woman after taking some pictures of Zahira in the setting sunlight.

"Wow I didn't! Temple of Transition Pillar of Birth! Whoa that's powerful," she said looking at the pictures of her lover.

The moment felt like a free fall. Zahira's heart was soaring like an eagle. She spread her wings into the soft desert wind and let the air envelope her with ecstasy. Just then the Earth Harp started to play. The sound instantly swept her out of her body.

The strings of the Earth Harp stretched from the Temple's gateway to it's highest peak. They were 120 feet long. Hearing them play was like listening to the desert hum and water sing. The sound vibrated through Zahira's chest like a universal orgasm. The entire front of her body was humming.

She stretched her arms back and felt her wings flapping in the wind. Zahira was truly manifesting light. She was raising the love from her heart to the sky. She was surrounded by a series of flashes. People had gathered to take photographs. While she could hear the clicks of the cameras she was no longer in her person. She had slipped into a band of stars and let the love from the Temple rip through her body and into the twilight. She became a portal, a star gate. She offered one message via this galactic connection.

"We come in peace," she whispered to the cosmos, "We come in peace."

◆

Astral Conception

Zahira watched the Man burn with her posse and then rolled out alone. She spent the entire night going from one massive fire to the next. She would see flames from across the Playa and she would jump on her BMX and peddle her heart out.

Zahira found the space that allowed her to connect with grace. After her first dance with the flames she switched dimensions all together. She was the turtle who would transcend galactic time and space to visit the fish. She was no longer moving through a physical plane. She was dialled into an energetic frequency that allowed her to dance with spirit.

She would greet each fire with a humble bow and then she would stand still until moved by a higher hand. She let the energy of spirit move her. It was beyond slow motion. It was like the air became water and her limbs were long strands of hollow reeds. Her movement was liquified and her body felt like stardust.

When she moved to the third fire she looked up to see her constellation smiling down upon her. She instinctively felt the wave of a child. She closed her eyes to greet this natural warmth and as she exhaled she felt the arms of her lover cradle her from behind. Her heart instantly started to hum. Nereo was there. She relaxed into his support and they started to sway from side to side. She felt him so clearly there was no mistaking his presence in this moment. She could even feel his fingers interlacing with her own.

Their hands moved silently towards the fire. Zahira could feel a bright wavelength coming towards them. They opened their arms and welcomed a light being into their cradle. Zahira's chin tilted down and she could feel the love of a child. She could feel the peace of their unit. They were all together. Their child had chosen them. She pressed her hands into her belly and started to hum. Her being was oozing with appreciation.

When the moment was right they released this love into the night sky. They welcomed their baby's spirit to drift away into the moon knowing they would all be together soon...

◆

The Temple Burns

Thank you for every single step I have taken along the way.
Thank you for every single step I have taken along the way.
Thank you for every single step I have taken along the way.
Thank you for every single step I have taken along the way.
Thank you for every single step I have taken along the way.

Zahira repeated this countless of times as she circled the flames of the Temple. The heat was exquisite. Only a select few could embrace the inside circle with her. She had transcended the heat with spirit the night before. Tonight she welcomed the glow and began her ritual. She walked the entire circumference of the burn holding her dusty gold moon boots.

"Thank you for every single step I have taken along the way," she smiled at her favourite pair of boots.

She had worn these boots to every burn over the last ten years.

They had danced, skipped, jumped, biked, run, spun, swirled and twirled with her. They had carried her every single step along the way. They were her favourite pair of footwear to date and they were on their second year of being duct taped together. *It was time* to say goodbye.

She finished her steps at where she felt the Pillar of Birth once stood. She wanted to honour the place where she had created a symbol of her love for Nereo. She stood before a tower of giant crackling flames and brought her hands to her heart, "Thank you for every single step I have taken along the way. I feel so blessed. I offer my love to the Temple of Transition and with this offering I am ready to start walking beside another."

Zahira threw her gold boots into the belly of the fire and let out a sweet giggle. She is ready, but the most amazing thing is…*he is too.*

Their time has come.

◆

"In the vibration of appreciation all things come to you. You don't have to make anything happen. From what you are living, amplify the things you appreciate so that it is the dominate vibration you are offering and then only those things that are a vibrational match to that can come to you. Then sit back and know, "You ain't seen nothing yet!!!"

~ Esther Hicks

◆

Home Sweet Hendrix

Zahira was the first one out of customs this morning. She deliberately got a seat at the front of the plane so she wouldn't have to wait for everyone to get off. She knew that after three weeks of zero unicorn the last three minutes before seeing him again would be highly charged.

When the sliding glass doors opened to the waiting room she had a big smile on her face. She scanned the room and realized he wasn't there. She didn't even flinch. She knew he was close, she could feel it. She sent him a text and he said he was waiting upstairs by the international arrivals gate.

Zahira took the elevator up with the same excited smile glued to her face. Again the doors opened and she scanned the room. She was looking for his tall lean frame, but what she found was a short stubby Hendrix wearing overalls. His ginormous head was peering over a railing and he was holding a welcome home sign in his hand.

Zahira belted out with laughter, "No way!"

She instantly walked over to Hendrix. Her best friend was nowhere in sight. She knew he was watching her and she rolled her cart slowly around laughing and calling out to him, "Yer ha-larious!"

Then he appeared before her, stepping out from behind a pillar. She felt an instant wave of peace. It was like seeing a sunset appear out of nowhere. They stood still and took each other in for a moment and then he came to embrace her. He swallowed her with his arms and she sunk her forehead into his heart. She instantly started to coo.

They were so completely lost in this moment that they were oblivious to the small fan club that was beginning to form around Hendrix.

"Excuse me," said one of the flight attendants in her uniform, "we hate to bother you, but could we have our picture taken with this.... this..." she said with a loss for words. She was pointing at their dear Hendrix.

Zahira belted out with laughter, "Of course! Of course!"

They peeled apart from each other and went to work crowd control for their celebrity piñata. It was hysterical. Zahira laughed all the way home. It was perfect. She knew he would surprise her somehow. It was a perfect homecoming. She was so giddy she wasn't expecting what came next.

When she opened her bedroom door her jaw physically dropped and then her body did too. She literally fell to the ground and hid her hands in her face.

"You didn't!" she said as she uncovered her eyes, "No way you did. Oh my god. *Are you for real?!!*" she covered her eyes again. She wasn't sure if she was dreaming or not, but every time she uncovered her eyes he was standing above her, "You didn't? Oh my god you really did! You painted my room lemon yellow?!"

"That's the best reaction ever," he said smiling gently.

She was still curled into a state of disbelief on the floor. He had listened to her secret wish and he had made it come true. He had paid attention to her idea of equating sunshine to luxury. Her unicorn not only painted her room into sunshine, but he bought her zebra print bedding too!

"Oh my god, do you *really* exist? Is this really happening?! Am I dreaming?!? You painted my room. You *actually* painted my room..." she shouted with disbelief.

They spent the rest of the morning talking, staring and smiling. They barely even kissed. Zahira marvelled at their connection. It is like nothing she has ever known before. It is beyond a sexual desire, it is more about being in awe, amazement and appreciation. It is more about figuring out if she is dreaming or awake. The couple has connected from the inside out and the result is an intrinsic love affair.

◆

Let's Talk About Sex Again

"You kissed him?" asked Nereo in a surprised tone.

"Yeah I made love with him," Zahira replied in total honesty. They were talking about a hip hop star. She had no reason to lie. It happened just before she and Nereo started dating. She never mentioned it to Nereo or this story because she doesn't need to share *everything*.

Nereo's face dropped and he slid under the covers.

"What? What's wrong?" Zahira asked feeling confused.

He didn't reply. He was quiet and clearly upset. Zahira just assumed it was jealousy. She was wrong.

"I just never really respected groupies," he said in a reserved tone.

"What?! That's *not* what it was like. First of all *he* asked to talk *to me*. I was oblivious to him. He was the one who tracked me down," she said feeling offended.

"Yeah I know, but you still met him and slept with him in the same night," Nereo said.

"I am *not* a groupie," she repeated with clear force. "It was an mutual interaction between a man and a woman. That's it. What's your problem?"

"This is my own shit I'll deal with it," he said not wanting to talk.

"Okay, but I think talking is always helpful. I know things are great between us, but these little snags also deserve our attention," Zahira said in full support.

He was silent for a long while. Zahira gave him space and time to express himself. She was feeling confused by his reaction. He was clearly very upset.

"I just really feel that love is the most important thing and making love is sacred," he started slowly. "For me it's what should happen after two people connect on a very deep level. I believe in exploring the layers of a person before connecting sexually. Sex should be the cherry on top of the cake."

Zahira was touched by his honesty. This man is so special, so unordinary. She resonated with what he said. She felt it was both valid and important, "I agree that sex is a sacred thing, I really do. I understand what you are saying and I am not disagreeing."

"I had a one night stand once and it made me feel hollow. I just don't respect it. I know this is my own problem," he said assuming responsibility for his emotions. It was clearly a deeply emotional subject for him.

"I grew up with a lot of guilt surrounding sex," Zahira started. "Having sex was associated with feelings of shame. I was extremely protective of my sexuality as a young woman. I was one of the last of my friends to lose my virginity. I was always the one preaching about self-respect. Sex was something that I could not do freely."

Zahira paused, she was trying to find her truth on this subject, "As I got older the coin flipped. I suffered a lot of guilt because I *wasn't* having sex. I felt guilty for turning men away because I wasn't interested. It was excruciatingly difficult to get in my space. I really isolated myself. I spent a lot of time feeling frustrated and alone. It was like I couldn't win, I felt guilty for having sex and I felt guilty for not having sex. It wasn't until I went to India that I allowed myself to explore the casual relationship in a healthy way. For me it was very liberating. I was making decisions from a place of clarity and confidence. It was not about getting drunk and losing my personal power. It was not about being desperate or insecure, in fact it was the opposite. It was about empowering myself as a woman to explore my sexuality from a place of awareness. I have not done anything to disrespect my body or my spirit," Zahira said in a soft and quiet tone.

Nereo seemed to respond to this truth, she could tell he was starting to feel better. They were lying on her bed now. She was smoothing her hand across his face. She was feeling grateful for this chance to communicate her sexual history.

Zahira understands Nereo's need for a deeper connection. She feels his sacred touch. She is so lucky to have found this rare and precious man. She has never felt so honoured by another. Her casual relationships have been wonderful and insightful, but the depth she shares with Nereo reflects the depth of her new awakening. The harmony she has found within herself is reflected by his own attuned self. He mirrors true love and truthful living.

Nereo is what Zahira believed in before she gave up. She had spent so much time waiting for a man who could touch her beyond the flesh that she eventually felt delusional. Her years of feeling frustrated were released by the Pomelo. He encouraged her to find a starting point with a man, a place to open the door to romance. The Carpenter Kid gave her an opportunity to practice this opening. She was able to explore her sexuality in a casual healthy relationship. The Cheeky Monkey was also a great teacher in uncommitted affection. His need for freedom inspired her own. It taught her not to lean on another, to be free and to set others free.

All three of these lovers have been special in their own way, but none come close to the depth of her existence with Nereo. She hears what he says about needing a special connection. She hears it loud and clear. She also applauds it. It resonates with a place deep inside her heart. She admires his heightened sensitivity and his soulful conviction.

Zahira does not have any regrets. She is grateful she has had a chance to explore her sexuality from a clear and confident space. She feels lucky to have met such beautiful men on this journey and to have shared herself with them. They have *all* been her teachers.

Until she met Nereo she did not know what it was like to rise in love. Their connection has taken her beyond what any casual affair could conceive of. Her higher self gratefully surrenders to him. She feels honoured to be in his presence. She can give herself completely to this man and he can connect with the most subtle layers of her existence. He can caress her spirit, whisper to her heart, cradle her emotions, inspire her mind and pleasure her body. She has not fully shared herself with *anyone* until Nereo. Only Nereo has found a communion with every level of her being.

Talking about all of this brought the two lovers closer together. Nereo was open to hear her truth. Her words had soothed him into a place of understanding. She wrapped him in her arms and they fell asleep feeling closer than ever.

◆

"Accept your sexuality — it is part of you! and a tremendously important part. You are born out of sex. Each cell of your body is a sex cell. Sex energy is your life energy! — respect it, it is a gift from God. Understand it. Be more and more meditative about it. But drop all prejudices, drop all condemnations because when you carry a condemnation you cannot understand a thing. Drop all judgements. Sex is sex — it is a pure natural energy. With great acceptance, love, respect, meditate over it. Go deeper and deeper into it to see what exactly it is. And in that very seeing you will be going beyond it.'

~ Osho

◆

On this Harvest Moon

"I will give you something that nobody else can. There is no name for it. You can only point your finger at it and wonder. You cannot put it inside of a box, but you can feel it. There is no price tag attached to it, you cannot find this in Walmart," Nereo said in a solid sexy tone.

Zahira fell deeper into this man. They were sitting next to a fire. Her legs were draped over his and their faces were touching. Their hoods were forming one. It looked like they were melting into each other. Zahira felt as though they were the only two under the stars. They were at the Harvest Moon Festival. The night was young.

After they left the fire the two danced like no one was watching. They twirled and swirled and made invisible love. She could feel his touch inches away from her flesh. She could sense his spirit smelling her scent like a wild and graceful creature of the night. They were ignited into stars so vivid Zahira could see them.

The next morning their bodies made love next to an old oak tree. It was the first time Nereo had experienced being naked in nature. It was the most natural and beautiful moment imaginable. It was a sunny Sunday afternoon. The fall air was cool, but not crisp. Their bodies were warm and electric and they were both smiling.

"The family tree," Nereo said as he smoothed his hands across the old oak.

Zahira's heart kicked back and opened wide. The word family hit her like a cosmic jolt. She stood and walked into a golden clearing in the forest and raised her arms to the sky. She welcomed the sun to fill her being and she felt a flood of warmth showering upon her. She could feel a light in the palm of her hands. It felt like the same spirit they cradled at Burning Man.

"Thank you," she whispered as she slowly lowered her hands to her heart.

Nereo gently carved their initials in the tree. Zahira stood still. She was bathing in the sunlight and she was memorizing the moment.

Her body felt like cascades of serenity and bliss. Her entire being was humming the song she has been singing to the moon for years. She couldn't help but wonder if a seed had been planted beneath the wise branches of their family tree.

◆

One Month Later

"Oh my god," Zahira whispered to herself. She was in the washroom at work. Her stomach instantly started to flutter and her knees went weak. She had just taken a test. "*I'm pregnant!*"

◆

Baby Bomb

"How are you?" Zahira asked feeling excited to share her news. After taking her pregnancy test she had hopped on a plane to LA. She went to spend time with Flower and her Ayahuasquero. She had no time to write about her trip and no time to tell Nereo her news. She couldn't imagine a better way to be reunited.

"Well it was a big weekend for me. I realized a lot of things. I am most certainly in love with you. I am certainly in love with life and I am also feeling a lot of love for myself. I ran into my friend who is a dad and I asked him about fatherhood again. He said that it really is amazing, but has really taken away all of his free time as an artist," Nereo replied.

"How did that make you feel?" asked Zahira feeling slightly anxious. She grabbed his hand and placed it on her heart. It was beating really fast. *Was he really bringing up this subject!?* He had no clue what she was about to say.

"It got me thinking about whether or not I am actually ready to be a dad. I also know if it happens it will be a blessing. I was teaching in a biology class today and the kids were watching a video and the video was all about reproduction and then it flashed to a screaming baby in a super market aisle. It was to promote wearing condoms. It made me…'

"I'm pregnant," Zahira interrupted him.

Nereo's mouth dropped and his eyes went wide, "What?"

"I'm pregnant," she smiled with a slightly nervous bite of her lip.

His face was frozen into a pure joyful shock. He pulled her on to his lap and wrapped his arms around her. He started laughing, "Oh my god!"

"I know," Zahira whispered into his earlobe.

"Oh my god!" he said again smiling and laughing. "This is totally meant to be."

"I know," she whispered again.

"I've gotta get that crown!" shouted Nereo with pure delight in his voice.

Zahira cackled with laughter. Her whole body flooded with joy. She smattered him with kisses. She could not have prayed for a better response.

◆

Moonstruck

"When you have some free time can we light some candles and meditate together? I wanna find a way to honour our baby's spirit," asked Nereo.

"Oh my god you are amazing. Yes. Yes. Yes. I love it," Zahira said swelling with gratitude for this man. They were holding each other basking in the glow of their news.

"Thank you," he said as he pulled her closer.

"You are going to be such an amazing dad. You have the gift of being present. You spend time with everyone who is in front of you. You really pay attention. You will be so amazing with this baby," she assured him. "I just want you to know that we don't need to worry about anything. We love each other and that is the foundation I can work from. If I was unsure about you this would be a bit terrifying. I don't feel any fear I only feel love."

She kissed him and continued, "All we need to do is give thanks for this amazing life and everything we need will come to us. How do you think you ended up here in my arms?! Abundance doesn't flow where there is stress. Abundance flows to gratitude. We are already rich."

"Okay," he said still holding her close, "we can do this."

"Can we keep this our own secret for now?" she asked him.

"Yeah I like that idea. Let's not tell anyone until we agree to do so," he said fully on board.

"Perfect it will give us some time to let it all sink in," she said.

They sealed their deal with a kiss.

◆

Love Letter

Dear Nereo
Life is meant to be loved together and apart. I am now complete with you next to me. I have loved myself to a place of peace, but there will always be a place reserved for you, for true love, the kind of love that requires no thought, the kind of love that recognizes it's own existence, the kind of love that is prepared to work hard and relax through all of life's changes and challenges. We will get through everything together. I am yours.
~ xo Zahira

◆

Fragile These Hearts Are.

Zahira sat alone in her kitchen. She was watching herself weep. She had been weeping for days. Her heart had a little crack in it. She put it there. Who else could?

Two nights ago Zahira waited for Nereo to crawl into bed with her. He had said he would be hers before sunrise. She woke up several times in anticipation of his arrival. She was giddy to feel his warm presence slide in next to hers. When 8:30am rolled around she was up for good. She was not upset, but she was starting to worry. When he arrived at 9:30am he started by saying he had something to talk about.

"First I want you to know that my lips are reserved for yours. They have not touched another," he said as he grabbed her hand.

Zahira felt her heart sink. She knew in this moment who he was with. She knew it was a friend who looks at Nereo with hearts in her eyes. She knew that they had spent the night together. She was right. He was honest about their interaction, they spent the night dancing and talking.

"We talked about us mostly," Nereo said trying to make Zahira feel better. "She asked me if you were the only one for me."

"What did you say?" Zahira asked.

"I took a minute to really think about it and my answer was you," Nereo said hoping this would make her feel better.

It didn't. It broke Zahira's heart. He needed *a whole minute* to wonder if his pregnant lover was the only one for him?! It shattered Zahira to hear about his hesitation. Even though his final answer was yes, it still shattered her.

It turns out Nereo had been heavy with his questioning heart all week. He got swept away with this woman and found himself needing to put it in check. They work at an after-school art gallery together. Last week a student said they would make a good couple. It was enough for Nereo to question the couple he was in even after she gave him their news.

So as she writes she cries. She cries because it was so unexpected. She cries because she felt so sure with this man, she felt nothing but sure. It was the reason this pregnancy was so joyful. The two are not married, they have no home and little money...but they did have an unwavering love. Now their love has been questioned and her entire foundation is crumbling. She is watching herself dissolve into fear. She is careful to love herself through the whole thing. She has been crying all day, but she has also been talking to herself.

"Please don't be too dramatic about this. What is this *really* about?

Is this hormones? Is this you being too unrealistic of life and of love? Is this you being too dependent on another?"

She decides it's a little of all of these things. She does not want to see him right now. She needs to get her shit together. She can't stop weeping. She needs to find the strength to be on her own two feet. She has a baby to think about. This is what really makes her cry, she is now responsible for another.

She heard everything he said to try and make it up to her. He was so sincere, but it felt empty for her. When she thinks about him right now she doesn't giggle and blush like she did three days ago, she just wants to cry now. She just feels sad. They were meant to spend Sunday honouring this life they have created, instead it was spent in tears.

Nereo has questioned their love and his doubt is contagious. She feels it now. She is now questioning. She is questioning their relationship. She is questioning his sincerity. She is questioning the book she is writing. She is questioning her ability to be an independent mother. She is questioning how hard she is being on him. She is questioning her questioning.

She must take responsibility for her sadness. She must own it. It is hers. No one can make her sad but herself. Her idealistic expectations, her storybook romance and her lust for a perfect ending are all reasons she feels shattered. The devastation she has felt from such a minor infraction is terrifying her. Part of it is because she is not alone anymore. She has a life in her belly that needs love even when she is sad. She is not able to walk away so easily now. She doesn't want to feel stuck. She doesn't want him to feel stuck either. She wants them both to be free to choose to be together.

She needs to trust if she is going to be with him, but she can't do this until she trusts herself to be okay *no matter what*. She needs to reconnect with her most powerful self. She needs to tap into her unconditional love. She must find the space where she needs no one and gives thanks for everything. She needs to relax and let clarity sink in.

◆

Letters

Dear Nereo
After a long night of drinking and partying together why did you choose to go back to the studio to be alone when you knew I was waiting for you? When you knew this woman was making you doubt us? When you knew that I am with your child?
~xo me

~~~

My love,
Maybe read this when you have time to really read it and not be interfered...

Language is complicated and sometimes we misinterpret what the other person is trying to say to us. So i'm hoping (ring fingers crossed) I can make sense out of what may not make any sense at all. What was running through in my head?

I'm trying to look at everything r a t i o n a l l y and with sincerity and honesty. Okay...going back a bit...if I can retrace where the questioning started...

When you told me you were pregnant I was speechless. My jaw instantly dropped (as you witnessed first hand), my eyes popped out of my face. I really was excited, I was happy! My heart was pounding. I was surprised and not surprised at the same time... and honestly I was also a little spooked.

Where did that fear feeling come from? Why was it there? What the hell did I have to be so afraid of? This is a time for celebration! ~ not for over contemplation I thought to myself.
~~~

Like wow...this is it!...This is really it...I'm going to be a dad.. whoaaaa!!!

So many emotions hitting me all at once.

I could see me with someone who I really do love so so much. Someone who is very special to me, very kind, very LOVING, *and supportive of me as an artist and of me as a human being. Someone whom I feel sees my soul. Someone who has been able to connect with me on so many levels and someone who I feel strongly about. It's a very rare thing... beyond my physical self. I am sooooo soooo lucky and so I'm even confused now.*

Why did I question us? Why did I allow myself to carelessly be carried away into a night of talking, hanging out and practicing hip hop dance routines?? Maybe it was greed? Maybe it was from a fear of losing that freedom to just get up and go wherever and whenever I please?

Today I realized upon talking with my friend that the attraction that kids see in adults isn't always right or on the money. Sometimes their idea of a good pairing is seeing two people with cool haircuts that kinda match or clothing styles that seem similar to each other. A kid entertained the idea of a good pair and we both saw a possibility in their idea.

But what do they know about you and I? And now I'm thinking where were they when I wasn't drinking wine and when I was one with nature and myself and perfectly perfectly aligned with you? But it's not what I think... it's about what I feel. I feel that I would like to be more open and honest with you and provide answers for both of us that make sense.

I am begging for forgiveness.

Forgive me for letting my head get in the way of my heart.
Forgive me for wanting to feel careless, a feeling that made me feel free in a way and not tied down, the feeling of having no responsibilities and just being a kid.

This is a transition I'm going through.

I've always said that behind a great king is a great queen. I feel that this love is what i've wanted for a very long time. A love that I have discovered through having love for myself…and in this very moment…right now…it is what I still want very much.

Life is about finding a balance. Part of me feels that it is not wrong to stop and question. Perhaps it is not such a bad thing?

On the other hand, I'm looking at it the same way people believe in a god or a higher power, you don't think about it you just BELIEVE it. I also used to say, and still say, that magic and magicians are powered by their believers. If people didn't believe in magic there would be no such thing.

So again forgive me for being a human being who is just figuring out life.

Forgive me for not feeling like I need to apologize for being real about everything. I do sincerely apologize for not being honest right from the beginning of when I began to question, but I myself didn't know what I was feeling or why?? I just let myself get carried away to a point where I became a little… confused.

The fact that it took sometime to figure this all out and create a mess along the way and a little crack in your heart, I know caused a lot of hurt for you and for myself too, but may it be a lesson in learning. No one is perfect. We move at our own pace.

I am learning about myself everyday and I feel that these hardships can only make me stronger and in doing so can make whom I love stronger if they're willing to put up with me and learn with me. Today I went for lunch by myself and was waiting in line behind this father and his baby boy. The baby kept smiling at me, he couldn't take his eyes off of me. I couldn't help but feel warmth from that smile.

I FEEL that if I were to pass on this gift, position, opportunity (so many things) to be loved by you and bring a child into this world with you, it would be one of thee most regrettable things in my life. I'd be pretty messed up.

I know the feeling of being free and single and having no one to answer to, but at the same time I've been through that. Some of it is really great, but companionship and love are just as important to me. Both are good. There just needs to be a healthy balance.

My friend knows how I feel about you and I know she respects that line. She even suggested not hanging out anymore, but I think that's not right. There is a lot I learn from other people and I need that from time to time.

Right now I just want us to heal.

Peace Love and Light
Try to enjoy your day.
- ME

~~~

DEAR NEREO
Once upon a time there was a unicorn who told me to 'believe it,' so I did. I believed it with all of my heart, with every cell in my body and every strand of my soul I believed it. He was my magician and
~~~

when I looked at him all I saw were stars and sparkles and light, a blinding beautiful light.

But I guess that's why they say love is blind, because one small fracture and the entire illusion is shattered. As the smoke clears I see what has been standing there all along...a human. A human who is living and speaking his truth. A human who is honest. A human who loves me.

When I told you about our baby I mentioned that I wasn't afraid. I wasn't afraid of anything because our love was so strong. It was all I needed to know. It was all I needed to be brave and sure and excited.

Once you questioned our love I had no choice but to do the same. I have spent the last two days with so much fear weeping through my body. It has hollowed out my heart and emptied my well. My unquestioning love for you was what gave me such faith in being a new mom, in becoming a family.

I can only weep for so long before I slap my tears into strength. My tears became anger. I wanted to show you that I can do this without you. I realized that I don't want to be a sure thing anymore. There is nothing alluring about a sure thing.

Perhaps that is the ticket to living in the moment. To know that nothing is for sure. There are no guarantees, there are no promises. Everything in life changes. We don't know what the future holds. All we have is now.

My anger has been enlightening. I could not feel so much anger and sadness if I did not totally love you. Total anger and total love exist together. They are both beautiful. While I no longer want to be a sure thing, I am sure that in this moment I love you like I love myself. I love you like I love our child.

Osho says that hate does not destroy love it only destroys the staleness of it. It is a cleaning and if you understand it you will be grateful to it. If you can be grateful to hate then nothing can destroy your love.

I am grateful the illusion has been shattered. I am grateful reality has come to us so soon. It is okay to become out of tune with each other. It will keep us growing and learning and bonding. The joy is in finding our way back. This has been a blessing. I am fully awake now.

It was important to spend time away from you. I needed to find the power in myself to do this alone, to feel independent and strong and brave. I found the space where Zahira will always be a surviver. I will always be my own best friend. I will always give myself what ever I need. I will always feel loved. I will always be blessed by the magic I believe in.

Yes I still believe in magic. I don't want to live with out it. I believe it is fuelled by the essence of awe. I believe it blooms from gratitude and unconditional love. I believe it comes from the same stars that this baby is falling from.

I believe in a higher power. I believe in a higher self. I believe in a higher us. I believe in unity. I believe in us as a family. I believe I have found a man who is not afraid to be honest, who is not afraid to share his own fears. A man who is willing to hurt me to keep truth talking. This is a great thing, this is true love.

I want you to know that I believe in aloneness. Real love is helping the other to be free. I respect your individuality. I also respect your friend and I have no ill will towards her. Of course you should remain friends with her. Friendship is sacred. I don't want to imprison you because then I myself would be in prison. Real love makes us individual. I am only here to give you wings not strings.

So while I see a man before me I also see a God. I do not lust for you, I honour you. This has not changed, this will not change. I feel your divinity. I am not here to get from you I am here to give. Loving you makes me rich. Thank you.

I am sorry it has taken me so long to come to this point. It is a sign that I am human too. While my 'fairy tale' has burst, I still believe in happy beginnings.

I would be honoured to keep writing this story with you. I hope to continuously find new ways to love you. I hope the mystery that is our beings remains alluring. I hope our love can be a constant adventure.
~ I am honoured to be your queen, all my love, Zahira

◆

The man's point of view from:

The Natural Pregnancy Book

"One point to keep in mind is that doubts are common and most men experience them. Am I ready to be a father? Will this child interfere with my life? Can I afford this child? Do I really want to be in a life long relationship with this woman? Will the child be healthy? It is okay to let yourself ask these questions and others. In fact it is probably healthier in the long run to begin to face your shadows at the outset rather than to deny them,"
~ Tracy Romm

◆

Gold Stars

Nereo text: I have something for you, for us.

Zahira: Ok I am free

He showed up as she was getting out of the shower. She was so happy to see her best friend sitting on her bed. It was their first chance to connect since their letters. He was holding an Etch-a-Sketch. She climbed across the bed to see what he was writing. The image on the screen said:

Eye Am Ready.

She laughed and smiled and hugged him. She loves the idea of an Etch-a-Sketch. It is a toy that she played with as a kid. You can make an image and then just by shaking the toy upside down the image erases and a fresh screen appears.

She likes this as a metaphor for life and love. Creating something new each moment. She has wiped her heart clean of all pain and it is once again radiating nothing but pure love for this man. She meant what she said, she doesn't want to get from him she wants to give to him.

He pulled something out of his coat pocket and started to pat her dry with it. When she realized it was a baby bib she started laughing even harder. Her smile was cracking her face in two. He reached into his coat and pulled out the matching outfit.

"No way! No way! Where did you get this?" she half shouted. She was so excited that her lover was showing up with adorable baby clothes.

"I did a performance up north in the spring. My friend has a shop there and he said I could take whatever I wanted so I grabbed a sweater for myself and this. I knew I would need it one day," he said smiling at her excitement.

"You picked out baby clothes in the spring? That's crazy!" Zahira took his face in her hands and kissed it. She kissed it over and over again and said, "Thank you."

"Thank you. Sorry it took me so long to get to this point, but I am ready," he said with reassuring love in his eyes.

The two held each other for a long time. It was like a lifetime had passed between them and they were closer and stronger than ever.

"I am really proud of us," Zahira said. "I think we did really good. We didn't yell at each other and we kept the communication flowing.

We stayed true to ourselves and we stayed true to each other."

"Yeah I agree," he said looking at her with a warm and open gaze, "We did great."

"Oh wait," she said as she ran to her dresser, "I think we both deserve one of these!"

And she placed a gold star on each of their cheeks.

◆

The Work Continues...

"Where have you been?" asked Zahira. He was an hour and a half late. She had been expecting him to join her at 11pm and it was now 12:30am. It was the grand opening of her brother's new club. Her whole family was there. Everyone had been asking where Nereo was. Zahira had no answer.

"I was at the Fairmont having a glass of wine," replied Nereo.

"The Fairmont? With who?" asked Zahira feeling disappointed.

"My friend," he said as he grabbed her hand.

Zahira's heart sank and her hand instantly lost its grip. He was with the woman who was at the root of all of her pain last week. It was too much in this moment. He could have been anywhere else, but he was late because he was with her.

"I was talking about us, about our baby," he said sounding hopeful.

"*You told her I'm pregnant?!*" Zahira said not ready to believe it.

Nereo's face dropped. It hadn't occurred to him that this was a big deal, but it was. The two lovers had made a pact with each other. They agreed not to share their news with anyone until her second trimester. They agreed that if this needed to change they would consult each other first. It was their special secret, now his friend knew too.

"Oh my god I'm so sorry," he stammered. "I'm so sorry. I just really needed someone to talk to and she was really happy for us and oh I'm sorry. Are you okay?"

"Well give me a minute," Zahira said feeling her heart pounding. "You show up here late and then I find out it's because you were with her and then you tell me that you've broken our deal? That's like getting punched in the face three times in a row. I don't know what else to say right now."

It was noisy and crowded in the club. Zahira felt a bit trapped. She was cornered back into disappointment. She didn't want to be feeling this way. She didn't want to feel so out of balance with her lover. She was relying on clarity to keep it all in check, but her heart was clearly deflated.

"I gotta get out of here," she said grabbing her coat.

"Okay I'm coming," he said.

The two left the club. Nereo put his arm around her and they walked in silence. Zahira was trying to find a quick way to make this not a big deal. She was trying to find the place in her heart that was able to simply smile and shrug it off. She was watching herself carefully. She was exhausted and sad.

"Do you want to get out of town?" he asked while driving home.

"Now?" asked Zahira.

"Yeah let's just drive somewhere," Nereo said sounding hopeful.

"Well I would need to go home and change. I'm not dressed for an adventure," she said looking at her fishnet stockings and frilly booty shorts.

"Okay well let's go to your place and grab some gear," he said steering them in that direction.

They arrived at her house. It was one in the morning. They sat in silence in her driveway. Zahira was contemplating his idea. She had to admit she liked it. Her house would be full of people. Her sister and her friends were coming to sleep over after the bar. They live out of town and Zahira had opened her home to them. Her roommates were also up playing board games. Zahira was not prepared to socialize. She knew they needed time alone. She knew it would be better to escape together.

"Okay let's do it," she said.

He smiled and looked relieved. They went inside to make a quick get away. Zahira changed into sweat pants. She put on the kettle to boil some water for ginger tea, she packed left overs into a lunch cooler, she gathered bedding and candles, her wing and her Osho book. They were out of the house and on the road in less than twenty minutes.

They drove the first hour in total silence. They decided they would return to the Seven Sisters area, the same place where he had surrounded her in a heart made of stones, the same place where they had first talked about babies and being a family, the same place where he told her to 'believe it'.

"What are you thinking right now?" Zahira finally asked him.

"I'm the worst," he said feeling sorry, "I can't believe I shared our secret when we both agreed we would wait to tell people. I really needed someone to talk to and it just came out. I was excited. She's my best friend and she is happy for us."

Zahira was wavering between sad and fuming mad. She was watching herself carefully. She was working through things with patience.

"How are you doing?" he asked looking over at her.

"Well," she said with a big sigh, "I just feel like things are imbalanced now."

"Imbalanced? What do you mean?" he asked.

"Well now there are three of us that know about this. It just doesn't work for me. I guess maybe we should just start telling people. I can't stand the thought of her knowing and not my closest friends and family. It will drive me crazy," Zahira said.

"What about the first trimester thing? Don't you think we should wait a bit longer?" asked Nereo.

"I think I would feel differently about this if you had told one of your buddies, but you didn't you told *her*. This fucking woman who came out of nowhere. *Your best friend?!* Why didn't you mention her name when I asked you who your best friend was? I've never heard you talk about this woman until last week and now you refer to her as your best friend? I thought you asked me to be your best friend!" Zahira said with a raised tone.

It was straying off topic, but it was where her head was going. She was upset. She was feeling pissed off and so she kept talking, "I just can't believe that you told her. My mom doesn't even know and *she* knows?!? Do you know how hard it was for me not to reach out to anyone last week? I was devastated, but I didn't talk to *anyone* because I couldn't tell them the whole story. I had to work through everything on my own."

Nereo was feeling even worse. She could tell by the look on his face. She was just being honest about her disappointment. He had broken their trust. It wasn't a small secret it was a big one, perhaps the biggest. Zahira's phone rang. It was her sister.

"Where are you?" asked her sister.

"I'm in Beausejour," Zahira replied, "Where are you?"

"Beausejour?!! What are you doing in Beausejour?!" her sister shouted in surprise.

"Well Nereo and I needed a quick escape so we just packed up the car and left. Didn't you get my note? I left it on the kitchen counter," Zahira said.

"We're locked out! We're at the back door and it's locked," said her sister sounding confused and upset.

"Oh my god, oh my god, I'm such an asshole. I totally forgot to leave the door unlocked. I am so sorry. Shit, fuck, okay, I'll call my roommates just give me five minutes," Zahira said hanging up the phone.

"I'm such an asshole," she said out loud as she started frantically dialling.

"So am I," said Nereo.

Zahira tried calling both of her roommates. Her heart was absolutely sinking. She knows they don't wake up easily. She has been locked out before banging on the door and calling their phones and neither one has gotten up. She was starting to panic. Her sister and her four friends were waiting outside. They had nowhere else to go. Zahira was already an hour out of town. Just then her sister called her back.

"They are not answering the door. All of our shit is inside. What the fuck are we supposed to do?!?" her sister was clearly upset and was sounding panicked.

"Okay okay... I'm gonna try one of their girlfriends. They are both sleeping over. Just give me two more minutes. I'm so sorry. Just give me two more minutes," Zahira pleaded.

Zahira's sunken heart was now breaking. Her sister never asks her for favours. Zahira had been so happy to accommodate all of her friends. Now she had totally fucked them over. Their car keys and their over night bags were locked inside the house, they would literally have nowhere to go. Zahira's anger was building. She was so mad at herself. She was on her third attempt at calling her roommate's girlfriend when she completely lost it.

"Fuck!" she yelled at the top of her lungs while kicking the dashboard. "Stop the car."

She opened the door and jumped out before he could come to a complete stop.

"Hello?" she heard a small voice on the other end of the phone.

"Oh my god hello?!? Hello? Are you there?" Zahira's desperation was about to be rescued.

"Are you okay?" asked a sleepy voice.

"Oh my god my sister and her friends are at the back door! Can you please let them in?!" asked Zahira feeling instant relief.

"Oh of course, no problem. I'll be right down," replied the angel who saved the night.

"I love you. Thank you," Zahira said hanging up the phone.

She called her sister and told her help was one the way. Zahira apologized for everything and told her she would call her in the morning. She hung up her phone for the last time and found herself standing under a cold canopy of brilliant stars. She was wearing her socks and the highway was wet, but she didn't care. She exhaled a big beautiful sigh of relief.

When she got back to the car Nereo was sitting with his head on the steering wheel. He had tears streaming down his cheeks. Zahira didn't say anything. She picked out a CD and chose her favourite song. She cranked the stereo, put on her boots and climbed back out into the night. She walked around to his door, opened it and pulled him out. She kissed his chest and wrapped him in a huge hug.

The two lovers began to slow dance on the dark highway. It was three in the morning. The air was crisp, the stars were glimmering and their hearts were healing. They didn't speak they just danced. They held each other close and danced.

Zahira felt sorry for the way she had exploded. It surprised even her. She reached a point where she could no longer take it. She lost it and then she instantly felt better. She knew her outburst had shocked Nereo. He had never seen her angry before. To be honest Zahira hasn't lost it in years, she can remember kicking a garbage can about four years ago, but apart from that her anger rarely gets the best of her.

After their song was over they split apart. Zahira went to pick another song and Nereo went to lie in the middle of the deserted highway. She put on 'That's Amore' by Dean Martin. The scene was eccentric. Zahira felt light and grateful. Her outburst was like a release valve, her tension had completely vanished. Nereo still had some emotions to work through so she let him be.

When he was ready he found her again. He wrapped her in his arms and they rocked together in silence. They were apologizing without words. The love and the gratitude flowing between them was like a gentle wave cleansing their hearts.

"I'm not sure what to do now," he said feeling a lingering concern.

"Well you can kiss me," Zahira said with her chin tilted to the sky.

He bent down and gave her a slow soft gentle kiss.

"I was thinking about our news. What do we do? Do we tell people?" Nereo asked.

"Well we don't have to decide right now," Zahira said giving him a squeeze. She could sense that even though he shared this news with one friend, he wasn't ready to share it with the world. "Why don't we see how our day goes tomorrow? We can make a choice when it feels right."

The last bit of tension seemed to unfurl from his chest. He sighed and hugged her. They had once again met in their most human forms. They had once again found serenity in their struggle. They were moving through their fairy tale with real life love and acceptance.

The two decided that it was time to rest. They were both exhausted. They were emotionally drained and it was now almost 4 in the morning. They found a dirt road and pulled over. Zahira lit a candle and poured them some hot ginger tea.

Even though they were tired they stayed up talking for another hour. They talked about being human and being real. They talked about being not human and feeling unreal. They talked until they were almost sleeping. They folded the seats of Paris to make a bed and then they folded into each other until ten in the morning.

◆

THE SPIRITUAL CATALYST

"This is the awakening. The point at which we stop dead in our tracks and decide that the fight is over. A kind of serenity is born of this acceptance. We see that 'happily ever after' is never a place that can be found in the world that surrounds us. It is only a state that becomes from within."

~ TEAL SCOTT

◆

HONEST EGGS

"I'm starving," were the first words that came out of Zahira's mouth. It was ten thirty and her stomach was growling.

Nereo sat up with out hesitation. He moved towards the steering wheel.

"Wow? Just like that! You can get up and get going just like that?" she smiled and pulled him back into her arms.

The two lovers had slept on a mattress that was stretched across their car seats. It was a tight fit, but it made for great cuddling. The sun was shining and the frost on the windows was melting. It had been a long night and they deserved a big breakfast.

"How are you feeling?" he asked smoothing the hair from her forehead.

"Well my mind has a few things running through it, but I am sure I will feel better after I eat something," she said honestly.

"Okay let's get you some food," he said getting up for the second time.

She let him go this time and crawled up front to join him. They had a big day ahead of them. They had plans to hike into paradise, but first they would fuel up on some bacon and eggs.

They found a perfectly quaint small town dinner. Zahira ordered hot water and Nereo ordered a hot chocolate with whipped cream.

"Ooh hot chocolate and whipped cream," she cooed, "It's gonna be a great day!"

They sat side by side like they always do in restaurants. She put her feet up on his lap and they chatted openly and honestly about their night. Zahira brought up everything she needed addressed. Nereo responded with his truth. It was like a debriefing, a decompression. It was the final stage of their resolution. It was a perfect way to start the day. They cleaned their plates and their slate.

◆

You Fell From the Sky

Zahira and Nereo arrived at their destination. They organized their gear into bags and set out on their hike. The crisp fall air was complimented by a warm golden sunshine. It was a perfect Sunday to lollygag through the woods. Zahira could feel bits of city tension unfurl as they meandered with a slow and easy pace.

They chose to walk off the beaten track. It made for a private forest romance. They moved slowly and gracefully together. He was wrapped in blankets and she was wearing mukluks and a giant faux fur coat. They were hardly your typical hikers. Their gear consisted of a found walking stick, a picnic and a lighter to start a fire.

They stopped several times along the way to embrace and absorb each other. Nereo's attentive affection was filling Zahira with peaceful pleasure.

"Wow your eyes!" he said as he was looking deeply in them, "Wow! Wow! They look like sunflowers! I have never seen that before. They are amazing. You are amazing. Thank you for being my teacher," he said as he planted a soft kiss on her lips.

"Thank you for being mine," she smiled feeling warm and loved.

When they found their perfect place they laid out their blankets, lit a fire and curled into each other. They were lying on a smooth rock using a fallen tree as a back rest. They had a view of a slow October river. The sun had disappeared, but the flames of the fire were bright and warm. They had found their palace.

"Are you comfortable?" she asked as she nuzzled into his chest.

"This is so perfect," he said.

She pulled out her wing and dusted his forehead. She wished for him to be free, to be peaceful and to be present. When she was done she fell asleep on his chest. The two lovers woke together to smile at their scene.

"You know I read somewhere that a true king and queen can find happiness living in a hut. When you can find happiness in a hut you can also find it in a palace. It doesn't work the other way around, being born in a palace doesn't mean you will find paradise in it," Zahira shared.

"I like that," said Nereo. "Do you think that the more you appreciate the simple things in life the less things will come to you?"

"No I believe the opposite," she said. "I believe the more gratitude you have in this life the more life will offer you."

"Yeah that's what I believe too," he said.

"I also think that even the smallest amount of gratitude can transform a life. Everyone has the power to live the story of their dreams," Zahira reflected.

"I don't think your book should have an ending," Nereo said thoughtfully.

"That's funny I was thinking the same thing. This book was supposed to end in India, but it wasn't until I got home that all of my teachings started to sink in. My cravings went away and I had nothing but gratitude remaining. Then I met you and now this baby has arrived. Now I think this is just the beginning again!"

"That's how your book should end. It should end as The Beginning," he smiled.

"I was thinking the exact same thing," she smiled. "Hey can we find a way to make an offering for our baby? A way to acknowledge his presence? A way to welcome this new being into our lives?"

"Like what?" he asked.

"I don't know, maybe we can write a letter on some birch bark and then burn it. Do you have a pen?" she asked.

He looked in his pockets, "No but we can think of something. I like that."

"Maybe we can do something here and then we can stop at the Petroforms on our way home. We can make a medicine bundle for the temple, a sacred offering," Zahira suggested.

"Yeah okay let's do it," he said fully on board.

Zahira went for a walk to see if she could collect some objects for their bundle. When she returned Nereo was creating his own beautiful message on the stony earth. He was putting the end of his walking stick in the fire until it started to burn, then he would take his massive flaming pen to the rock face and use the charcoaled tip to write a message on the earth.

Zahira watched him repeating this process with diligence and patience. Each letter required another trip back to the fire. He was working slowly and with love in his heart. Zahira could feel hers melting in this moment. She knew it was important for him to find his own way to connect with his baby's spirit. She pulled out her camera to video tape the moment. She let him work in silence.

"It's beautiful," she said when he was finished.

The message read: YOU FELL FROM THE SKY. Then he drew a heart with a single star inside of it.

"The baby is going to see this video one day," he said softly.

"Yep," smiled Zahira.

Nereo looked into the camera and said, "I want you to always love yourself, love yourself and love others. You are wise. You will do some great things in the world, that is what you are destined to do. You came from a special place, you are here to do some special things. Live a beautiful life so that others can live a beautiful life through you," he paused for a moment and finished with, "Love life."

Zahira turned the camera on herself, "Your mom came up with that last bit."

"Yeah," Nereo smiled. They both laughed.

"Welcome home," Nereo finished.

The two lovers kissed. The moment felt fit for a fairy tale, a real life fairy tale filled with heartaches and disappointments, truth talking and peaceful resolutions. A true tale filled with symbols and offerings.

"I think it's really important to work beyond the rational mind. The bible is written in metaphors because it connects with a higher self. Using these kinds of creative offerings is a way of telling our subconscious and super-conscious we are paying attention. It is a way of communicating with divinity," she said admiring Nereo's work.

She was laying on the stone next to the heart he had drawn. She was feeling grounded and soulful, grateful and serene.

"This baby is so wonderful to choose us as parents," she said with a lazy smile. "He is coming to be our greatest teacher. I think you and I have incredible talents, but this baby is going to blow us both out of the water."

Nereo laughed and hugged her, "I can see it! I can see it!"

The two sat in silence for a while. The sun was starting to set so they decided to start hiking back. They gave thanks to the elements and cleaned up some litter that was there when they arrived. They made a plan to find some objects for their sacred bundle on their walk back.

They strolled slowly with their arms around each other. They collected three acorns that looked like they were curled in a fetal position and found an arrangement of leaves on a stick that looked like a rose. Zahira gathered some fresh green fallen pine needles and a piece of birch bark.

"Wow look at the clouds! They look like cotton candy!" Zahira cheered as she pointed to the sky.

They could see the sky through the tree line and it was turning into a beautiful sunset. What they didn't expect was the most exhilarating sunset of their existence. The sky turned from soft pinks and blues to a burnt orange colour. The two started to pick up their pace. They wanted to get to the trail head so they could have a clear view.

"Wow! Wow!" Nereo was shouting and half running. The sky was almost neon. It looked like it was going to catch on fire.

"Oh my god!" Zahira said feeling genuine surprise. "Oh my lord this is intense!"

They made it to the clearing and they stood with their jaws dropped. The sky was electric orange. The clouds were so low they felt like they could reach up and grab them. The colours were so intense it was causing them both to shout in appreciation.

"Wow this is definitely amazing! To write you fell from the sky and then have the sky do this?!?! This is definitely our child!" cheered Nereo.

It was a magical moment. Both of them felt it. It felt like a wave from their child's spirit, like a 'hey guys got your message!' Zahira and Nereo were blown away. They looked like two kids at a magic show. They were frozen in a state of awe.

They stood motionless until the last trace of orange vanished from the sky and then climbed back into Paris with out saying a word. They were both utterly speechless. Zahira wrote a message on the piece of birch bark she had found. It read:

EARTH AIR FIRE WATER & SPACE
Thank you for this time and thank you for this place
Thank you for this life that is about to join the human race
We love you with all of our hearts
in all of our ways
for all of our days
Namaste

◆

ZEN FOX

"The very first time I came down this path there was a butterfly waiting for me at the entrance. I put my finger out and it crawled on. It stayed with me all the way to this sacred rock up here where people leave offerings," Zahira said.

The two lovers had arrived at the Petroforms. They were carrying a sacred medicine bundle to honour their unborn child. The light was fading from the sky and the air was crisp. The forest was quiet and meditative.

"It felt like a really beautiful greeting," she continued, "like the spirits were welcoming me. It was so special."

The two stopped dead in their tracks. Just as Zahira completed her sentence a fox appeared before them. It was standing next to the sacred rock which was covered in offerings of tobacco and cloth. The three beings were frozen in time. No one made a move. They were all aware of each other. The moment felt crystallized.

"Oh my goodness," Zahira whispered.

The fox sat down and stared at the couple. He was less than three feet away. He was eating dinner and seemed to enjoy having their company.

"Wow… hello Mr. Fox," Zahira whispered. "It's an honour to be here."

The fox was looking at her. He seemed calm and curious. He was adorable. He was red in colour with a super thick fluffy tail.

"Hi there," said Nereo crouching low to the ground. He put his hand out in a soft welcoming gesture.

The fox moved in closer and sniffed Nereo's hand. He was comfortable and calm. They all were. It was a perfectly zen moment. There was nothing but an effortless focus on the present. The fox's arrival felt a gift from the ancestors, a way of saying 'welcome.'

When it was time to move on the fox circled once and then vanished gracefully into the night.

"Holy!" Zahira cheered. "That was unreal! A fox doesn't have to show himself unless he wants to. Wow that was crazy special!"

"Wow!" Nereo echoed, "I've never seen anything like that before. He was so cute. I want to take him home!"

Zahira laughed, "Come on let's find the temple before it gets too dark."

They walked hand in hand along the Canadian Shield. Zahira explained that Petroforms are outlines made with stones. They can be shaped like; snakes, turtles, pregnant women, thunderbirds, medicine wheels etc. Some people believe they are star gates.

"No one can date how old the Petroforms are because they are rock placed on top of rock. There is no way to do an archeological dig," Zahira explained. "We did some ceremonies here with my Shaman from Peru, Maestro Flores. He found a space that he believes is the point of genesis. He feels this area is a star gate where the Mayans came through."

"Wow that's crazy," Nereo said feeling in awe of everything.

The area felt sacred beyond time. In the fading light it took on a surreal effect. When they found the temple Nereo gasped at the view. The trees were draped with cloth and medicine bundles. The sun faded fabrics hung like quiet messengers from their branches. There was no wind. Everything was still. Zahira felt an ancient silence in the air.

They approached the circle of stones and stood still before entering the West gate. It was a moment to pay respect and offer thanks. They both closed their eyes and felt the cool air around them. Zahira held their bundle next to her belly. She tuned into the most subtle breeze. When it ceased she felt ready. Nereo took his time. When he opened his eyes he too was ready. They entered hand in hand.

"Do you want to walk in a circle around the whole thing before we pick our tree?" she asked in a whisper.

"Yes," he said with an equally soft tone.

She handed him their bundle. It was his turn to put his love into it. They made a loop around the trees passing the North, East and South doors. When they made a complete circle she said, "Okay let's go find our tree."

They walked slowly into the centre of the temple. The fabrics draped around them seemed stoic and proud. They felt like humble ancestors, alive but in a different realm. It was like walking into another dimension, one that does not connect with the rational mind, one that encourages a connection to spirit.

"Hey what about this one?" she said pointing to a little baby tree amongst all of the Grandfathers and Grandmothers.

"Perfect," said Nereo without hesitation.

It was a very young sapling. It had twigs rather than branches. It seemed to be standing alone in the crowd. It was the only tree that had not been decorated with honour. Nereo took the bundle from his heart and began to tie it with some tall pieces of grass. When it was secure they let go and held hands in a circle around their baby tree.

Zahira can't remember what they said at this point. She knows that it felt like a ceremony. Not a wedding, but a commitment beyond religion. It was a union of spirit. Nereo would speak a sentence and she would repeat his words. When it was her turn she would speak and then he would echo her. She really can't remember what they said, it was like she evaporated into the hollow twilight that seems to surround her in moments of pure sacred reflection.

She knows she cried. She cried tears of disbelief and relief. It was a moment that she will always remember. A moment that would have pulled her through so many lonely nights had she known it was coming. A moment that she prayed for as a woman over and over and over again. A moment that she had completely released upon returning from India.

She was standing under the stars with the father of her unborn child welcoming it's existence. It was a time to remember. They were giving thanks and sharing love and offering support. They were recognizing the sacredness of parenthood. They were bonding into a family. She is going have a family. Wow she needs to write that again - *She is going to have a family!!!*

Her baby has arrived and he has chosen his father wisely.

"What do you think of the name Fox for our baby?" Nereo asked.

"Yes! I love it!' Zahira cheered.

"How about Zen Fox?" Nereo added with a thoughtful smile.

"Perfect!" Zahira said as he gave her a soft kiss, "It's perfect."

PART 10

Sacred Union

◆

Out of the Blue into the Green

A year ago Zahira set the intention of traveling with her parents. She has kept true to the importance of this commitment. They are taking a family trip to the Amazon! She realizes this seems a little out of the blue, but Zahira has been so involved with her love and her life she has hardly had time to write about it!

Her shaman Maestro Flores has a centre for medicinal plants in the heart of the Peruvian jungle. It is a humble indigenous sanctuary with a powerful international vision. People from around the world travel to connect with Maestro's rare and powerful knowledge. It is a place to heal and transform, it is a gateway between ancient teachings and modern times.

Zahira has been to the healing center before. It is an extremely remote paradise that comes with its own set of challenges. She is a bit surprised her parents have agreed to go. It is *way* off the beaten path and her parents are more accustomed to comfortable travel. However, they are extremely open minded and ready for an adventure. Zahira is thrilled at the opportunity to bring them to such a spiritual destination. It will offer them all a chance to unplug from the world and plug into their most soulful selves.

As luck would have it a small crew of Zahira's closest friends have decided to join her family. The Winnipeg crew includes; her Ayahuasquero, the twin Ravens (and their mom!) and Zahira's best friend Coco.

It will be great to have their close crew on board because Zahira and Nereo are going to have a sacred union ceremony. They have asked Maestro to preform a blessing for their love as well as for the spirit of their unborn child.

Her next entry will be from the heart of the amazon...

◆

Tropical Flavoured Rainstorms

Zahira and the crew have arrived. She is exhausted from their long journey. She left Winnipeg two days ago. It was a full day of flying just to get to Lima and then another small plane took them to a smaller town where they met their guides. They spent the afternoon wrapping their gear in plastic, purchasing rubber boots and then began their epic trek into the jungle.

Zahira found the car ride extra challenging with torrential rain. It made the red clay roads slick, thick and hazardous. It was pouring outside and the windshield wipers on the car were useless. The bumpy terrain was too much for the small car that seemed to be held together with duct tape. They blew a tire within the first ten minutes. The driver took his shirt off and went out into the tropical storm to change it. Zahira had no choice but to laugh. Her pregnant exhausted body was hungry, wet and far far from home.

Zahira's mom and dad were in the car in front of her. She had concerns about their well-being. They have a marvellous sense of adventure, but Zahira was feeling like the concerned parent. She was worried about their comfort. The twists and bends on the slick mud roads were making her nauseous. She hoped her mom and dad were fairing better.

She also knows her dad has a fear of water. The next leg of their trek would be to climb into a low wooden boat without life jackets. They would travel upstream along a tributary to the Amazon river. She imagines the fast brown waters are home to all sorts of hungry creatures.

When she caught up to her parents at the dock they were in good spirits. They were hovered under a small wooden shack wearing army green rain ponchos and lemon yellow rubber boots. Zahira had to laugh at the sight of them. She gave them both a huge hug.

"This would be a perfect commercial for why you should always hire a travel agent," joked her dad.

Their guides loaded their boat with all of their gear and the crew climbed in one at a time. Her dad appeared quite calm, but Zahira was still concerned about his blood pressure. He is good at masking his nerves. He was cracking jokes and avoiding eye contact with the water. Everyone else seemed quite relieved to be on the boat. It was a much smoother ride than the car.

The final leg of their journey was on foot. The rain had completely erased their path into puddles. They moved slowly and cautiously. Zahira appreciated movement. Her body had grown stiff from their long journey. The jungle hike was challenging, but instead of allowing herself to become short of breath she took long slow inhales and lots of breaks. The jungle was alive with the fresh rain fall. Zahira found the sounds of unseen creatures to be loud and welcoming.

When they made the final steep downhill climb into the valley Zahira's heart sighed a familiar gasp. The healing centre is nestled next to a river of boiling volcanic waters. The steam created from this heat creates a heavenly effect. Zahira felt instantly at peace.

They all arrived to base camp safely. Zahira immediately peeled out of her wet clothes and into some cozy dry sweat pants. She plopped into the first hammock she found. Her body was heavy and tired.

"We made it baby!" she said to her belly before passing out cold.

She woke to eat potatoes and rice. She is now scribbling her story next to a lantern. She is missing the comforts of home, but she has enough experience to know that this will pass. In a matter of days she will gracefully sink into these simple surroundings.

◆

Happily Ever Now

Zahira woke up to Nereo stroking her belly. He was sitting in a halo of soft white light. The mosquito net cast a sweet calm glow around them. He was looking down at her with love in his eyes. He was speaking without words. She simply smiled at him and closed her eyes. The rain started to fall on the tin roof of their jungle hut. It went from a soft whisper to a thunderous boom. Zahira was in a bubble of contentment.

They lingered in bed for hours not speaking. He was stroking her skin softly, she was dozing in and out of realities. She would close her eyes and dream and she would open her eyes and feel like she was still in one.

Nereo instinctively began massaging her hip. Zahira was surprised to note that it hasn't troubled her like it did before they met. Her time with her lover has transformed her on so many levels. Her body doesn't ache the way it used to. Nereo's touch has been so loving and genuine, there is no attention to technique or treatments. Just his simple loving touch has healed her like no other.

Eventually Zahira felt a need to stretch her body so she finally spoke, "Do you want to go and lay next to the river?"

Nereo just smiled and raised the netting. They rolled out of their halo to join their crew. They were lounging like Gods and Goddesses on long slabs of warm stone next to the rushing waters. The effect of the steaming waters was epic. It looked like a set from a make believe movie about heaven. The vapour from the boiling river was hanging thick in the air like sparkling clouds. They appeared to be floating.

Spending time next to the water was transformative. The hypnotic sound of the rushing waters combined with the warm steam was incredibly powerful. Zahira's mind felt like it had been emptied. Her body felt renewed and some how purified. Her spirit felt warm and connected, like a soft shawl around her shoulders.

Zahira relaxed further into appreciation. She felt like she had fallen from the pages of existence. She was losing interest in writing, she felt too humbled to even try and keep up. *Was she really getting married here?* This would be the perfect place to honour her love for her King and their unborn child. As little girl who loved Cinderella, Zahira could not have dreamt a more beautiful kingdom for a Sacred Union.

◆

Proud Daughter

A big highlight of Zahira's trip has been watching her parents adapt and embrace. Their accommodations are modest to say the least. Their huts have thatched roofs with paper thin walls and screen windows that have holes big enough for bats to fly through them.

"How you doin' dad?" she asked him as they were saying in some hammocks.

"Well this journey has been very different than anything that I have ever done, but it's pretty close to what I expected," he said with his classic easy tone.

"The trek in is pretty wild huh?" Zahira half asked half stated.

"Yeah. You wouldn't call it terrifying, but… well I was unsure that bloody car would even hold up! To me it was bordering on the brink of the ridiculous to the guy behind the wheel it was just another day doing his job. He didn't give a shit," he reflected with a wise warm heart.

Zahira laughed as Coco joined them.

"How you makin' out? How is your room?" Zahira asked her.

"I'm gonna love that little room," she laughs with determination. "Definitely had a little freak out over the mattress and the potential of having bed bugs. I had a slight panic that I wouldn't be able to rest until I'm back in Winnipeg, but now that my bed is made I feel so much more settled into this place."

"Oh good I'm glad," Zahira smiled at her friend. She was so grateful to have her here. What great fortune! Her best friends and her parents would be present for her Sacred Union with Nereo. She felt super blessed.

"Where will the ceremony take place?" asked her dad reading her mind.

"In here. This building is called the maloca. Maestro designed it himself," Zahira replied.

The maloca is a beautiful structure that acts as an indigenous temple. Maestro uses it for purging and healing ceremonies. It is also where every one communally gathers to eat lunch, sway in hammocks, read books and share knowledge. It is where Zahira and Nereo will receive their shamanic blessing.

"Maestro will most likely be around to talk to us in the morning. I would love for you to get some medicine for your blood pressure and glaucoma," Zahira said with her fingers crossed behind her back. She was hoping her dad would be open to trying alternative remedies.

"Okay," he replied nonchalantly.

"Oh yay!" she smiled and hugged him.

Zahira loves her parents so much for being here. Her profound respect for them is growing deeper. She prays they will leave this experience with more vitality and youth. She prays the indigenous plant medicines will inflate them with health. She prays they make a stronger connection to their higher selves.

Zahira is so glad she kept her commitment to travelling with her parents. She just can't believe they ended up in the middle of the jungle...for her wedding! Holy shit! Just typing those words blows her mind.

◆

Six Months Pregnant in the Amazon

Zahira is thick and pregnant and has been queasy all day. She went from bliss to bloated over night. She is currently trying to eat a plate of eggs and potatoes. It is the driest most dull dinner imaginable, but she is actually enjoying it. Even if she had a choice she would have picked the plain food in front of her. It is perfect for her tender belly.

It has been an adventurous day for Zahira and Nereo. They spent the morning lounging next to the river smoothing hot towels over each other in the rain. They were exchanging prayers for each other's well being and were so lost in their intimacy they didn't see the water rising up around them. When the hot water swallowed Zahira's feet she looked up to see the rocks around them were quickly disappearing. The currents were strong and intense.

"Ow! Oh shit!" she said feeling a sweep of panic. "We can't go back the way we came!"

The boiling water was rising quickly and the two had to act fast.

"Let's go straight up," Nereo said pointing to the bluff above them.

Nereo scaled to the first ledge and pulled Zahira up just in time. The water was rising and devouring what little stone they had left. Zahira's parents were fortunately watching from above and met them with rubber boots and hugs. They looked extremely concerned. The couple had narrowly escaped a flash flood of boiling water.

Later in the day they decided to hike to where the water was much cooler. Their Ayahuasquero lead the way with a bright smile and a dull machete. The trek through the slick thick jungle mud was challenging. The rain had created a series of mudslides that made it hard to get good grip. Zahira had to use her hands to pull her way up through some steep trails.

By the time she arrived up stream she was panting and profusely sweating. Her bellyache had made it difficult to control her breath. It was totally worth it though. She was able to submerge her swollen belly into a current of cold liquid. She felt her nausea disappear and she almost cried from relief.

◆

Once Upon a Now

It is raining outside. The steam from the river rises and the water from the sky falls. Zahira is still itchy, but her body has no choice but to relax in these surroundings. This scene begs for nothingness. It echoes the place within herself that is permanently still, calm and clear.

The conversation in the maloca is light. Nereo is drawing, Coco is reading and her mom is swaying in the hammock. She thinks her dad might be napping. She feels less concerned about her parents being here. They have embraced this experience wholeheartedly. She is so proud of them.

It is a beautiful thing to have them at this healing centre. It feels surreal and so real all at once. It was a wish she had made years ago when she was first here. She recalls thinking about how much they would benefit from such a sacred setting. Her rational mind deemed it impossible (as if her parents would trek into the jungle!) but her heart was hopeful. She remembers letting her silent wish go into the vapour of the boiling river, now they are here.

Head zero heart won.

◆

Déjà Vu

"What would you say is important for people to know about this place?" Zahira asked Coco.

"This place is all about being open to another way of seeing things. You must be open to different perspectives even if they are far from your own. Trusting the process of these ancient traditions is a part of the healing process. If there is no trust there is no healing," Coco replied without hesitation.

Zahira smiled and instantly thought about her time in the Ayurveda hospital. She is certain she uttered those very words.

◆

Father of the Bride

"Okay so I talked to the Mexican healer and he is going to play drums as I walk you down the aisle," says her dad as he poked his head in her room.

"Oh okay! That sounds great," smiled Zahira.

She was sitting at her desk practicing what she wanted to say to Nereo. Their union was scheduled for early evening. Zahira felt calm and normal. She was even about to start her laundry.

"Maestro will open the ceremony, then you and Nereo will exchange words, then your mom and I will speak and then you will throw your flowers," he said feeling confident he had organized the whole thing.

Zahira let out a grateful laugh, "Flowers?"

"Yes I told Coco she is your maid of honour and she in in charge of flowers and when you throw them she is going to catch them so she is next!" her dad smiled.

Zahira cackled. She loves her dad so much. She is realizing in this moment that this is a big day for her parents, their middle child is getting 'married.' They are such good sports. They are doing their best to make this moment special and to honour it for what it is: a sacred union between two lovers who are about to embark upon the greatest journey of their lives—parenthood.

◆

Jungle Love

"Maestro has asked if he could move your sacred ceremony to Saturday at 3," informed the Mexican healer as he found Zahira next to the river.

She had been quietly contemplating what she wanted to say to Nereo.

"Oh of course," she said as Nereo joined them.

"I was just coming to tell you," he said with a soft smile.

"Yeah it's perfect," Zahira said with a bright outlook.

Zahira instantly saw a chance for the two lovers to secretly elope. Nereo instantly agreed! They left the river's edge and went to cleanse their bodies under a cool stream of water. When the stars appeared they silently slipped into the night. They nestled into a private paradise next to a hot flow of rushing water.

They sat quietly for sometime listening to the strong currents and becoming hypnotized by their steady power. Zahira was the first to speak. She was ready to say what she had been practicing. She even had some cheat sheets written on the palm of her hand. Nereo teased her about it, but she didn't even look she just spoke from the heart. They both did.

The couple spent hours truth talking with one another. It was beautiful. Zahira said everything she could possibly imagine she would want to say to a lover on her wedding day. She heard everything she could have possibly wanted to hear as well. They exchanged truths with open hearts. It was magical. It was how she imagined it to be before she left home, just the two of them alone with the spirits of the amazon drifting all around them.

"I feel like the stars and the river are the greatest witnesses we could have for this sacred union," she smiled as she exhaled into his shoulder.

They both felt as though they were being heard by each other and by the cosmos. It was the steam rising up all around them that felt like spirit was listening intently. The words they exchanged were clear and loving, but it was the quality of the air between them that felt pure and real, humbled and honoured.

She feels she said everything she wanted to say, but she can scarcely remember his words to her. It was like the moment they shared at the Petroforms when they met their fox and tied their sacred bundle. It's as though the words were too precious to capture, too golden to be blackened by ink.

She knows that he spoke of balance and that his idea of true love is finding someone who is ready to continue the balancing act, finding it within the self is a constant practice...

She pauses from writing to investigate a gigantic clear bug with wings that has attached itself to their mosquito net. She is on the outside and Nereo is on the inside. She tries to photograph it while holding her flashlight in between her teeth.

"Hey Nereo can you remember what you said about balance?" she asks as she returns to type next to candlelight.

"Life keeps on moving and changing. When we reach the point where we feel like we have found our centre it doesn't stop there. There will be days when we get knocked off balance, where we get thrown off, and I think that true love is helping each other get back to that centre," he replies with a calm steady tone.

"Perfect," she says as she blows out her candle. She is done recording for the day. She is ready for sleep. She will carefully avoid the giant beetle and crawl into the arms of her lover.

◆

River of Truths

Zahira and Nereo have been making love with their words all day and night. Last evening they eloped and tonight they repeated the process. They returned to the river bank to purge and share.

"I think there is a part of me that is afraid of being a mom," Zahira said somewhat surprising herself. "I just know that right now I have full confidence with myself as an individual, I know that I can care for myself and I can keep my life fresh, exciting and healthy. I can keep a romance alive because I can keep myself satisfied," she continued with tears in her eyes, "I guess I have a fear that if I lose myself in motherhood I am going to lose you too. I don't want to lose us."

Nereo held her quietly and wiped away her tears.

"Wow I didn't even know that was there," she said after sometime. Her tears and her fears surprised her. They had been lying in some distant dormant place, a place that she was not conscious of.

"Who needs a tobacco ceremony," he said referring to the action in the maloca. "We are purging everything right here with our truth, our words."

Zahira laughed and it was gone. She spoke it and was free of it. She feels Nereo's love, it is strong and deep. He is not afraid to meet her in the place of truth. She gets to be both woman and child with this man, she gets to feel both safe and vulnerable. On every level he meets her, recognizes her, acknowledges her and reflects her.

"There is a part of me that doesn't want you to share our whole story in your book," he confessed. "I think there are parts that make me look like a bad guy."

"I don't think so," she said honestly. "I think the part where we go through that intense period is really important to leave in. I think it is human and I think everyone can relate to it. I think we dealt with it beautifully. I also think it's important to share pain as well as pleasure.I believe sharing our shadows makes it easier for others to understand and embrace our light."

"I agree. I just want to be clear about the night that I was out with my friend. It wasn't like you were totally out of the picture, I was talking about us. Also the dancing that we did was just practicing hip hop dance routines. It wasn't romantic," he clarified again.

"Okay baby I'll make it clear," she assured him.

"I read your whole manuscript," Nereo admitted.

"You did!?" Zahira asked quite surprised, "Where? How?"

"There was a copy of it on the memory stick that you leant me," he replied.

"So how did it make you feel when you read it?" she asked him.

"Well...first I read our part, King Nereo, then I approached the rest of it as though I were reading the novel of a friend. I didn't want to read it as someone who has ownership of you. It's in your past. Reading about your sexual encounters was interesting. It made me want to write about my own experiences. I'm glad I read it before it gets published. I feel confident that I am not bothered by it."

Zahira exhaled and released a bunch of kisses,"Oh that makes me so happy!"

Zahira was relieved. She imagines most men would not want to hear such detail about their lover's past (let alone have her share it with the rest of the world!). She has found a man who is secure in his being, a man who is both confident and relatable.

"You have a very special quality," Zahira whispered, "just having your presence in a room alters it. You have an otherworldly essence and yet you are so attainable and personable. People want to be your friend, they want to hear what you have to say. You have a humility and grace that makes your truth easy to swallow and relate to. It is a very powerful gift you possess."

"I love you," he said as he hugged her with a strong sincerity."I feel like you truly see me."

"I feel the same way," Zahira smiled.

"I received a lesson about love and lust in my dreams, lust being something outside of what we share. It was very clear that it is up to me to protect this love," he said with his arms around her.

"I think it is a matter of protecting, respecting and honouring it. I also think that when a person becomes dissatisfied in a relationship it is because they are dissatisfied with themselves. When one starts to stray it is because they have started to stray from themselves. When we first met neither one of us were looking for anything, we were both so content to just be existing. We are together because we enjoy each other's company. If we weren't looking for anything when we were on our own I don't see why we would start looking for anything while we are together," Zahira said.

"That makes perfect sense," he responded.

The two went back and forth and back and forth with more

truths. They dug deep and shared wide. Everything felt very natural and safe. They were sharing from a place of self-love and love for one another. Once again it felt as though the river could hear their whispers and would carry them into their future. They will be reminded of these moments when the currents of their lives grow strong. They will be reminded to let go of one another so they can continue to flow together.

◆

Sacred Union

"Oh my," said Zahira's mom holding her hand to her heart, "I think I'm going to cry."

"I think I am too!" said Zahira as they hugged.

It was moments before her sacred union with Nereo. She and her mom were watching the shamans crossing a small thatched bridge to reach the maloca. For the first time this week they were all dressed in their ceremonial attire. They had on long ancient robes with beads and feathered crowns. The sight of them walking in single file ushered a silent reverence into her heart. Her skin tingled with goosebumps.

Maestro's wife came to greet her with a warm hug. She was taking charge of explaining certain traditions. It was very important that Zahira and Nereo pick a godfather and godmother for their union. They each needed a guardian for their love. They easily chose her Ayahuasquero and Coco. Their role is to watch over their union and to support them through the ups and downs.

They were organized into couples and put in order to walk down the aisle. Zahira and her dad would go first followed by her mom and Ayahuasquero and then Coco and the Mexican Healer. Nereo would be waiting for her inside the maloca.

She linked arms with her dad and gave him a big smile, "Are you ready?"

"Alright!" he said with a cheer.

The force of power Zahira felt when she stepped through the threshold of the maloca was enough to stop her dead in her tracks.

She was instantly in awe of what she felt. She needed a moment to absorb every special detail. Maestro's daughter greeted her with a bouquet of flowers, the shamans were standing at the head table dressed in their ceremonial attire and her lover was waiting for her at the front of the room with the most beautiful smile.

She took a deep inhale and slowly started to proceed. She greeted her guests as she passed them. They all appeared to be enjoying this moment as much as she was. When she looked at Nereo she lost sight of everyone else in the room. He looked like a king dressed in black and gold. They locked eyes and her body instantly released a peaceful glow.

When it was time for her dad to give her away Zahira hugged him with all of her heart. She was aware of the significance of this gesture, it was something they had talked about when she was a little girl. She felt tears of love and appreciation flowing for this moment. It was time for her dad to give her hand to the father of her *own* child. She was ready. Everything felt natural and right.

Zahira and Nereo joined hands and acknowledged the wall of power before them. They were clearly standing in the temple of an Asháninka shaman. Zahira was tremendously humbled by the effort that their hosts had put into this moment. It was laced with care and tradition. It had a formal outline but was coloured by nothing but spirit. Everyone in the maloca could detect that they were experiencing something sacred and special. The moment felt incredibly real.

The altar was surrounded by four chairs. Maestro and his wife sat on one side and Zahira and Nereo were seated across from them. There was a long pause when they sat down, it was not an awkward silence it was a much needed inhale. Zahira wanted to absorb what was before her. It was a presence of graceful humble power. It was not the kind of power that makes you feel little, but the kind of power that makes you feel large.

Maestro introduced a plant that would give them a blessing for their love and for all of the world. He said it would offer them power for their union. He sprinkled the green bouquet with flower water and then shook it around the couple.

"All of my blessings for this couple in the name of the Son, the Father and the Holy Spirit," he said in Spanish.

He then went to Zahira's parents and all of the other guests and did the same. The maloca filled with a sweet aroma. The sound of the shaking plant was hypnotic and soothing. It offered a moment for Zahira to turn around and absorb the whole scene. Their international and local guests were seated in two rows facing each other. Maestro was walking around the room blessing each and everyone of them.

When Maestro returned to the altar they were given a gift from two tribes; one from a neighbouring Amazonian tribe the other from the Shipibo tribe. Maestro then offered his heart to Zahira and Nereo as well as all of the other guests present. He explained that true love looks very simple, but it can be very challenging. His blessings were not only for the couple and their unborn child, but for *everyone* in existence.

Maestro finished by saying, "May your love be an example for all of mankind and for all of the world."

His wife then offered the couple two gifts from the healing centre. They were wedding bands to wear on their wrists. Zahira's was bright and colourful and Nereo's was darker in colour. She gave them each a small wooden bowl that she filled with rice. This was to symbolize a home that will always have food. Zahira and Nereo accepted the gifts with open hearts.

Then it was time for Zahira's dad to speak.

"Do you know how to say 'wow' in Spanish?" was the first thing he asked his translator. The crowd laughed and he continued, "I don't know how many ceremonies I have attended in my life, but this has to be the most beautiful. I believe that a special occasion deserves a special location. For Zahira and for Nereo this is a very very special occasion and there is no doubt in my mind that we are in a very special location. To all the guests gathered here today I would like to thank you for travelling all the way to the middle of a peruvian jungle to be with Nereo and Zahira. I know that the invitations they sent to you mentioned that you would be staying at a 5 star hilton, but how else were we to entice you to such a beautiful isolated place?"

Everyone in the maloca laughed. Zahira's dad has a lot of

experience in giving speeches and she knew that he would be adding some humour to their occasion. It was comforting to have his classic Canadian dad speech amongst the sacred indigenous blessing.

"Besides it's spiritual nature, there is a second reason why this is such a perfect place for a sacred union ceremony," her dad continued. "It's saving me a lot of money. The thousand dollar outfit my wife would have been wearing at home is a lot more expensive than the two dollar outfit she has got on today."

Zahira groaned out loud, "Dad!"

She was hoping that his translator wouldn't translate that last joke, but he did so with a big chuckle and everyone laughed again. Then her dad turned to face her and Nereo.

"To you Zahira, I always wondered who your life partner would be. As you matured your suitors came and went. As they did I would say to mom, 'ah! maybe this is the one?' 'No no', your mom would say. Then the next one would come and I would say, 'maybe this one?' and mom would say 'no no no'. And then along comes this man, Nereo, and I say to her, 'is this the man?' and mama smiles and says 'yes.'"

Zahira felt Nereo squeeze her hand and her dad continued.

"With you and Nereo the saying that opposites attract couldn't be further from the truth. You two see the world through the same set of eyes. Your creative, loving, spiritual natures are mirror images of each other. I am so happy for both of you and in a few months I will be even happier when you introduce Fox into this world and complete your cycle of life. So to both of you, mom and I and everyone here want to wish you nothing but the best in life. Follow what your hearts are telling you and I know that you will enjoy a spiritual happiness that most people can only dream about. Congratulations."

Everyone in the maloca clapped and both Nereo and Zahira stood to give her dad a huge hug.

"Thanks dad," she whispered in his ear, "you're the best."

Then Zahira's mom got up to give a short and sweet thank you in Spanish. It was so sweet it almost needed a Spanish translator! Zahira was beaming with appreciation towards her mother. She had so much love for her in this moment. She could see that their hosts also appreciated her mom's attempt to communicate in their language.

It was touching and lovely and both Nereo and Zahira gave her a long hug when she was done.

The moment was followed by a beautiful song from her Ayahuasquero while the Mexican Healer accompanied him with a soft beating hand drum. Zahira closed her eyes and felt everything. She felt a current coursing from Nereo's hand to her heart. She felt the warm soft tropical air kissing her cheeks. She felt how real everything was.

When her Ayahuasquero finished singing Zahira opened her eyes. It was her godmother's turn to speak. It was a bit of a surprise to Coco, she had nothing prepared.

"I've been in love with Zahira for 8 years," began Coco feeling a bit nervous.

Zahira looked at her and mouthed the words, "You'll do great."

Coco giggled and continued, "I too had seen her with different suitors in the past and I always wondered who in the world was out there for such a radiant, beautiful, incredible woman. When I first saw her with Nereo I knew before she knew that he was the man she had been waiting for. So from the very beginning of their story I have got to witness and love both of them together. These two inspire people to believe in true love and I am so happy for you both."

When it was Zahira's turn to speak she felt like she had no words. She was so grateful that she and Nereo had exchanged two nights of truth talking because in this moment she was in complete awe. Anything she could have written on the palm of her hand would seem little and silly, instead she started with a huge thank you to those before her.

"Wow. I feel like I have very few words to say. I am completely overwhelmed with how beautiful all of this is. It has far superseded my imagination. I want to thank Maestro and your beautiful wife and everyone present for the love that I can feel in this room. You've really recognized this day as being special for us so thank you," she said addressing the room.

"And to my Nereo," she said as she turned to look at him. They both stood and interlaced hands. She giggled and kissed him lightly on the lips.

"Thank you for being here in this moment, right here right now," she started with a slow clear confident tone. "Thank you for the love that you have found within yourself and for the way you honour yourself. Thank you for mirroring that to me. I believe that true love is about honouring one another to grow together and to grow apart. I pray before all of these witnesses; the river, the air, the vapour, the plants and these beautiful shamans... I pray that I can help you stay on your path. I love you. Thank you."

It was short and sweet, but for Zahira it felt like a direct communion with her divine self. Her words came without thought, they simply flowed from a higher consciousness. Then it was Nereo's turn speak.

He stood for a while just looking at her. There was nothing rushed about the moment. He was waiting for the words to come. Just like Zahira he started with gratitude for the occasion, "Thank you everyone for being present and for those who are not here, my mother and father and for everyone around the world who knows how important this love is to me, who recognize how big this is, thank you."

Nereo took another pause to direct his entire focus on Zahira. She was so calm and so clear that her toes weren't even twitching. They were both barefoot and completely grounded.

"I believe this love is guided by a very high force, a very powerful force," Nereo began, "I believe that we will grow strong together because we have been able to connect with each other on many levels; the physical, emotional, mental and spiritual. We both recognize our power as individuals. This love between us is also powerful."

He paused again, "There are many challenges in life and I believe it is about finding a balance over and over again. I have found my centre and I know you have too. I have no fears, I've learnt to let go of you."

Nereo smiled and acknowledged Zahira's belly, "I believe that this child will only help us survive our love," and then he laughed, "I can talk forever about this! I really love you."

The two joined foreheads and let time elapse around them. Zahira felt like she had arrived home. It brought a flush of tranquility through her body and mind. The world grew quiet and a great sense of ease enveloped her. She even saw stars while they lingered here.

She doesn't know how much time had passed, but when the moment was right they pulled apart to speak her mantra. They had rehearsed this part. Nereo had memorized it and they shared it with a slow and meaningful pace.

"Earth air fire water and space,
thank you for this time and thank you for this place.
Thank you for letting us be a part of the human race.
We love you with all of our hearts, in all of our ways,
for all of our days. Namaste," they said in perfect unison.

Everyone clapped for the couple. The official part of the ceremony was over. Then Zahira threw her bouquet just like her dad imagined. It fell flat on the floor and Zahira looked at Coco and shouted, "Dive!"

Coco grabbed the bouquet and everyone laughed. The shamans came and hugged the couple one by one, then they went around the room and acknowledged and hugged each of their guests. There was a joyful and festive feeling in the maloca.

To Zahira's surprise the chef brought out a cake they had baked in their rugged jungle kitchen! It had their names hand written on a piece of paper and placed on top. It was so sweet and it tasted delicious. Zahira and Nereo fed each other and once again everyone clapped.

Zahira was delighted by all of the effort that had been put into this occasion. She was smiling from the tips of her toes. It felt more like a wedding than she had imagined. She really got married! It was the most untraditional yet universal wedding she has ever attended. The best way she can describe it is...*real.*

◆

"To me, the whole of nature is the greatest temple to honour. Apart from listening to the plants the hardest part is how to go forward, how to behave as human beings. When we are humble we open more hearts. What we can try and do is practice a little love every day. It is useless to speak of love today if we loose it tomorrow. Love is simple, but keeping it can be difficult. We can maintain and follow our paths with love. We need to march beyond what is expected of us."

~ Juan Flores

◆

Sacred Reflections

"The one thing I do think is so essential to some type of a union is having witnesses to it," Coco comments. "I liked that everyone on this property was there. It was a super random tossed salad of attendees. It's like all of these people from around the world are suddenly witnesses to your wedding. They will go off and scatter and sprinkle these seeds. It's really cool. It's too bad Nereo's parents were not in attendance."

"I would like to thank all of you for making this journey. I know that your invitation said that you would stay at a five star hotel, but how else were we to lure you here?" Nereo laughed recreating her dad's speech.

They all started cracking up. Zahira started recording their conversation.

"Man I've got a lot to learn!" cheered Nereo. "Your dad is the greatest."

"There is so much beauty we get to bring with us from just one short week in the jungle," remarked Coco. "One of my favourite parts about the ceremony was watching the smile on Maestro's face. He was so happy and so proud to be there. When your dad started talking Maestro was totally cracking up!"

Nereo lost it again, "Man I wanna see the video of your dad's speech and watch it every night. I got so much to learn about making speeches. I am so happy to be a part of this family."

"I felt incredibly honoured to be there beside you two," Coco started, "but even just to be in the presence of the people who are caring for us and treating us with such generosity. I felt like we were family. Maestro took it upon himself to get his whole force involved; all of his tribesmen, his wife and his daughter who turned out the be the flower girl, the cook who baked the cake, the shamans who were in their full uniforms. Everyone was involved… chickens were slaughtered for heavens sake!" she said referring to their first non-vegetarian meal since they had arrived. "To me it just shifted everything into place as far as how I have been trying to process this experience. The whole entire framework of this place is rooted completely and entirely in love."

"It really was amazing. It felt like a formal shamanic ceremony mixed with moments of a classic Canadian wedding. I really wasn't expecting that! How would you describe my face?" Zahira asked Coco with curiosity.

"You were in shock and in awe and looking around," Coco replied. "You were overwhelmed and super humbled by it all. When you were listening to Nereo I couldn't take my eyes off you because your eyes were so focused and open, big brown eyes, so much love flowing through them, so encouraging even as he was speaking. Your face was beaming with loving openness. I thought, wow she is beautiful."

"Aw thanks. How did you feel about everything Nereo?" Zahira asked placing her hand on his own.

"I was happy, really happy. I didn't feel nervous. I felt comfortable. I felt like we were getting married for the third time, like three days in a row! The first night we talked I already felt that my body mind and spirit were connected to you. I think that as long as you and I continue to acknowledge and connect our spirits we will continue to be blessed in each other's presence… with or without out a ceremony. I think that's the most important thing. The ceremony was to include others into our world," he replied.

"Was there a highlight for you?" Zahira asked her new husband.

"When our Ayahuasquero sang and all the talking was done for a minute I had a moment to collect myself and breathe. It was a good moment. I had flashes of our evolution; of dancing with you, of being in a prairie field with a camera, of going tubing with your family. I had an image of me tearing the first time you did your healing work on me, brushing away my worries with your wing, then I opened my eyes and I had another flash and it was you holding my hand under the maloca roof."

"Wow that's amazing," Zahira blushed, "how did you feel in our moment of silence with our foreheads touching?"

"I felt like nothing could come between us. I felt like every other night when we are forehead to forehead the only difference is that there were people watching," he replied.

Just hearing those words made Zahira's heart hum. She feels the same way. When they connect their foreheads Zahira melts into Nereo and sees stars. She loses time continuum and a sense of self.

"After we spoke our prayer," Nereo continued, "I looked over at Maestro and he had a smile on his face. He was slowly nodding his head as if to say...yeah they've got it. I felt it hit home for him. It probably felt good that there are people out there who are conscious and in tune with spirit and the world around them. I think he knows and feels that we are both people who are able to embrace the simplicities of life and not be over taken by distractions."

"Well said," Zahira beamed and typed his words into her story.

"Going into the ceremony I didn't expect any of this. It really was a wedding!" Nereo cheered. "It felt great. I know I don't need a ceremony to say I love you, but I really feel like the union of our spirits has been acknowledged."

"Me too," Zahira smiled and sealed her words with a kiss.

◆

Moon Honey

The honeymooners are in paradise. They left the jungle and reversed their tracks back to civilization. This time the trek seemed almost light and effortless. The whole crew was floating with appreciation for their experience. They landed in Lima and celebrated with an ocean view dinner. Their itchy legs, empty stomachs and tired bodies were restored and pampered.

Zahira and Nereo have been indulging and embracing the concrete jungle. They have landed in a brilliant love nest. Zahira has spent the last two sunsets naked with her lover in their breath taking honeymoon suite. They have floor to ceiling windows, their own private balcony and a shower with glass walls overlooking the magnificent ocean. The entire room has a clear view of her favourite healer.

Zahira can gage a good year by how many visits she has had with the toes of the ocean. A year ago today she left the Ayurveda hospital in India to say goodbye to the sea. She has *definitely* had a magical year. She has travelled from the princess of the Arabian to the South Pacific Ocean. She has gone from being grateful and single to pregnant and in love! Life has a funny way of unfolding. Her neighbour Harry was right!

There is nothing to worry about,
what's next is next.

◆

So What's Next?!?

First comes love, then comes marriage *then* comes the baby in the baby carriage! The newlyweds have returned to Winnipeg with a warm glow around them. Zahira is oozing with love for her life. She is in awe of how her story has unfolded. She has a baby in her belly! Her life is about to drastically change.

Motherhood! Zahira feels ready but can't comprehend what that even means. She is grateful she has had so much time to indulge in her own well being. She feels she has filled up her cup enough to overflow into another.

As Zahira reflects on the past year she connects with a few

important realizations; self awareness, gratitude and relaxation have been her greatest gifts to self. While she cultivated these gifts on her travels, her real journey began when she landed home. Her homecoming allowed her experiences to settle into understandings. Her ambitions have been annihilated in the most liberating sense. She is simply grateful to be floating in the currents of existence. She has relaxed into total realization. She has surrendered into a balanced view.

Her sacred union is a reflection of this surrender. She didn't find the man of her dreams, she is living in her most awakened state. By connecting to the phenomenon of her consciousness she met a man who has connected with his. They are not living in a fairy tale they are living in real time. They are both wide awake and celebrating life.

Zahira feels the love she shares with Nereo is possible because of the love she has nurtured from within. Her self awareness and self-love are reflected by her King. And while the love has grown from within, it feels like it is coming from a higher place. It feels like a love that belongs to everyone. It is a love that has no name, no beginning and no end in sight.

◆

And so it was written

"Wow! Wow! Wow!" squealed Zahira.

"What?" asked Nereo looking up from his own book.

"I'm just reading my manuscript and came across a quote from one of my teachers in India. Remember the Belgian Lightworker I did the mandala with?" she asked.

"You mean the mandala you did in the sand? The one where you explored your deepest self?" asked Nereo.

"Exactly! Well the healer who was guiding that process actually said:

'When the Queen and the King are married in an act of pure love, when their energies are balanced and they can flow freely into one another and become one, then the Golden Child is born.'

I had no idea when I heard those words how prophetic they would be!" Zahira cheered in amazement.

Nereo smiled and moved to hold her quietly. Zahira rubbed her massive belly and smiled at how her story has unfolded. It feels almost miraculous. Well it is miraculous. She has a divine life inside of her who is due any day now! She is excited to meet her child, but she feels a small wave of sadness for the end of this book.

She can't help but breathe in these last few moments of romantic freedom with a nostalgic heart. She knows that their romance will continue, but it will inevitably shift. She is determined to keep her connection with her King. She knows that these final few days pre parenthood are incredibly valuable and precious. Nereo recognizes this too.

"These are special times," said Nereo reading her mind out loud.

"I know," sighed Zahira.

His words hit her with a profound impact. They seemed to awaken a deep reverence for the significance of this time. Zahira started to cry.

"You are hands down the most amazing chapter of my life. This romance we share is more awe inspiring than any other experience I've ever had. I am really going to miss it," Zahira softly sobbed. She nuzzled her nose into Nereo's neck. "Thank God I have taken the time to write it all down."

◆

Gonna Make You Sweat

Both Zahira and Nereo feel their baby is about to make his grand entrance. She is so positive it is a boy! The moon is full tonight and Venus is in transit. The stars have aligned and they are feeling ready but not rushed.

Today felt like the last piece of the puzzle being clicked into place. Nereo was fortunate enough to experience his very first Sweat Lodge. The invite came with perfect timing right down to the weather.

"My name is Buffalo Warrior," said the Elder who was leading the Sweat. "People tend to pray for themselves, but if we all learn to pray for each other our prayers will be more powerful. When you feel suffering think of your brothers and sisters. You may have thoughts where you feel panic and doubt, pray for your brothers and sisters. If you feel pain it does not have to be your own. If you pray for your brothers and sisters in the lodge you will also have twenty people praying for your needs. It is simple math," he said with great wisdom.

Zahira appreciated this introduction. It resonated clearly with her heart. She would patiently wait outside of the lodge. She was there to support her lover and to expose their unborn child to the sounds of the drums and the powerful essence of spirit.

"Take some tobacco and offer it to the fire," she whispered to Nereo as they were lining up to enter the Lodge, "I love you."

He kissed her and then joined the men who filed in one by one. It would be a tight squeeze. The lodge was small and the group was large. She watched him enter with a calm expression and remarked how he reminded her more of a lion than a unicorn in this moment.

Zahira watched the helpers carefully draw the Grandfather stones from the sacred fire. They were white hot. The helpers used a pitchfork and great caution to place seven stones inside the Lodge. As they sealed the doors the Thunder Birds began to roll. Zahira felt her toes twitching with excitement. The air felt electric and powerful. The rain would soon come.

The moment the ceremony began the first drops were felt. Zahira instantly embraced the idea of getting wet. She wanted to stay close to the sounds of the Sweat. She put her shawl around her shoulders and took out her wing. She began to feather her belly to the rhythm of the chanting and drums.

The rain came with more intensity as the Sweat progressed. It felt as though the elements were responding to the ceremony. Zahira felt a great sense of peace and honour wash through her. She stood to embrace the heat of the fire and let the mud sink between her bare toes. She swayed back and forth tapping her belly and moving to the beat.

She tilted her cheeks to the rain and whispered, "Please cleanse this body to prepare us for birth."

As the final round was coming to a close the rain began to slow.

The east door opened and the steam billowed out of the small dome. It looked like a spaceship landing from Mars. As the first few participants began to emerge the rain stopped completely. There was a pause. Nereo was taking his time and when he finally appeared so did the sun. He looked like a warrior and Zahira's heart instantly started to hum.

He took some tobacco and offered it to the fire. Then he came to greet her. They stood for a long time without exchanging any words. She could feel the love pouring from his being. They both had their eyes closed and could clearly see each other's spirits. When they opened their eyes they were both crying.

"I am so grateful that you have come into my life," he said with the most genuine expression.

Zahira said nothing. She sunk into his chest and softly sobbed. She could feel the significance of this event. Nereo had been given a chance to be reborn. She could feel his transition. His skin was refreshed and glowing. His breath was relieved and his heart was beating quickly. He was holding her tightly.

Zahira will soon be experiencing her own transition and he will be there to support her. The birth of their child will be a rebirth for herself. They are all moving through this passage together. She sees them all clearly united on the other side. She sees how powerful they will become through this process.

They are ready.

It is time.

◆

Labour of Love

Zahira sunk deep into her being. Her arrival at the Birth Centre was calm, but her departure was a bit more intense. The midwives sent her home because she was only two centimetres dilated. They also told her she would have to have a hospital birth because they found a bit of meconium in her discharge. It means the baby had its first pooh and there was danger of him or her inhaling it. They said it was important to have a specialist on hand who was skilled at clearing the air waves.

"Are you sure I should leave?" Zahira asked the midwives after they had done a smudge. Her contractions were four minutes apart and they were growing stronger. She was on all fours and having a hard time lifting her head. Her eyes were closed.

"You could be at two centimetres for the next 24 hours. This is only the beginning of your labour. You need to relax as much as possible and save your strength," said one of three midwives on hand.

Zahira wanted to say '*there is no fucking way* I am going to be like this for another 24 hours,' but she kept her mouth shut. She knew instinctively this baby was coming sooner than later.

The midwives made a plan to come and check on her in four hours. Zahira also knew this would be too long to wait. She didn't say anything. She left without an external struggle. The one inside was enough to occupy all of her energy.

They got to Coco's who was acting as her doula and she immediately put her in the shower. Zahira couldn't stand. She was on all fours. Coco was holding the shower head over her sacrum and Nereo was holding her hand. She was squeezing it tightly during contractions. She started to make unrecognizable sounds from her body. She was moaning with pain.

"It's okay Fox," she whispered reassuringly to their baby, "Mama's okay. You are doing great little buddy."

Inside of her head Zahira was wondering how to turn all of this pain into pleasure. She had watched an orgasmic birthing dvd and had high hopes of managing her pain by simply relaxing. This proved to be more difficult in practice. *Every cell in her body* would clench during contractions. This is most likely why they are not called expansions.

"Your mom called and she is really worried," said Coco with a gentle tone. "She really feels that you should be at the hospital. She said because your water has broken and the midwives detected meconium that you should instantly be admitted to the triage."

Zahira absorbed this information but could not respond. She knew her mother was anxious, but Zahira felt no immediate panic.

She had to trust that she and their baby would be fine.

"Do you want me to call our midwife and see what we should do?" Coco asked.

Zahira nodded her head and sunk deep into another contraction. She could trust her midwife, but more importantly she could trust her own body to know when the time was right to make a move. She was not going to let anything pull her out of her concentration. She had read that women and wild animals can move backwards in labour if they feel fear. Zahira was only interested in moving forwards. Her focus was absolute and she knew she was progressing quickly.

"Open… open," Zahira kept saying between moans. She was coaxing her cervix to dilate.

Coco returned with news, "Our midwife says that if you move to the hospital too early they will want to induce you. She wants to ensure you that you are safe and she will be here in a few hours to check on you."

Zahira knew her body well enough to know that she would need attention before then. Her contractions were growing longer and closer together. Coco was timing them and giving her the most incredible hip squeezes. Zahira had never felt such relief and such pain all at once. Nereo was by her side holding her hand. He was calm but she could feel a genuine concern. She can only imagine how hard it would be to reverse their roles and see him groaning in pain.

After three immensely intense contractions Zahira moaned,"Okay we're going to the hospital."

With out wasting anytime her team had her out of the shower and dressed. Zahira had still not opened her eyes. She was aware of the transfer, but she was deep in her zone. When they got to the hospital their midwife was waiting for them.

"We are going to take her to do an internal assessment," said her midwife to the nurse.

"Does she need a wheel chair?" asked the nurse.

Zahira shook her head. She couldn't imagine sitting down. She needed to stay bent forward. As she was slowly moving down the hall her legs dropped and she let out the most intense sound she has ever made in her life.

"Oh Zahira! That sounds like a push," exclaimed her midwife.

"Don't start pushing here," snapped a nurse with an aggressive tone. "You can't have your baby in the hallway!"

Nereo put a protective shield between herself and the nurse who was now bringing her a wheelchair. Zahira could feel her papa fox snarling for her. It made her feel safe. He was even wearing a fox tail and a tank top with a fox logo that he designed. He was like her personal mascot! Zahira got on the wheelchair backwards. She put her knees on the chair and held onto the handles.

Once again the nurse snapped, "You can't do that! That is not acceptable."

Both Nereo and Coco shouted, "She's fine!"

They wheeled her into the room and Zahira got on the examination table. Her midwife checked her cervix.

"Oh wow Zahira! It looks like you are ready to have this baby!" she exclaimed with surprise, "You are already at eight centimetres, maybe nine. You've been working hard."

They instantly moved Zahira to a private room. She crawled onto the skinny bed and stayed on all fours. She grabbed Nereo by the chest and planted her face into his body. He was the most amazing pillar of strength for her in this moment.

"Zahira we need to put you in a safer position. Can you crawl to the back of the bed?" asked her midwife.

"No," Zahira said with an absolute tone, "I want Nereo." She was gripping him with her entire being, "Babe can you take your shirt off?"

He whipped his shirt off in seconds. He had apparently been thinking the same thing. His bare chest felt like a vortex of love and light. She slid deep into that vortex and into transition. Her contractions were one on top of the other. Zahira lost all sense of pain. She lost all sense of everything but Nereo and their love. He was there for her, solid and deep and calm.

"Find your rhythm," he whispered to her, "You are doing great."

Zahira pulled Nereo to her lips and gave him a long soft kiss. She felt a passion and presence so deep she could have kissed him for hours, she instinctively knew however it was time to start pushing. Somehow her body seemed to enjoy this part. She flipped over on to her back, vacuumed strength from their vortex and pushed it down and out from the top of her abdomen. Her moaning grew silent and she even started to smile and coo.

Her entire team was encouraging and supportive. She could hear the comments of how well she was doing, but it was Nereo and his silent prayerfulness that was powering her and their child.

"You are doing great Fox," Zahira whispered once again, "We are almost there."

Zahira was able to fully relax her body in between pushing. She felt the most incredible euphoria in these moments. She opened her eyes for the first time and looked straight into Nereo's. He was gently crying with the most joyful and tender tears she had ever seen. Everything else blurred from existence. In this moment it was just the two of them. It would be the last time she would look in his eyes before they would cross the threshold into parenthood. They were both ready.

"He's coming. Our Fox is coming," Zahira said holding his gaze and squeezing his hand.

"It's time," he said with a peaceful kiss, "Let's do this."

Zahira turned her focus on to their baby. It was time for him to enter the world. She put her hand to her forehead slipped into the centre of her being. She let out a clear breath of intention and drew upon the energy that was available to her from all of her most powerful loved ones around the globe. With two solid pushes Fox arrived safely to planet earth.

Their little prince and greatest teacher had arrived. He was instantly placed on her chest. Zahira looked down in pure awe. She could feel Nereo's arms around them both. Their son was shining.

"You were right," Nereo said with a giant grin, "It's a boy!"

Zahira had no words. She was exhausted but clear. She had moved through an undefinable vortex. She was now on the other side and she was holding her child. Her time to be a mom had come.

The Fox family has arrived.

The Beginning.

Epilogue

◆

Zahira always has this feeling after a movie or a book that she wants to know what happens to the main characters. She always wants the story to go on and on after the couple meets and falls in love. Because this book has taken her so long to self publish, she has both the luxury and courtesy to do this for you. She knows how it turns out *after* the happy ending.

Fox is going to be 2 years old in two weeks! He is beyond the light of Zahira's life, he is the beacon. She follows him around with hearts in her eyes. He really does radiate a royal quality. He waves to everybody and he loves to connect and make people smile. The earth is his stage and he wants everyone to play on it. It so beautiful to watch him move through the world.

Zen Fox is also magical and mythical. He has two different coloured eyes! His right eye where he holds his knowledge is full of wisdom and is a startling clear blue. His left eye where he holds his love is so kind and beautiful. It is warm and brown and is secretly Zahira's favourite.

Her Unicorn is still glowing and never ceasing to amaze her. He just texted her this new business plan that he has.

Nereo: I'm starting a lemon aid stand called Arctic Fox. It is a drink stop and Fox is the owner. I'm one of his top employees and graphic designer. Gonna be so much fun.

She can't believe she actually married a man who is in to making lemon aid stands! It's crazy because when she was Nereo's age she also had her own kool-aid stand. She set it up in the middle of downtown Winnipeg and gave away a free liquorice straw with every purchase. Now she gets to have a kid *and* a husband to play with.

But their happy ending isn't with out hiccups and heart aches. Zahira's transition into motherhood wasn't as graceful as she had hoped. It was really fucking hard actually. But she wrote an entire book on it so you can read all about it.

She is also thinking of writing a side book called *How to Live with a Unicorn*. She is learning that Unicorns have a vehement need for freedom, are not exactly practical and they shed. That being said they are absolutely real and utterly magical partners.

Living with Nereo has eliminated fear in regards to time and money. The result is quite liberating. Together they are aligned with a wealth of experience that feels like gold. They are financially broke, but Zahira secretly wonders if the publishing of this book will bring her the monetary wealth that her German Tarot reader predicted...

And so it is written.

Author Niki Trosky

Niki Trosky is an artist creating global change through; empowering photo shoots, sacred healing retreats, yoga parties, innovative school curriculums, public speaking events and writing.

Trosky's adventures have stretched across five continents bringing her endless creative inspiration and valuable life experience. Through speaking, film, photography and writing Niki has shared some of her most intimate moments with the world. Her desire to bare all comes from the earnest hope of helping others learn from her fumbles and findings.

Trosky's gift is to create intimate connections with her audience through poetic expressions of tangible beauty and transparent truth talking. She believes that wisdom is just observation and the first place to start looking is the self. Her work simply reminds us to love life.

Niki enjoys creative collaborations and would love to hear from you.

WWW.LOVELIFEPRODUCTIONS.COM